COMMON GROUND?

Acknowledgments

The editors acknowledge both our institutes, Campion College and the John Paul II Institute for Marriage and Family, for their ongoing support while we undertook this project. We acknowledge the attitudinal research undertaken by Sexton Marketing, professional editing provided by Louise Ann Mitchell and Sr Anne O'Connell, RSJ, marketing assistance from Mary Drum, publicity by Alan Davidson and the decision to publish by Fr Michael Goonan, SSP, and St Pauls Publications, and their patient dialogue on many aspects of the work including the title. We also acknowledge review of the text and helpful suggestions by the Hon. Christine Campbell, Member of the Victorian Legislative Assembly and of the Australian Labour Party, and member of the Board of Directors of Caroline Chisholm Pregnancy Support Agency. Finally, we express our gratitude to Alison Fleming and Dr Mary Walsh for their sustaining love, patience and tolerance.

Common Ground?

Seeking an Australian Consensus on Abortion and Sex Education

Edited by

John Fleming PhD
Nicholas Tonti-Filippini PhD

ST PAULS

COMMON GROUND?:
Seeking an Australian Consensus on Abortion and Sex Education
© Selena Ewing, John Fleming, Helen McConnell,
Brigid McKenna (Vout), Marcia Riordan,
Nicholas Tonti-Filippini, Mary Walsh,
for their respective contributions.

First published by St Pauls Publications 2007

National Library of Australia
Cataloguing-in-Publication Data:

Common ground? : seeking an Australian consensus on
abortion and sex education.

Bibliography.
ISBN 9781921032646 (pbk.).

1. Abortion - Moral and ethical aspects - Australia. 2.
Abortion - Australia - Public opinion. 3. Abortion. 4.
Sex instruction - Moral and ethical aspects - Australia. 5.
Sex instruction - Australia - Public opinion. 6. Sex
instruction. I. Fleming, John I., 1943- . II.
Tonti-Filippini, Nicholas. III. Title.

179.760994

Published by
ST PAULS PUBLICATIONS — Society of St Paul
PO Box 906 Strathfield NSW 2135
http://www.stpauls.com.au

Cover design by David Henley

Printed by Ligare Pty Ltd

ST PAULS PUBLICATIONS is an activity of the priests and
brothers of the Society of St Paul who place at the centre of their
lives the mission of evangelisation through the modern means
of social communication.

Contents

Contributors

Dr John Fleming, as President of Campion College, works with young people and has presented regular popular commercial radio talkback programs over many years, principally in Adelaide, South Australia. He is also a bioethicist and widely published in that field. He was a foundational member of UNESCO's International Bioethics Committee, which produced the Universal Declaration on Human Genome and Human Rights. He is a member of the Vatican's Pontifical Academy for Life, the Gene Technology Ethics Committee (Commonwealth of Australia), and a member of the Council of the National Museum of Australia (Commonwealth of Australia). He has previously served the South Australian Parliament as a member of the SA Council on Reproductive Technology, and was a member of the Medical Practitioners Professional Conduct Tribunal (District Court, SA). Dr Fleming is a Catholic priest, married with three adult children.

Dr Nicholas Tonti-Filippini is a well-known bioethicist and a senior lecturer in Bioethics at the John Paul II Institute for Marriage and Family. With his wife, Dr Mary Walsh, a medical doctor with a practice in family medicine, he was involved as a consultant in drafting directives for sex education for the Catholic Archdiocese of Melbourne. For several years he has conducted post-graduate courses for those who wish to become involved in marriage and sexuality education. He was a lecturer in medical ethics in the Philosophy Department and the Faculty of Medicine at the University of Melbourne, and in 1982 was Australia's first hospital ethicist at St. Vincent's Hospital, Melbourne, where he was Director of the Bioethics Department until 1990.

Dr Helen McConnell, PhD in Medical Science, has worked as a Senior Research Fellow in Cystic Fibrosis Centre at State Medical University in Sanct-Petersburg (Russia). Since coming to Australia she has completed a postgraduate course, Biotechnology of Life, at Monash University.

Selena Ewing is a researcher with a health/science background at Southern Cross Bioethics Institute in Adelaide and a Director of Women's Forum Australia. She has undertaken an extensive literature review on women's motivations for abortion and the resulting effects on their health and wellbeing.

Dr Brigid McKenna (Vout) is a medical graduate who is the Life Officer for the Catholic Archdiocese of Sydney. She completed a Masters in Bioethics at the John Paul II Institute.

Marcia Riordan is the Respect Life Officer for the Catholic Archdiocese of Melbourne. She is a science graduate and was a researcher with the Royal Children's Hospital Melbourne. She currently works to promote programs to achieve healing after abortion.

Dr Mary Walsh is a family physician, who recently completed a term as President of the Ovulation Method Research and Reference Centre of Australia. Dr Walsh works full-time at The Manningham General Practice in Melbourne and has interests in fertility and infertility care.

Introduction

In most western societies, the abortion debate is carried on between those who strongly advocate for a policy of abortion on demand and those who strongly advocate a pro-life policy in which abortion would be legally proscribed. Public policy decisions on the lawfulness of abortion are made either by the courts, interpreting existing law or by duly constituted legislatures acting for and on behalf of the community as a whole. In so far as the community as a whole is concerned, decisions are frequently made without reference to the wishes, desires and beliefs of the community.

Where legislatures are concerned, the abortion issue is most frequently treated as a 'conscience' issue such that each member of parliament is free to vote as he or she wishes. In most parliamentary democracies, the vast majority of voters seem to cast a vote for a party rather than an individual. That being the case it cannot safely be said that the state of public opinion on abortion is reflected through the members of parliament exercising a personal vote on the matter.

After establishing the context and recent history of the abortion debate in Australia, this work continues with an analysis of data concerning Australian attitudes to abortion and to sex education. Sexton marketing, an independent survey company, was commissioned to undertake a detailed survey of Australian opinion on abortion and on sex education.

The survey is unusual in that it was designed to distinguish between people's views on when abortion should be legally available and when it is morally acceptable. It also identifies areas of agreement that there may be among Australians, on the abortion issue and on the matter of sex education.

Social and medical perspectives are explored. The heart and mind of the Australian community is tapped – at professional, personal and societal levels. A detailed presentation of medical issues, including early intervention diagnosis, and associated issues of stem cell research and the abortion drug, RU-486 further inform the debate.

Two foundational tools to any movement forward are identified as 'sex education' and 'counselling'. Extensive research and practical experience are used to clarify the reality and possibility of both these arenas.

The final chapters review international law in this respect and analyse the moral question of proposing public-policy solutions that may not be ideal, but which have a chance of political success given the dominant attitudes within the Australian community.

While Australian society is deeply conflicted on the matter of abortion, there are nevertheless substantial areas of agreement, which would seem to indicate possibilities for well-founded public policy.

This book proposes a way forward in the area of public policy on abortion and sex education in Australia based on the strong areas of agreement within the community.

John Fleming
Nicholas Tonti-Filippini

Chapter 1

The context and recent history of the abortion debate in Australia

John Fleming

The abortion debate in Australia, across all jurisdictions, has been characterised by the confrontation of two mutually exclusive positions, the cases for which have been passionately advanced by their advocates.

On the one hand, supporters of legal abortion have emphasised the right of the woman to have control over her own body; the disadvantages women face when confronted with a pregnancy they do not want and which seems to challenge their life plans; and the dangers of illegally provided abortion which women will access in their desperation. Here abortion is seen as a necessary evil, a way out for women in desperate circumstances, a choice that should always be available for her, a choice that empowers her to take control of her life in circumstances that threaten her sense of who she is and what she wants to do with her life.[1]

On the other hand, opponents of legal abortion see in abortion the direct and willed destruction of the foetus, the unborn child, who is no less a human being than any other member of the human family. Since every member of the human family has natural rights, including the right to life, abortion should be rejected as the homicide of an innocent and particularly vulnerable human being. Some opponents of abortion may make an exception in the case of a life-for-a-life, that is, when the mother is in imminent danger of death. However, abortion opponents would also say that such situations need not occur in an advanced society such as Australia.

In reality, then, the abortion debate is characterised not just by the fact that the two positions are mutually incompatible, but also by the fact that each side finds it difficult to engage the other side, since they appear to be talking on parallel planes. One side is especially concerned with the woman's need for empowerment in a situation where she experiences a profound sense of powerlessness and alienation. The other side is concerned with protecting the lives of the innocent in a situation in which there is no one left, as they see it, to speak up for the weakest and most vulnerable members of society.

It is not fair to conclude that those who support abortion have no concern for the welfare of the foetus. Many supporters of legal abortion have made it clear that this is a serious consideration for them, as was exemplified in the television documentary, 'My Foetus'[2]. Nor is it true that abortion opponents have no concern for women, since it has been abortion opponents who have often been in the vanguard of private initiatives to offer distressed pregnant women alternatives to abortion and relief from their situation. But it is fair to say that the debate, or at least the way in which it has so far been conducted in Australia, has allowed these stereotypes to flourish, thereby creating mutual suspicion and misunderstanding.

How is it that the public debate on abortion in Australia has taken the form that it has? It is true that this is similar to other countries, but our research has suggested that this debate has gone on in Australia in a context where there is room for accommodation and progress on what has been one of the most divisive social-moral debates in modern political history. The key, we believe, is to be found in the genesis of abortion law reform in Australia in the late 1960s and early 1970s.

1.1 Public involvement in the debate

In tracing the way in which the abortion debate has unfolded in Australia, it is necessary to recognise that the legal status quo has been achieved, not by the public will or even demand, but by the courts and the parliaments. Put another way, change has been achieved in the most populous states in Australia (Victoria, New South Wales and Queensland) by judges liberally interpreting the meaning of statute law and, of course, without consultation with the community. An opportunity to have the High Court of Australia review lower court interpretations of the 'very liberal interpretation of the NSW law'[3] became available in 1996. That opportunity was ultimately lost when the matter that occasioned the review was settled out of court.

In South Australia, change was achieved legislatively after a parliamentary inquiry. Tasmania's parliament rushed through its abortion legislation in only two months. Western Australia had a sustained public and parliamentary debate that revolved around polarised ideological positions on the basis of an agenda set by politicians. The same was true in the ACT.

Where New South Wales is concerned, there have been parliamentary debates surrounding private members' bills, none of which were enacted as law. The same can be said about the Federal Parliament, of which more will be said later in this chapter.

The first point to be made here is that, until our study, very little information has been available which would show what the community as a whole believes should be the tolerable limits within which abortion is made available in Australia. Our study provides our politicians with a good guide as to the changes in social and public policy to which the Australia public could agree, in what is otherwise a very polarised and divisive debate.

Second, since the debate has been conducted largely in the courts and in parliaments, we have chosen to focus on these areas as providing an understanding of the nature of the abortion debate thus far in Australia, its consequences for the legal status quo, and its largely unproductive character.

1.2 The practice of abortion versus the law

Prior to significant changes in the statute law or to court interpretation of the law, it is difficult to find any reliable evidence of the extent of illegal abortions. Anecdotally, it would seem that in some jurisdictions doctors were practising abortion outside of recognised legal limits.

Where 'backyard abortions' are concerned - that is, illegal abortions carried out by private individuals not licensed as medical practitioners - it is almost impossible to get any real feel for what was happening prior to 1975. Such abortions certainly occurred, as hospital records have made clear. But hospitals would only have seen those cases where something went seriously wrong and the woman sought medical help. There would have been others as well. Maternal deaths from illegal abortions have now been eliminated as women seek abortion from medically qualified personnel who operate in appropriately antiseptic facilities. However, some women have suffered catastrophic injuries from the abortion procedure, such as a perforated uterus, raising questions about the appropriateness of private abortion clinics as an alternative to those procedures being carried out in a public hospital.

The number of 'backyard abortions' and the fear of a return to that period when they were carried out have had a significant impact on the nature of the debate. But evidence of the extent of the practice (as distinct from abortions being carried out illegally by medical practitioners) presented to the South Australian Select Committee on Abortion (1969) was equivocal. The police estimated that there was one maternal death every four years from these kinds of abortion, and that there were between five hundred and one thousand abortions carried out annually, some of which were legally performed for medical reasons. On the other hand, the Abortion Law Reform Association claimed that there were between 5150 (minimum) and 8900 (maximum) abortions in South Australia each year. The Association also claimed, on the basis of hospital data, that the estimated number of admissions for abortion due to illegal interference was 272 (minimum) to 515 (maximum)[4]. However, the official statistics for legal abortions in South Australia, after abortion had been largely decriminalised, show that there were only 1 440 abortions in the first year of the operation of the Act, 1970. It took twenty-four years (1994) for the reported legal abortions to get near the 5150 minimum in 1968 stated by the Abortion Law Reform Association, and it has never reached anywhere near the 8 900 they set as the maximum in that year. In fact the number of terminations in South Australia has never been higher than 5663 (1999).[5] But as late as 1990, the Abortion Law Reform Association figures were still being quoted as authoritative, despite the actual experience of legal abortion in government statistical reports.[6]

What does seem to be true, however, is that despite any formal legal restrictions that may, strictly speaking, apply, 'abortion is generally available in Australia and regarded as legal'[7]. Not only has abortion been freely available to Australian women at least from the middle 1970s; it has been paid for by Medicare.

1.3 Legal abortion - the facts

Since 1970, accurate statistical data on abortion has been kept in South Australia. The Northern Territory also keeps statistics, as does Western Australia, following the legalisation of abortion there in 1998. It has been sometimes alleged that pro-choice supporters of abortion are hostile to accurate information being collected. In some cases this may be true, but it is not universally the case. For example,

Women's Health Victoria, an organisation which 'upholds the tenet that decisions should be made by those most closely involved with them' and that it is 'appropriate that women make decisions regarding their fertility, including unplanned pregnancies, based on their life situations, personal views and beliefs', strongly supports the collection of accurate data. Women's Health Victoria has expressed concern that accurate data is not available and that Medicare statistics are not a reliable indicator because they do not refer to abortions that take place in a public hospital since no rebate is claimed. They conclude their discussion of the problems in this area thus:

> The health impacts of unplanned pregnancies, and the circumstances that contribute to their occurrence need further investigation. However, a lack of accurate data makes it more difficult to tailor interventions and offer the most appropriate services to individual women.[8]

The same organisation also supports the provision of 'unbiased, relevant and accurate information and support for women experiencing an unwanted pregnancy'.

It seems a pity that the abortion debate in Australia seems nearly always to be preoccupied with changes to the law, and carried on in an atmosphere of mutual distrust and animosity, and without recognition of the common ground identified in our survey, which is also in accord with positions stated by the 'warring' parties. It is also a pity that even a request for more accurate data should be automatically associated with an ulterior motive. In all the circumstances, it would be difficult to suspect Women's Health Victoria of such a motive when it makes a plea for better and more accurate information.

For an intelligent and thoughtful debate on any matter of public importance to occur, there is a need firstly to identify the facts. Since much of the debate on abortion goes on without the benefit of such facts as can easily be gathered, it is no wonder that more heat than light is generated. Apart from the essential philosophical and moral issues, which lie at the heart of the abortion controversy, there is a wide range of other issues, which could be addressed if all sides of the debate would agree to let that happen - a range of issues that concern most Australians - as our study clearly shows.

1.4 Setting the scene for the national debate

There are four major factors that have conditioned the social context for the abortion debate in Australia, and the way in which it subsequently unfolded in the following forty years. These factors are: *Bourne's* case; the development of the contraceptive pill and the sexual revolution; a major shift in the social, moral and cultural assumptions of Australian society; and developments in the feminist movements.

In 1938 in the United Kingdom, the first legal test as to whether or not any abortions were lawful occurred in the case of *R v Bourne*.[9] A fourteen-year-old girl was presented to a distinguished surgeon, Aleck Bourne. She was pregnant after being pack raped. Bourne carried out the abortion after first having publicly announced that this was his intention. He was charged under section 58 of the Offences Against the Person Act 1861. Justice Malcolm Martin McNaghten ruled that the words 'unlawfully procuring abortion' in section 58 had to be understood to mean that an abortion is unlawful 'unless the act is done in good faith for the purpose of preserving the life of the mother'.[10]

It is important to note that McNaghten recognised that:

> The law of the land has always held human life to be sacred and the protection that the law gives to human life extends also to the unborn child in the womb. The unborn child must not be destroyed unless the destruction of that child is for the purpose of preserving the yet more precious life of the mother.[11]

McNaghten then went on to determine what constituted 'preserving the life of the mother' for which he gave three separate criteria. The first criterion was when the woman 'was in danger of instant death', and the second was when there was no danger of instant death but 'there was a danger of health such that life might be lost'. But it was McNaghten's third criterion, which was used to cover the case before him.

The third criterion covered the situation where there was no danger of instant death and no expectation of loss of life, but such a serious challenge to the woman's health that her life may become intolerable.

> As I have said, I think that those words ought to be construed in a reasonable sense, and, if the doctor is of the opinion, on reasonable grounds and with adequate knowledge, that *the probable consequence of the continuance of the pregnancy will be to make the woman a physical or mental wreck*, the jury are quite entitled to take the view that the doctor, who, in those circumstances, and in that honest belief, operates, is operating for the purpose of preserving the life of the woman.[12]

The McNaghten decision was described in the *Australian Law Journal* of October 1938 in these terms:

> It is difficult to overcome the feeling that his Lordship in taking this step was responsible for some judicial, and possibly judicious, legislation. His summing up, however, seems to be the only present judicial statement of the law on this subject.[13]

This is, perhaps, a polite way of saying that McNaghten was making new law. Suffice it to say that this English case strongly influenced the way in which Australian judges were to interpret the law some thirty years later.

But the really important thing to note here is that McNaghten held *both* that the life of the 'unborn child in the womb' was 'sacred' and had 'the protection of the law', *and* that the life of the mother was 'more precious' than the life of the child such that its protection was of greater legal, moral and social significance than that of the child. The grounds for protecting the woman's life and for legal permission to be granted for the destruction of the 'potential life of the unborn child' were cast quite widely.

The later debates over abortion in the United Kingdom and in Australia were to be couched in terms of the 'right to life of the unborn child' versus the greater importance to be attached to the life of the mother; whether the foetus is a child or merely a 'potential life'; and the extent of the grounds which could be described to provide the legal limits for abortion. *Bourne's* case introduced all these arguments as central to the abortion debate, arguments which have been pursued by leaders of all sides to the argument ever since.

From the 1960s changes occurred in Australian society that were to advance the call for more ready access to legal abortion. The development of the contraceptive pill greatly encouraged the sexual revolution that was to engulf most Western societies. Seemingly freed from the necessary link between sexual intercourse and procreation, many Australians embarked upon a lifestyle characterised by greater sexual permissiveness.[14] But the use of the contraceptive pill and other forms of contraception, did not provide fail-safe methods to prevent conception, where unforeseen pregnancies were concerned.

In 1969, the Abortion Law Reform Association in South Australia, in a submission to the Parliamentary Select Committee on Abortion, was already arguing the connection between failed contraception and abortion.

> Today the contraceptive pill is widely prescribed by doctors. Having delegated this responsibility to them it seems very logical that society should allow them competence to advise further on abortion *when contraception fails.*[15]

Thirty-five years later, a major South Australian study graphically confirmed the reality of failed contraception as a key indicator for abortion requests.

> Women presenting for termination reported problems with contraception more frequently than women presenting for antenatal care. Even so, a quarter of the women in the antenatal group reported problems, and more than half of those in the repeat termination group did so. Further, women in these termination

groups reported failure of the method more frequently than those in the antenatal group (40 per cent compared with 16 per cent). This appears to be a factor in repeat termination, although reporting bias may be a consideration.[16]

Even more significantly, the same study found that 'sixty-four per cent of women presenting for termination with unplanned pregnancies stated that they had been using a contraceptive method, and two-thirds of them attributed the pregnancy to failure of the method'.[17]

Two matters deserve comment here. First, the idea that abortions are mainly carried out on inexperienced teenagers is not supported by the data in, for example, South Australia. That data shows that 23.1 per cent of reported abortions were carried out on teenage girls. Twenty to thirty year olds had 47 per cent of the abortions and the thirty-plus group had 29.9 per cent. It would seem that the teenagers are the smallest of these three groups. Second, the strategy of more sex education and information on contraceptives seems not to have worked, with more experienced women having more abortions than less experienced; 64 per cent of women presenting for abortion stating they were using contraceptives; and two-thirds of them attributing the pregnancy to method failure. Clearly, new approaches need to be devised if we are to see a reduction in unwanted pregnancies and a reduction in the number of abortions.

In addition to the sexual revolution, and in many ways inextricably linked to it, have been:

- the significant cultural shift in Australian society characterised by increased wealth and prosperity for the many;
- claims to greater personal autonomy and individual rights;
- the decline in attachment to the Christian religion and the influence of the Churches;
- significant increases in experimentation with drugs;

- significant increases in unemployment rates; and
- the rise in pre-marital cohabitation.

In this situation more and more people are claiming the right to make their own personal moral decisions, while at the same time increasing demand for services, which would assist individuals who as a consequence found themselves in situations of personal and social distress.

A crucial part of the great social reformist movements of the 1960s and the 1970s was the women's movement. The women's movement covered a raft of particular philosophical, social and political views, but one objective generally held by the leadership was the achievement of greater access to legal abortion. Abortion was crucial to the feminist agenda because it freed women from what some advocates saw as domestic servitude and gave them greater opportunity to find fulfilment apart from that defined in terms of marriage and children. That meant the possibility of achieving not only better access to workplace and career, but also equal access to workplace and career. Feminist influence was strongly felt in political parties, in the various state parliaments, and in the professions, especially in education. With much of the abortion debate centred on the right to life of the child versus the rights of the mother, it was the women's movement that provided the strongest advocacy for a 'woman's right to choose'.

1.5 Abortion law reform 1968–2002

Bourne's case opened up the possibility that if there were 'unlawful' abortions there must be 'lawful' abortions. The other critical development in English law for Australian purposes came almost thirty years later with the passing of the Abortion Act of 1967 at Westminster, which codified in statute law what those 'lawful' abortions would be. There was immediate pressure in Australia to follow suit, especially in South Australia, Victoria and New South Wales.

It is important to recall how the law was reformed in different jurisdictions. In Victoria and New South Wales, judges decided what constituted a lawful abortion. These decisions were made at first instance and were not appealed. In South Australia (1969), Western Australia (1998), the Australian Capital Territory (most recently, in 2002) and Tasmania (2002) the parliaments shouldered the task of reform. But in each of these states except South Australia, this only came about when parliamentary action was forced upon legislators by peculiar events. It only came after a long period where, in the wake of the Victorian and New South Wales court decisions, the existing laws had not been enforced.

As we shall see in what follows, however, in each case the same elements were in play in shaping the final formal position at law, namely:

- abortion was, in general, unlawful;

- the foetus or unborn child was protected in law but not at the expense of the mother's right to life; and

- in exceptional circumstances abortion would be counted as lawful; (those exceptional cases having regard mainly to the circumstances in which the mother found herself).

1.5.1 South Australia

The first legislative initiative to legalise abortion in Australia occurred in South Australia in 1968–1969. After five months general discussion inside and outside the parliament, the then Attorney General, the Honourable Robin Millhouse (Liberal Country League), introduced the Government's Bill for an Act to amend the Criminal Law Consolidation Act, 1935-66. In his second reading speech Millhouse explained the background to the Bill. At the latest Liberal Country League (LCL) conference a resolution had been passed requesting the Government to examine the law on abortion in SA to see whether or not it should be altered to conform broadly to the new law passed in the UK. Millhouse was then approached on the matter by the Abortion Law Reform Association who also wanted changes to the law to provide for abortion on demand. The Government decided to set up a Select Committee of the Parliament to examine the issue, the new Bill being the trigger for that reference.[18]

Interestingly, in his second reading speech, Millhouse referred explicitly to the '1938 Bourne case' in great detail, before reading directly from a document published by the Church of England's Assembly Board for Social Responsibility. The document, *Abortion and Ethical Discussion* (1965), defended the right of the unborn child to live as the primary and general intention of the law; referred to the foetus 'as potentially a human life'; saw the problem of abortion in terms of 'weighing the claims of the mother against the claims of the foetus and vice versa'; and concluded there were 'certain circumstances' in which abortion could be justified.[19]

The debate that ensued in South Australia revolved around the degree of legal protection owed to the unborn child, the moral status of the foetus especially as compared to that of the mother, and the breadth of meaning that could be attached to the idea of protecting the woman's physical and mental health. When it was passed, the new law defined the meaning of 'preservation of the life of the mother' far more widely than *Bourne*. McNaghten had spoken in terms of the 'probable consequence' of the continuance of the pregnancy, which would be to 'make the woman a physical or mental wreck'. In addition to the provision of abortion when 'the termination is immediately necessary to save the life or to prevent grave injury to the physical or mental health of the pregnant woman' (*Bourne*), the SA law allows doctors to perform an abortion if, in their opinion, the continuance of the pregnancy 'would involve greater risk to the life of the pregnant woman or greater risk of injury to the physical or mental health of the pregnant woman than if the pregnancy were terminated'. The determination of risk could also take into account 'the pregnant woman's actual or reasonably foreseeable environment'.

The South Australian Act, which has never been amended, also went beyond *Bourne* by providing, among other things, for individual doctors and nurses not to be involved in abortions on the grounds of a conscientious objection, and for abortion on the grounds of foetal abnormality.

1.5.2 Victoria

In the different political and legal context of the State of Victoria the legal definition of a lawful abortion was determined in the Supreme Court. In Victoria at that time, there seemed to be 'uncertainty' as to the meaning of the law on abortion since, although abortion was being increasingly widely practised, prosecutions tended to be unsuccessful. This was in large part due to the unwillingness of doctors to testify against colleagues who had been charged, and reluctance on the part of the judges to punish women in desperate circumstances.[20] So in 1969 a test case was set up by the Victorian Branch of the Australian Medical Association and the Attorney-General's Department to bring the matter before the courts for clarification.

In the event, Justice Clifford Inch Menhennitt ruled in the matter of *R v. Davidson*[21] to define what, for the purposes of the state of Victoria, were legal abortions. Menhennitt came to similar conclusions to those of McNaghten in *Bourne*, but his reasoning was different. Menhennitt applied the principle of necessity[22]; that is to say, the principle that makes lawful what would otherwise be unlawful in cases of imminent peril.[23]

In his application of this principle to Victoria's law on abortion, Menhennitt ruled as follows:

For the use of an instrument with intent to procure a miscarriage to be lawful the accused must have honestly believed on reasonable grounds that the act done by him was:

i. necessary to preserve the mother from serious danger to her life or her physical or mental health (not being merely the normal dangers of pregnancy and childbirth) which continuance of the pregnancy would entail; and

ii. in the circumstances, not out of proportion to the danger to be averted.

The Victorian law, as interpreted by Menhennitt appears to be at once less liberal and yet more liberal than the South Australian law. It is less liberal in that it makes no provision for eugenic abortion and requires abortion to be provided only in an emergency, in a situation of serious danger to the mother. But it is more liberal in that it provides no limit as to when an abortion can occur as against the twenty-eight week limit under the South Australian Act.

In July 2000, three senior medical staff at the Royal Women's Hospital were stood down for conducting a late termination at thirty-two weeks. The procedure followed the discovery that the foetus was affected by dwarfism. The mother was believed to be depressed, even suicidal, on learning of her unborn child's condition and demanded the termination. Despite there being a Victorian statute for the crime of child destruction in which miscarriage is procured after the child has become viable, the hospital referred the matter to the coroner. The Deputy Coroner found that there was not a reportable death. This decision has since been supported in a report to the Victorian Parliament by the Parliamentary Law Reform Committee. The report supports the view that the Coroner does not have jurisdiction to investigate stillbirths (babies born dead after twenty weeks). The report admits that its conclusion abrogates the Act in favour of a common law view, and is contrary to legal advice from the Solicitor General. The effect of this advice is that no action is to be taken to prosecute the crime of child destruction that is defined in the Victorian Crimes Act.

1.5.3 New South Wales

In 1972 New South Wales District Court Judge Aaron Levine, handed down a decision in *R v Wald* which, like Menhennitt, applied the principle of necessity to the abortion law to determine which were lawful abortions. He followed Menhennitt and went beyond him, adding that there can be 'economic, social or medical' reasons constituting 'reasonable grounds upon which an accused could honestly and reasonably believe there would result a serious danger to a woman's physical or mental health' from continuing with the pregnancy.[24]

Much later the grounds for abortion in New South Wales would be further widened. In 1995 Acting Chief Justice Michael Kirby of the Court of Appeal provided a more liberal interpretation of the law in his detailed discussion of his reasons for rejecting a restrictive interpretation of the Levine judgment, handed down at first instance in a civil case by Justice Peter Newman in the Supreme Court. Kirby offered:

> a reinterpretation of the Levine ruling according to which the meaning of 'unlawful' abortion is in effect determined by a doctor's subjective beliefs about when an abortion is appropriate, based on that doctor's assessment of the impact of the social and economic factors on the health of the woman seeking abortion. His approach therefore arguably legitimises the provision of abortion services 'on request', but only if those services are provided by doctors who consider that abortion should be provided on request because forcing a woman to continue with an unwanted pregnancy would inevitably have a negative and serious impact on her mental health.[25]

1.5.4 Australian Capital Territory (Federal Parliament)

On the 8 March 1973, two Victorian Members of Parliament, D.C. McKenzie (ALP) and A.H. Lamb (ALP) gave the required formal notice of intention to introduce into the Federal Parliament a Private Member's Bill to liberalise existing abortion legislation in the Australian Capital

Territory. Until 1988 the Australian Capital Territory was governed by the Federal Parliament. Thereafter it was granted self-government.

The McKenzie-Lamb Abortion Bill provided for abortion-on-demand and provoked considerable public debate. In the end the Bill was defeated on 10 May 1973 with twenty-three members voting in favour of the Bill and ninety-eight voting against.

C.R. Matthews (ALP) supported by D.L. Chipp (Liberal) moved a motion on 28 August 1973, which called on the government to set up a Royal Commission on Abortion. This motion was successfully significantly amended by J.M. Fraser (Liberal) and F.E. Stewart (ALP). The following year Prime Minister E.G. Whitlam set up a Royal Commission, but on lines much more in keeping with the Matthews/ Chipp original motion. Given that two of the three Royal Commissioners were already on the public record as supporters of a more liberal approach to abortion, it was not surprising that the Commission recommended that 'abortion should be free of legal regulation when performed by a registered medical practitioner at the request of the woman up to the end of the twenty-second week of pregnancy'.

On 11 October 1978 Senators S. Ryan (ALP) and D. Grimes (ALP) moved a motion 'to disallow the Australian Capital Territory Termination of Pregnancy Ordinance 1978'.[26] That ordinance contained a ban on the establishment of abortion clinics in the Australian Capital Territory. The Ryan/Grimes motion was defeated 36 to 24, with senators exercising a conscience vote.

With the sharp increase in the numbers of abortions and the advent of Medicare, it would only be a matter of time before the question of abortion funding became an issue. For opponents of abortion, Medicare payments represented an involvement of the people in general for what they regarded as a seriously immoral act. Moreover, they argued, if a woman wanted to choose an abortion she should accept the cost if the procedure was simply elective. On the other hand, pro-choice advocates saw Medicare funding as crucial to ensure not only that women had ready access to abortion when they judged they needed one, but equal access for the poor.[27]

Nevertheless, on 15 August 1978, S. Lusher (National Country Party) gave notice of his intention to move a motion directing the Government to cease the payment of medical benefits for abortion. Lusher had two main concerns: the increase in the rate of abortions in Australia, and the cost in terms of medical benefits payments. Lusher's motion went through three versions. He began with a motion that would have banned all Medicare payments for abortion. Ultimately, though, the final form of his motion was as follows:

> That this House requests the Government to introduce legislation which will provide that:
>
> medical benefits shall not be provided by the Commonwealth for the termination of pregnancy unless the termination was performed to protect the life of the mother from a physical pathological condition and that the life could be protected in no other way;
>
> where medical expenses are incurred in respect of a medical service specified in the Medical Benefits Schedule which could include the termination of pregnancy, the doctor who performed the service shall be required to certify to the Department of Health that:
>
> > i. the operation was not performed to terminate a pregnancy but for a stated, other purpose; or
> >
> > ii. if the operation was performed to terminate a pregnancy, it was carried out in order to protect the life of the mother from a specified physical pathological condition and that the life could be protected in no other way.[28]

A detailed account of this debate is available. Suffice it to say that the Lusher motion exposed the irreconcilable differences between the two sides. Opponents of Lusher argued that his motion, if passed and acted on, would cause discrimination against the poor, interference with state laws, sectarianism and the suppression of a woman's control over her own body. Supporters of Lusher saw his motion as a call to the Federal Parliament to reaffirm the 'sanctity of life' principle, which, if applied, would eliminate Medicare payments, thereby reducing the numbers of abortions that would be carried out in the country.

B.D. Simon (Liberal) moved an amendment to the motion eliminating all words after the first 'that' and replacing them with these words:

> [That] this House is of the opinion that the Commonwealth Government should not pay any medical benefits for or in relation to the termination of pregnancy unless the procedure is performed in accordance with the law of a state or territory.[29]

This amendment was duly passed. The Federal Parliament reminded the nation that the lawfulness or otherwise of abortion was an issue determined by the States and Territories, not by the Federal Parliament. The whole episode, with the heated passions that it excited in the community, was a reminder that the issue of access to lawful abortion roused deeply held convictions. Other abortion related issues received very little attention in the heat of the battle, given the terms in which the battle was being fought.

1.6 Essential elements of the abortion debate

The terms of the abortion debate in Australia were framed by laws, unchallenged until 1969, which protected the foetus from destruction in all cases except when the mother was in imminent risk of death. What changed this was a shift to an increasingly broadened consideration of the circumstances – physical, mental, emotional, social, and finally, financial - in which the woman found herself. No wonder, then, that the debate quickly polarised around the issue of whether there were any circumstances so desperate, in a wealthy country like Australia with an excellent health system, which would justify abortion. Those who held to the primacy of the right to life of the unborn child generally argued that there were no circumstances that would justify a direct abortion. Those same people argued that an indirect abortion, subject to certain criteria, would be justified and that such a provision took full account of the hard cases affecting the life of the mother.[30] Those who held to the primacy of the mother's right to choose argued that there was no one better placed than the woman to judge her personal circumstances; that control of one's own life and fertility was a right the exercise of which would empower women. These people also argued that abortion was, of course, always a difficult choice for a woman to make. Nevertheless it was her choice to make and hers alone.

That these two polarities dictated the nature and scope of the argument became especially clear in the later abortion debates that took place in Western Australia, the Australian Capital Territory (ACT) and Tasmania. In all three cases the major debates took place in parliament. These debates exemplified the polarisation, which is characteristic of the discussion when there is so much at stake, and when the proponents of each case so passionately believe in the rightness of their cause that compromise is effectively impossible. The fact that the community was largely in 'the middle ground' was, at that time, unknown to the major protagonists, both of whom adopted a 'winner-takes-all' mentality. This is said without judgment. It is easy to understand how this happened and why. But it has been largely unproductive and, as our study now makes clear, is certainly unrepresentative of the opinion of the larger sections of the community.

After the ground breaking reforms of the late 1960s and early 1970s, abortion continued to be dealt with differently in different states and territories. In Queensland the clarification as to what would be counted as lawful abortions was decided in the courts. In Western Australia, Tasmania and the ACT the clarifications and changes in the law in relation to abortion were decided in parliament. We use the debates that occurred in the Western Australian and ACT parliaments to exemplify the *nature* of the abortion debate in Australia, its uncompromising character, its acrimony, and its polarisation around the 'right to life of the unborn child' and the 'right of a woman to choose'. Such is the nature of that debate that any suggested compromises are seen, rightly or wrongly, as no more than attempts by the other side in bad faith to undermine sacrosanct and absolute principles.

By setting out the kinds of arguments used in the parliaments, it will become even clearer that those two polarised positions do not accurately represent the positions adopted by most Australians as is evidenced by our research. It should be noted here that in all the parliamentary debates in the federal, state and territory parliaments, members of parliament have been given the opportunity to vote according to their conscience. Since little reliable information on public opinion was available to guide politicians, it meant that how they voted was almost certainly in line with their personal opinions.

1.6.1 Queensland

The Queensland Criminal Code, section 292, makes it clear that abortion is not the equivalent of murder or manslaughter of the unborn since 'a child becomes a person capable of being killed when it has completely proceeded in a living state from the mother, whether it has breathed or not, and whether it has an independent circulation or not, and whether the navel string is severed or not'.

Nevertheless, doctors and health workers who perform abortions are liable, under section 224 of the Code, to prosecution and imprisonment for fourteen years, and a woman who intends to procure her own miscarriage by the same means is guilty of a crime and liable to imprisonment for seven years.[31]

However, section 282 provides an exception where the abortion is carried out to preserve the mother's life. According to Nicolee Dixon there were indications that

Queensland judges during the 1980s were moving to the view that section 282 'provided a defence to a charge of "unlawful" abortion, provided it met the requirements of the Menhennitt ruling'.[32] This matter was clarified in *R v. Bayliss and Cullen* in 1986.[33] District Court Judge Frederick McGuire approved the Menhennitt ruling as applying to Queensland but did not go as far as adopting the more liberal approach of Levine in *Wald*. In fact McGuire expressed concern that Menhennitt lacked sufficient certainty and clarity and that it was up to a higher court or the parliament to make any definitive ruling about the law in relation to abortion in Queensland.

In acquitting Bayliss and Cullen, McGuire pointed out that the parliament did not approve the termination of pregnancy merely because the woman wanted to end the pregnancy, that is, the parliament did not approve abortion on demand.

> The law in this State has not abdicated its responsibility as guardian of the silent innocence of the unborn. It should rightly use its authority to see that abortion on whim or caprice does not insidiously filter into our society. There is no legal justification for abortion on demand.[34]

Dixon has observed that it is clear from the decision in *R v Bayliss and Cullen* 'that abortion on request is not permitted in Queensland'. She summarises the legal position in Queensland in these terms:

> It would appear that to obtain a conviction of a medical practitioner, the prosecution would have to prove the following beyond reasonable doubt–
>
> 1. the doctor did not hold a reasonable belief that the procedure was necessary to preserve the woman from serious danger to her life, or serious danger to her physical or mental health (which, in NSW, but probably not in Queensland, would allow consideration of economic or social factors as well as health factors) which may operate throughout the pregnancy or after the birth of the child; or

2.   the doctor did not hold a reasonable belief that the procedure was proportionate in the circumstances to the need to preserve the woman from the aforementioned serious danger.[35]

Dixon wants us to further note, as we have above, that under Queensland law the foetus is not a person until after it has been born.

There is currently no wish by the Premier or Leader of the Opposition to see legislative changes to the law on abortion in Queensland despite the changes recently made to the law in the ACT. Since abortion is widely practised in Queensland, as elsewhere in the country, the Premier no doubt sees a debate over legislation in his State as achieving little except to bring on another furious battle between the two major antagonists including members of his own Government.

1.6.2 Western Australia

In February 1998 two Perth doctors were charged with having procured an unlawful abortion. The charges, the first laid in Western Australia for almost thirty years, were highly suggestive of a trigger event being constructed to make the attainment of abortion law reform easier to attain.

Abortion doctors staged a 'strike' to pressure the parliament to regularise by statute what had become the widespread practice in the state.[36] In March 1998 Cheryl Davenport introduced into the Legislative Council a private member's Bill for the decriminalisation of abortion. In May 1998 the Acts Amendment (Abortion) Act 1998 was passed. The effect of this was to 'remove from the WA Criminal Code certain offences relating to abortion' and to amend 'the Health Act 1911 (WA) to regulate abortion procedures'.[37]

The terms in which Davenport introduced the Bill were these:

Can we live with our conscience if we, the politicians [of Western Australia], in failing to change the law, witness women dying or sterilising themselves unnecessarily because access to a safe, legal medical service is denied?[38]

The debate which followed was accordingly both polarised and acrimonious. The pending charges against the two doctors and the threatened abortion doctors 'strike' provided an emotionally charged context which was always going to make a cool and reasoned discussion impossible.

1.6.2.1 Men's right to participate in the debate

An issue arising within this debate is the question of the right of men to participate. Our survey shows that most Australians (76 per cent) believe men have an equal right to public comment. But in the Western Australian Parliament a number of men felt they needed to apologise for their lack of qualifications to speak. Ken Travers (ALP) not only felt unqualified to speak, he asked his partner Trish Cowles to write his speech.[39] Similar sentiments were expressed by Tom Helm (ALP)[40], Barry House (Lib)[41] and Greg Smith (Lib). Smith stated:

> I am prepared to say it is not in the domain of a man to comment on abortion because I have never had to experience carrying a child to full term nor the trauma of an unwanted pregnancy … I do not have the right to force a woman to go on with an unwanted pregnancy.[42]

The difficulty here is, of course, that it calls into question whether the parliament really passed the Act and whether, and to what degree, some male members abrogated their responsibility as duly elected representatives of the people. If a man is disqualified from comment on the basis of never having experienced a pregnancy or an unwanted pregnancy, what of the women who voted who had either never been pregnant or had never experienced an unwanted pregnancy? Should they have disqualified themselves as well?

1.6.2.2 The right to choose

The main argument in favour of the Bill was a woman's right to choose abortion in any circumstances. This was backed up by the unsupported assertion that the majority of Western Australians were of this opinion. The argument was, of course, disputed, but in the end, backed up by a fear of 'backyard abortions', it proved decisive. While no objective evidence was offered to support this fear members seemed to accept that deaths from unhygienic 'backyard abortions' were the only alternative to liberal abortion laws.

1.6.2.3 Reasons for abortion

Among the many reasons given which justified ready access to abortion were contraception failure, financial stress, relationship instability, unwanted pregnancy, disability in the child, medical reasons (physical and mental health of the mother), mother's life at risk, rape and incest, sex selection for disability, and women will seek abortion whether it is legal or not. Late term abortions were also accepted by the parliament when the mother or child has a 'severe medical condition'.

1.6.2.4 Conditions under which abortion should be provided

Pro-life members, a minority, offered some amendments that were rejected by the majority pro-choice members. These included an amendment to make coercion an offence. There was also strong opposition to the proposition that mandatory counselling be provided. While there was agreement on the need for women to be fully informed, there was little agreement on what information should be provided and how it should be delivered. In a debate, characterised by an attitude of 'winner-takes-all', the majority was in no mood to accept the amendments put to them by the minority even though, as we now know, there was broad community support for those amendments. Even in the area of informed consent, a legal requirement before the carrying out of any medical procedure as part of the doctor's duty of care,[43] there was a tendency for the majority to see such a requirement as a measure to prevent abortion being made as widely available as possible. Mandatory counselling was seen by its opponents as a 'destruction and not an augmentation of women's rights'[44], as putting 'obstacles in the way of women seeking that choice' and wanting 'to constrain, harass and frustrate them when they face very sensitive and difficult decisions'[45], an 'insult to women'[46], and in any case something that simply would not work.[47]

1.6.2.5 Deep divisions in the parliament

The final comments made by members of parliament showed how deep the divide was between those who supported the Bill and those who opposed it. This divide was evident across the main political parties with proponents and opponents of the most liberal abortion law in Australia to be found in both major political parties.

Diana Warnock (ALP), supporter of the Bill, said this: 'This parliament has, in a very tolerant and profoundly Australian way, decided to let women make their own personal moral decisions about this agonisingly personal matter.'[48] Warnock was backed by Michael Board (Liberal): 'I am reluctant to force my view onto other people. From the outset, for me, that has been the issue at the heart of the debate ... nobody has been able to tell me how we can force a woman to carry a child she does not wish to carry.'[49] On the other hand Michelle Roberts (ALP) expressed dismay at the unwillingness of pro-choice members to accept compromise. She labelled them as 'zealots'.

> According to zealots, it is her choice, no matter her state of distress, no matter the duress that she may be under from her boyfriend or husband, no matter whether she has been informed of her options or their consequences, and no matter that the decision to terminate is irreversible ... The zealots want no checks or balances. They

resist propositions that doctors should certify in writing that the woman concerned has been appropriately counselled, or that her life or the life of her child is in medical jeopardy.[50]

Ms Roberts was in turn backed up by William McNee (Liberal). 'The Parliament is about to pass the worst legislation in the world ... Members may suggest that the Bill has been dressed up a little. I say it was dressed up begrudgingly. It took a long time to get a few concessions.'[51]

1.6.3 Australian Capital Territory (ACT Parliament)

In 1992 the Parliament of the ACT repealed the Termination of Pregnancy Act, which restricted the carrying out of abortions to public hospitals. This was followed by the establishment of a freestanding abortion clinic. Pro-choice groups in the ACT believed that the 'battle for women's reproductive freedom' had been 'largely won'.[52] But in 1998, Paul Osborne (Independent) introduced the Health Regulation (Maternal Health Information) Bill, which was subsequently passed. This Act had a number of important features:

- abortion had to be performed by a registered medical practitioner in an approved facility;

- the woman had to be offered counselling;

- before an abortion could be performed information was required to be given to the woman about the risks of abortion and the risks of continuing with the pregnancy, in addition to certain other information contained in the Act including the probable age of the foetus;

- there had to be a 72-hour 'cooling off' period after the information session was completed;

- a Regulation required pamphlets to be prepared which would contain pictures of the developing foetus at different stages of gestation.

Immediately after the 2001 elections, when a new government had come to power, the Speaker, Wayne Berry

(ALP), introduced two abortion law reform Bills. There was a Bill to repeal the 1998 Act and a Bill to repeal sections 42-44 of the Crimes Act 1900 to remove abortion from the criminal law. On 21 August 2002 both Bills passed by the narrow margin of 9 to 8. The parliament went on to make amendments to the Medical Practitioners Act 1930 'to ensure that abortion would only be carried out by medical practitioners in registered facilities and that health workers with a conscientious objection to the procedure would not have to take part in them'.[53]

The situation in the ACT now is that abortion is to be treated like any other medical procedure. It is no longer unlawful, and may be performed at public clinics on pregnant women up to twelve weeks gestation. After twelve weeks an ethics panel is required to review the case.[54]

Looking at the debate itself, the polarisation of beliefs among the Members of the ACT Legislative Assembly was extreme. Wayne Berry (ALP) stated that supporters of a woman's right to choose had to be 'vigilant about protecting well into the future any gains that are made'. On the issue of a woman's right to choose, Katy Gallagher (ALP) stated her position as a *Credo* (creed):

> *I believe* that women have the right to make choices about their own health.
>
> *I believe* that women have the right to determine if and when they want children, and how many.
>
> *I believe* that women have the right to decide in what circumstances they find it acceptable to have a child and what circumstances they do not.[55]

On the other hand, Gary Humphries (Liberal) pointed out that in 1995 he had 'introduced legislation which interfered with women's right to make decisions about their own bodies', legislation which had been supported by women's groups across the ACT as well as every member of the Assembly, and that legislation was 'to outlaw female genital mutilation'.[56]

Vicki Dunne (Liberal) wanted statistics on abortion to be collected to test whether or not 'Mr Berry's regime for making abortion safe, legal, accessible and rare is working'.[57] But Berry was against the collection of statistics because he thought the information would be used to 'punish women for having an abortion'.[58] He also thought that with the small population in the ACT, and the small numbers of late-term abortions in the ACT the collection of statistics 'would come close to identifying people'.[59] Roslyn Dundas (Democrat) thought that abortion should be 'treated like any other procedure'. While she did not mind numbers of abortion being reported she objected to a 'regulation that requires reasons for abortions to be publicly stated'.[60] John Hargreaves (ALP) also opposed the keeping and publication of statistics on abortion because:

> If you want to know the statistics on the number of ingrown toenails which are fixed, you can find out because keeping the statistics is an automatic part of the process, but you will find nowhere in the legislation a requirement for somebody to tell somebody else about the number of ingrown toenails that have been chopped in this town and in any case they would be inaccurate because some abortions occur in hospitals but are reported under another name.[61]

The mistrust of the Dunne proposal was exemplified by Kerrie Tucker (Greens):

> I am assuming that this provision [requiring reporting of statistics] is actually about trying to reduce the number of abortions, because that is what Mrs Dunne and other people say they want to see happen, as do I and, I think, as do most people in this place ... But if we are really serious about this subject, let us not put people's information on the internet and let us not have every three months ... let us look at the social condition that creates unwanted pregnancies.[62]

There was no agreement either on the issue of informed consent. The Bill proposed to repeal the provision of a booklet showing pictures of the developing foetus, providing information on the risks to the woman of an abortion and other matters. Vicki Dunne argued in favour of retaining the information booklet because medical practitioners had failed to fully inform women facing an abortion, that the 'commonest gynaecological operation, one that we dislike' had been delegated to doctors less qualified than gynaecologists or obstetricians to do the procedure, that 'we have not ensured that the highest standards of practice have been available or reviewed, nor have we seen to it that adequate counselling and contraceptive advice has been made available'.[63] Dunne also wanted it to be clear that abortion providers should not be the ones to provide the statutory information that would fulfil the requirements under *Rogers v Whitaker*.

John Stanhope (ALP), supported by Simon Corbell (ALP), responded by arguing that a special requirement was not necessary since doctors were already under the *Rogers v Whitaker* requirement for disclosure to fulfil their obligations to a patient. Roslyn Dundas was suspicious of the motives of those who wished to retain the informed consent provisions. Since anti-abortion campaigners believe that the right choice is not to have an abortion, what these people assume is that women will not have an abortion if provided with the adequate information. That being the case, she said, it is only 'a small jump from there to saying that the only information that is adequate is that which leads to a decision not to have an abortion'. This she said was not 'truly informed decision-making'. Dundas further asserted that the woman who has reached the decision to have an abortion has already considered the physical and emotional consequences, and that, in fact, the measure to repeal this law was more than justified given that 'all this law did was increase the trauma and inconvenience for women who had made a decision to pursue termination'.[64]

Katy Gallagher said that the law, which Berry wished to repeal and which required women to be given certain information before they agreed to a termination, 'undermines the process of choice by undermining women, devaluing their choices, questioning the legitimacy of their decision-making ability, and by patronising them'.[65]

Dunne described the situation in the Parliament well: as a situation where members divided on 'pro' or 'anti' abortion lines had become adversaries.

> It is a matter of great regret that there is no meeting of the minds and no attempt at convergence. What we see instead is the grim process of gainsaying a harsh and brutal rejection of each other's views and the hurling of abuse, thinly disguised as parliamentary debate. I cannot help feeling that we dismay not only ourselves but our electorates when we do this, because, in truth, we are failing as legislators in a very real sense ... Good faith to me means, among other things, a search for commonality, a genuine attempt to identify affinities and accentuating the positives.[66]

Yet the data in our survey indicates the real possibility of commonality, at least on some issues, in the abortion debate. It will require among politicians the same good faith that seems to be present in the community at large.

1.6.4 Tasmania

The law in relation to abortion in Tasmania was similar to the law in Queensland until the challenge to that law which occurred in 2001. Up until that time abortions were being carried out in Tasmania for reasons of serious risk to the mother's physical or mental health. This was the practice, absent of any judicial interpretations to clarify the law and despite the fact that the Tasmanian law did not include the phrase 'or upon an unborn child for the preservation of the mother's life', which had allowed the Queensland courts to rule that the Menhennitt judgment governed the interpretation of the law in that state.

In November 2001 a medical student alerted the police to the abortion practices in the Royal Hobart Hospital and asked them to investigate. As a consequence Tasmanian doctors refused to do abortions, with the government then making arrangements for abortions to be carried out by a doctor from Melbourne. The Director of Public Prosecutions advised the government that it might be aiding and abetting a crime.[67]

The Tasmanian Premier recalled parliament from the end of year recess to allow the Health Minister to introduce a Private Member's Bill to clarify the law in Tasmania. The debate again highlighted the polarised nature of the abortion debate in Australia. The Premier reportedly said that his main concern was women's rights, while the Deputy Premier, who opposed the Bill, commented that this was the only area of the law that approved the destruction of a human life because someone was financially stretched.[68]

In the event, the Criminal Code Amendment Bill (no. 2) 2001 was passed by both Houses on 20 December 2001, with the assent being granted on Christmas Eve 2001. The Bill inserted a new section that said that no crime was committed if the abortion was 'legally justified'. Abortion remains subject to the Criminal Code in Tasmania. Section 165 provides the conditions under which an abortion is 'legally justified':

> two registered medical practitioners, at least one being a gynaecologist or obstetrician, have provided written certification that the continuation of the pregnancy would involve greater risk of injury to the physical or mental health of the woman (taking account of any relevant matters) than if the pregnancy was terminated, and the woman has given informed consent, unless it is impracticable for her to do so.[69]

The woman is deemed to have given 'informed consent' if the medical practitioner has provided the woman with the facts about the medical risks of abortion as well as alternatives to abortion and if he has referred her appropriately for further counselling on other related matters.

The legal justification for abortion is similar to the laws which obtain in South Australia with the broad range of factors able to be taken into account being similar to what obtains in case law in New South Wales.

1.7 How many abortions annually in Australia?

An authoritative account of the difficulties in getting reliable statistical information on abortion in Australia was published on 14 February 2005 by the Department of Library Services of the Parliament of the Commonwealth of Australia.[70] In Appendix One the authors set out the status of abortion record-keeping in the states and territories. As the authors point out, 'South Australia is the only Australian jurisdiction which both collects and routinely publishes comprehensive data on abortions'. Less comprehensive data is collected in the Northern Territory and Western Australia, but this information is not publicly available. New South Wales keeps records on abortions in public hospitals but the data is not routinely made publicly available. Victoria collects some data but there is no publicly available material on all abortions performed in that state. The Australian Capital Territory used to require the managers of abortion facilities to report certain statistics to the Health Minister under the Health Regulation (Maternal Health Information) Act 1998, but that Act was repealed in 2002. And finally, in both Tasmania and Queensland, abortion record-keeping practices were unknown to the authors at the time of publication.[71] A dearth of reliable Australia-wide, publicly available statistical data on abortion frustrates a rational debate on the social and medical implications of abortion as it is currently practised.

The authors make two important conclusions from their inquiry:

> Each of the three publicly available data sources on abortion – Medicare data, hospital data and South Australian data – can be used to estimate, in fairly crude terms, the incidence of abortion. However, none of these, either singularly or in combination, can be used to quantify *accurately* the number of abortions which take place in Australia each year.

> Accordingly, calls for accurate or 'truthful' information on the number of abortions in Australia will not be able to be answered, unless modification of current systems of statistical collection takes place.[72]

Estimates of the numbers of abortions in Australia have been between 70 000 per annum and 100 000 per annum, with 90 000 being the mean between the two positions. Put another way it has been suggested that as many as 2 in 5 diagnosed pregnancies end in abortion, with an estimate of 1 in 4 pregnancies ending in abortions, being the more conservative and widely used estimate.

1.8 Some observations

This brief survey of the history of abortion law reform in Australia and the debates which have been conducted on the issue allow us to make a number of observations:

1. The criteria for 'lawful abortions' vary between the states and territories.

2. The likelihood is, that despite those differences there is, in fact, not much difference in abortion practice.

3. It is currently impossible to get *accurate* statistics on the number of abortions being performed in Australia and the reasons for them. To obtain an accurate picture of the current state of affairs there would need to be significant changes to the way abortion statistics are collected and made publicly available, perhaps along the lines of the South Australian model. Until that occurs much of the abortion debate must remain uninformed.

4. The parliamentary debates in the various federal, state and territory legislatures have strongly revolved around the 'right to life' and 'right to choose' polarities. Until the Southern Cross Bioethics Institute survey, knowledge of where the community stands on abortion has been quite incomplete. It would now seem that

some of the initiatives rejected in some parliaments were in tune with community expectations.

5. One of the reasons why some of the initiatives referred to in the previous point were rejected was because of the deep-seated mistrust between the major public protagonists in the abortion debate.

6. The abortion debate cannot be contained or frustrated by one side declaring itself to be the winner for all time.

7. Much of the rhetoric used in the abortion debate consists of 'assertions' and 'personal beliefs' which those who hold them do not always submit to critical scrutiny.

It seems to us that continuing to restrict the debate around the 'right to life' and 'right to choose' polarities is unlikely to produce outcomes which are in tune with what most Australians say they want where abortion is concerned. The range of abortion-related issues about which the community is concerned will continue to receive short shrift in the ideological battleground which has characterised the Australian abortion debate unless community leaders agree to find other ways through the abortion mine-field, ways which we have identified in chapter eleven of this book.

Chapter 2

Analysis of new data on Australian attitudes to abortion, pregnancy counselling and alternative ways to reduce the frequency of abortion in Australia

John Fleming

In the first chapter the attitudes of legislatures and parliaments within Australia have been exemplified by reference to parliamentary debates, legislative outcomes and case-law outcomes. But what is known of public opinion?

There have been a significant number of public opinion polls carried out to determine public attitudes to abortion and related issues. Those polls have given the supporters of a pro-choice position a fair degree of comfort that their views are shared by the wider community. But the vast majority of this research, such as it is, does not reach below the surface. It seems to be limited only to finding some measure of the degree to which Australians would agree with a broad proposition about abortion on demand. Some research has gone a little deeper, but not to the extent needed to get a real feel for the complexity of attitudes to abortion, which might assist our understanding of the preferences of Australia where social policy is concerned.

There are significant and identifiable limitations on the social research previously carried out in Australia. They include the following:

- It is not designed to distinguish between people's views on when abortion should be legally available and when it is morally acceptable, merely asking people whether they approve or disapprove of abortion in particular circumstances.[1]

- It only asks whether people think abortion should be legal in particular circumstances, perhaps presuming that this indicates moral approval or disapproval for abortion.[2]

- It has not measured the strength of this approval or disapproval.[3]

- Generally, it does not distinguish various situations in which people might approve or disapprove of abortion.

- There has been little or no attempt to ascertain what areas of agreement on the abortion issue there may be among Australians, focusing principally on the areas of disagreement.

The year 2004 was characterised by a new interest in the subject of abortion, partly fuelled by members of the federal parliament, and partly by the mass media. This debate, like most of those previously conducted in Australia, was dominated by the usual suspects and conducted at full volume. Lost in the debate was any reference to the views of the community as a whole, and the more so since very little about those attitudes was known.

The key questions, which were of interest to the present writer, included the following:

- How far, and to what extent, do Australians support the decriminalisation of abortion, that is, abortion on demand? Are the attitudes of Australians to be simply described in terms of *for* and *against* legal abortion?

- How aware are Australians of the extent of contemporary abortion practice in Australia? Once that becomes known, are Australians satisfied with the rate of abortion?

- Do politicians and pressure groups accurately reflect the complexity of abortion views in Australia?

- Is there much support among Australians for a greater emphasis on alternatives to abortion? Or are Australians satisfied with the current status quo?

In November 2004 two of the contributors to this book, in collaboration with the Sexton Marketing Group, designed a major, four-stage research project to explore in depth the attitudes of Australians to abortion and to some other issues connected in one way or another to abortion.

2.1 First stage (quantitative)

The first stage of the research was committed to determining in as much detail as possible Australian attitudes to abortion, the strength with which those attitudes were held, and the degree of consistency with which those attitudes were held given various scenarios. This base-line data, would in turn, help determine the design of the subsequent stages. The funding for the project was made available by a businessman who wished to remain anonymous. The businessman concerned played no role in the research project beyond providing the necessary funding.

2.2 Study design[4]

The Adelaide-based Sexton Marketing Group was commissioned by Southern Cross Bioethics Institute (SCBI) in Adelaide, South Australia, to carry out a quantitative survey, using a stratified random sample of twelve hundred Australian adults, who were interviewed by telephone in the first two weeks of December 2004. The sample was comprised of adults eighteen years of age and older. Based on the latest Australian Bureau of Statistics (ABS) figures, the sample was selected to be proportionately representative of:

- each state's and territory's population in Australia;
- capital city and non-capital city populations in each state and territory; and
- the age and gender of the adult population.

With these stratification provisions, the sample was randomly selected from the published electronic white-pages telephone directory for Australia. A standard questionnaire was used to conduct each interview, using computer-aided telephone interviewing (CATI), and in accordance with the code of ethics of the Australian Market and Social Research Society of Australia.

Participation in the survey was voluntary. In order to avoid any selection bias towards adults interested in the topic of abortion, the survey was introduced as a survey on social issues, without specific mention of the topic of abortion. After agreement to participate, respondents were then given the option to decline to participate if they did not want to be interviewed on the specific topic of abortion. Three respondents declined to participate when informed that the survey may include questions on abortion.

In the case of non-response, each household selected to participate was called back, up to three times before being replaced. Ten per cent of all participants were re-contacted upon completion of the survey, to validate responses and check for interview quality - part of the requirements of the market-research quality-assurance scheme endorsed by the Australian Market and Social Research Society.

A stratified random sample of twelve hundred respondents yields a maximum statistical error of estimation of ± 2.6 per cent at a 95 per cent level of confidence. When examining the percentage of respondents who have answered a question in a particular way, it can be assumed that the sample percentage is within ± 3 per cent (conservatively rounded up) of attitudes within the general population, with a 95 per cent level of confidence in making that assumption. This also means that, as a broad rule of thumb, when comparing two percentages from this survey, a difference between them of 6 per cent or greater can be assumed to be a statistically significant difference, with a 95 per cent level of confidence in making that assumption.

It is important to note that the ± 3 per cent error of margin applies to percentages reported for the full sample (n=1200). If percentages are reported for sub-samples, the error margin increases, as follows:

Segment size	% Margin of error (95% confidence level)
900	± 3.3
625	± 4
400	± 5
300	± 6
200	± 7
100	± 10
50	± 14

Within these parameters, the results of this survey can reasonably be taken to reflect the attitudes to abortion of Australians generally.

2.3 Objectives[5]

The broad aim of the research was to generate a statistically reliable database of attitudes to abortion, with sufficient depth of analysis of public opinion to allow informed commentary on this issue. Depth of analysis has been secured by two particular aspects of the survey, namely:

- a sufficient number of detailed questions exploring public attitudes on numerous facets of the abortion issue; and

- a sample size sufficient to allow reliable segmentation based on different attitudes to abortion, as well as the strength of those attitudes.

The specific objectives of the research were to:

- identify public attitudes towards the proposition that women should have unrestricted access to abortion on demand;

- measure the level of support or opposition to selected arguments in favour of, or against, abortion on demand;

- measure the extent to which the public believes that women's rights, which are the foundation of the pro-choice argument, should be extended to include the right to have access to sufficient information to make an informed choice about whether to terminate a pregnancy or not;

- identify whether the public believes that abortion, under different circumstances, should be allowed by law, and separately, whether abortion in each of those circumstances is perceived as morally right or wrong;

- gain a measure of how positively people feel towards the choice for abortion compared with alternative choices; and

- gauge the extent to which people feel that community awareness of abortion issues should be increased.

2.4 Australians' attitudes to abortion on demand[6]

Respondents were given opportunity to say whether or not they were prepared to be interviewed on abortion, adoption, or penalties for serious crime. Those who did not want to participate in questions on abortion were thanked, and the interview went no further. The first two questions in the survey established the gender of the respondent and the age group to which the respondent belonged. Respondents were then asked for their general attitudes to abortion and two other social issues[7] before proceeding to in-depth questioning on abortion. Responses were then rated under the following categories: strongly agree, somewhat agree, neutral, somewhat disagree, strongly disagree, undecided/ can't say/no opinion, and declined to say.

The first question on abortion was as follows:

Q. 3: I will ask you now about some different social issues. Please give your own personal opinions, that is, how you feel personally on each issue. The first issue is whether women should have unrestricted access to abortion on demand, no matter what the circumstance. Do you agree or disagree with that view? [Is that strongly *agree / disagree or* somewhat *agree / disagree?]*

Table 1. Unrestricted access to abortion on demand.	
Response	**Total Sample** % (n=1200)
Strongly agree	37
Somewhat agree	25
Neutral	4
Somewhat disagree	15
Strongly disagree	19
Undecided	1
Declined to say	0
TOTAL	(101)

In summary these results show that, depending on how the question is posed[8] between 62 and 69 per cent of people think women should have unrestricted access to abortion whatever the circumstances; 27 per cent to 34 per cent disagree. This is broadly consistent with various polls over the past decade.[9] However, of those who support abortion on demand, only 37 per cent do so strongly; of those who oppose it only 19 per cent do so strongly. Nearly half the population (45 per cent) are moderate on the matter: 25 per cent somewhat agree, 15 per cent somewhat disagree, 4 per cent are neutral and 1 per cent is undecided.

When the abortion issue is defined as an issue about women's rights, a majority of the adult public (approximately 60 per cent) hold attitudes in favour of women's rights to have unrestricted access to abortion on demand with only a minority (less than 40 per cent) *strongly* agreeing that women should have the right to abortion on demand. But put another way, 63 per cent of Australians either oppose or are not strongly supportive of abortion on demand.

That support for personal choice (a woman's right) was a key factor in broad attitudes to abortion, and was substantiated by the answers received to question 6 (see opposite page). These results were checked by our commissioning questions through Newspoll in mid-April 2005. The first Newspoll question was this:

> *Q. 1: Do you agree that women should have unrestricted access to have an abortion on demand – no matter what the circumstances?*

Approximately half (51 per cent) agreed; slightly fewer (45 per cent) disagreed. A third (33 per cent) strongly agreed and a quarter (25 per cent) strongly disagreed. Sixty-seven per cent either opposed or were only somewhat supportive of abortion on demand. Forty-two per cent expressed 'moderate' views on abortion on demand, being either neutral or somewhat agreeing or disagreeing.

At about the same time (April/May) the Australian Federation of Right to Life Associations (AFRTLA) commissioned Market Facts (Qld) Pty Ltd to carry out a similar nationwide survey. In this survey the sample was asked 'Do you support abortion for any reason whatsoever, that is, abortion on demand?' They found that 59.8 per cent said, 'Yes'.[10]

Response	SCBI %	Newspoll %	AFRTLA %
Strongly agree	37	33	59.8
Somewhat agree	25	18	
Neutral	4	4	8.3
Somewhat disagree	15	20	31.9
Strongly disagree	19	25	
Undecided	1	n.a.	n.a.
Declined to say	0	n.a.	n.a.
TOTAL	100	100	100

Table 2. General attitude to abortion on demand.

2.4.1 Significant influences

Having ascertained attitudes to 'abortion on demand', we undertook to identify what had influenced these attitudes. The question was posed as follows:

> *Q. 6: I will now ask you a few extra questions on one of those issues, and for your interview it will be the topic of abortion. Please try to give open and honest opinions because we recognise that some people hold strong views but others do not, and there are many different views in the community. We are not trying to judge or influence your views in any way. You mentioned earlier that you (Refer to answer given in Q3. strongly/somewhat; agree/disagree) with the idea of abortion on demand. What has been the one most significant or important influence on you which has caused you to think that way?*

Of those who expressed support for abortion on demand, the two issues most commonly identified were 'personal choice' (42 per cent) and 'it is my right/a woman's right to choose' (25 per cent). By contrast, among those who expressed opposition to abortion on demand, there was a wide range of issues that received support in single figures. It is important to note at this stage that the strong support for abortion on demand should be understood in terms of the abortion issue being defined as a woman's right to have unrestricted access to abortion versus a denial of those rights.

The research then went on to explore other aspects of the abortion issue to determine whether Australians' attitudes to abortion so far reported are reflective of their attitudes to abortion per se, or whether they are more a reflection of Australians' attitudes to women's rights as an independent but overlapping issue, or some combination of the two.

2.5 How many abortions are carried out annually in Australia?

There are difficulties in arriving at reliable estimates on abortion rates in Australia. The only state which collects and reports abortion numbers each year is South Australia where, in the most recent year reported, there were 5417 abortions or 17.2 per 1000 women aged 15-44.[11] This figure rose steadily from 1440 or 6.0 per 1000 in 1970. The total number seems to have stabilised in that state over the past decade. It accounts for about 1 in 4 known pregnancies that are not naturally miscarried, the other 3 in 4 of which are carried to term. 'Repeat abortions', that is, abortions amongst women who had had at least one previous surgical abortion, were 38.7 per cent. Many commentators have attempted to discern the annual number of abortions in Australia by reference to procedures carried out under specific Medicare items.[12] On this basis the number of abortions has been assessed as 73 191 in 2003-04. However, these items also include claims for 'procedures which are not pregnancy terminations per se', procedures which are 'undertaken as a result of miscarriage, foetal death, or other gynaecological conditions not necessarily related to pregnancy'.[13] Medicare figures, even if they could be accurately divined, do not account for all abortions in Australia. Many abortions, which are carried out in public hospitals, do not appear in the Medicare data.

Each of the three major, publicly available data sources on abortion – Medicare data, hospital data and South Australian data – can be used to estimate, in fairly crude terms, the incidence of abortion. However, none of these, either singularly or in combination, can be used to quantify *accurately* the number of abortions that take place in Australia each year.[14]

This is not to say that the estimates of the annual number of abortions in Australia are not a useful starting point. Many commentators project from the available data an annual surgical abortion rate Australia-wide of somewhere between 75 000 and 100 000 per annum, with most tending towards the higher figure. The Australian Bureau of Statistics estimates that there were approximately 95 200 surgical abortions in Australia in 1996 - Medicare, public hospital and privately funded.[15]

For the purposes of determining attitudes to current abortion rates, our research used two different ways to express estimated abortion numbers, both of which are conservative and cautious since we wanted to avoid any suggestion of using inflated data in gathering information on what the community thinks. Accordingly, a round figure of 90 000 was suggested, together with a more contextualised estimate of 1 in 4 pregnancies not naturally miscarried, ending in abortion. With 251 200 births in Australia in 2003, 1 in 4 pregnancies ending in abortion would put the number at around 84 000 abortions per year.[16]

2.6 What do Australians think about the annual number of abortions?[17]

In this part of the research, respondents were given information about the number of abortions conducted in Australia each year, and then asked two questions in the light of that information. The two questions were as follows:

Q. 9: With approximately 90 000 abortions conducted in Australia each year, some people we have spoken to have the opinion that there are too many abortions in Australia at present and it would be a good thing if the number of abortions was reduced. Do you agree or disagree with that point of view? [Is that strongly agree/disagree or somewhat agree/disagree?]

and

Q. 10: If ways could be found to reduce the number of abortions in Australia but still give women the right to freely choose an abortion, do you think that would be a good thing or not?

The results indicated that 64 per cent of Australians think that 90 000 abortions a year are too many and that it would be a good thing if the number were to be reduced. This confirms a similar finding in some opinion polls.[18] Even amongst those who favour abortion on demand, most (46 per cent of those strongly in favour and 60 per cent of those somewhat in favour) thought 90 000 abortions per annum were too many. An even higher proportion of those neutral (79 per cent), somewhat opposed (81 per cent), or strongly opposed (91 per cent) to abortion on demand agreed that 90 000 abortions a year were too many and that it would be a good thing if the number were to be reduced.

This sense that there are too many abortions in Australia was further enhanced by the answers to question 10 in which 87 per cent of Australians supported the idea of finding ways to reduce the number of abortions while still preserving the right to freely choose abortion. This includes 90 per cent of those strongly in favour of abortion on demand, 95 per cent of those somewhat in favour, and 89 per cent of those who are neutral towards or somewhat opposed to abortion on demand. Given that more than 90 per cent of those who support abortion on demand also support efforts to reduce abortion numbers, any description of this segment of the population as pro-abortion is misleading. More accurately, they are genuinely pro-choice. This is in line with the rhetoric used by pro-choice lobby groups who have often insisted they are not pro-abortion but they are pro-choice.

It is interesting to note that those who were strongly opposed to abortion were less favourably disposed to measures, which might decrease abortion numbers if access to abortion remained unrestricted. Nonetheless this proposal won the support of two-thirds of this cohort (67 per cent). This can be explained in terms of this group's reluctance to maintain the current legal status quo in Australia.

What this means is, that while Australians may be divided in their attitudes towards abortion on demand, they are united in the view that there are too many abortions and that it would be a good thing if the number could be reduced. It also suggests that Australians are very deeply conflicted on abortion. The depth of that conflict became even more apparent in subsequent sections of the first stage of the research project.

In the third and fourth stages of our research, we again asked the same fundamental questions about abortion attitudes. These results were also checked by the Newspoll survey referred to above, which was conducted in mid-April 2005. The survey, put to a representative sample of twelve hundred Australians, asked the following questions:

Q. 1: Do you agree that women should have unrestricted access to have an abortion on demand – no matter what the circumstances?

Approximately half (51 per cent) agreed; slightly fewer (45 per cent) disagreed. A third (33 per cent) strongly agreed and a quarter (25 per cent) strongly disagreed. Sixty-seven per cent either opposed or were only somewhat supportive of abortion on demand. Forty-one per cent expressed 'moderate' views on abortion on demand, being either neutral or somewhat agreeing or disagreeing.

Q. 2: Government sources estimate there are approximately 250 000 births and 85 000 abortions in Australia each year. This is a rate of 1 out of every 4 pregnancies ending in abortion. Do you agree or disagree that the number of abortions is too high?

Sixty-five per cent agreed. Women (68 per cent) were slightly more likely to hold this view than men (63 per cent).

Q. 3: If ways could be found to reduce the number of abortions in Australia but still give women the right to freely choose to have an abortion, do you personally agree or disagree that this would be a good idea?

Approximately 8 out of every 10 (82 per cent) Australians supported finding ways to reduce the number of abortions, while still giving women the right to freely choose abortion. The majority (58 per cent) strongly agreed with this proposition. The following table shows a comparison of the results obtained on all four occasions.

Table 3. Abortion rate and a woman's right to choose.

Question	SCBI Stage 1 December 2004 %	Newspoll April 2005 %	SCBI Stage 3 October 2005 %	SCBI Stage 4 January 2006 %
Abortion rate Too high Not too high	64 36	65	61 39	n.a.
TOTAL	100		100	
Reduce abortions, retain right to choose: Support Oppose Neutral	87 7 6	82	63 9 28	88 6 7
TOTAL	100		100	(101)

2.7 What do Australians think of a woman who aborts?[19]

The real answer to this question is difficult to assess. However, question 11 invited people to say how they felt about women faced with an unexpected pregnancy who make one of four possible decisions.

> *Q. 11: On a scale of 1 to 5 where 1 means 'very negative', 2 means 'somewhat negative', 3 means 'neutral', 4 means 'somewhat positive', and 5 means 'very positive', what number from 1 to 5 reflects your feelings towards: women who have an abortion; women who raise child on their own; women who give up child for adoption; women who raise child with partner.*

Table 4. Feelings towards women's responses to unexpected pregnancies.				
Response	**Negative** %	**Positive** %	**Neutral** %	**Total** %
Have an abortion	13	28	59	100
Raise child on their own	7	63	30	100
Give child up for adoption	9	61	31	(101)
Raise child with partner	1	74	24	(99)

The data shows that Australians have a very much higher regard for women who do not abort their child. While many vote 'neutral' in all categories, it is only in the case of abortion that the 'neutral' category is by far the greatest and, unlike the others, is higher than the sum total of those with negative and those with positive feelings.

Table 5. Feelings towards women who have an abortion.				
Response	Negative %	Positive %	Neutral %	Total %
Strongly pro-abortion	4	43	53	100
Somewhat pro-abortion	5	27	68	100
Neutral	10	21	69	100
Somewhat anti-abortion	21	15	64	100
Strongly anti-abortion	38	11	51	100

What is to be made of this? Is it possible that many people, feeling it easier to express positive feelings than negative ones for fear of being seen to be judgmental, have 'parked' their vote in the 'neutral' category? If so, does that mean that the real sense of negative feelings where abortion is concerned has been masked? In any case, positive feelings for women who choose abortion are only 28 per cent, less than half of what is expressed for women who maintain their pregnancy. Here we have the first suggestion of a deep ambivalence in the community about the practice of abortion.

The reasons for this ambivalence become clearer as more questions are asked. For example, people were asked how they rated arguments presented in favour of abortion, and then a series of arguments used in opposition of abortion. The responses represent an interesting community perception on which arguments are persuasive and which are not. The questions posed were as follows:

Q. 12: I will now read to you some opinions that other people have expressed in favour of not making any changes to the current abortion laws in Australia. As I read out each opinion, please tell me if you strongly agree, somewhat agree, or are neutral, or somewhat disagree or strongly disagree with each opinion: abortion is a woman's right; a foetus is not a person; abortion is bad but sometimes justifiable; abortion gives women control over their lives.

Table 6. Opinions re pro-abortion arguments.

Argument	Agree %	Neutral %	Disagree %	Total %
A woman's right	69	4	27	100
A foetus is not a person	42	15	42	(99)
Abortion is bad but sometimes justifiable	70	8	22	100
Abortion gives women control over their lives	75	7	18	100

Q. 13: I will now read to you some opinions that other people have expressed against abortion. As I read out each one, please tell me if you strongly agree, somewhat agree, or are neutral, or somewhat disagree or strongly disagree with each opinion: 1 in 4 pregnancies aborted is too high; abortions for lifestyle reasons are less acceptable than for health reasons; women should consider all alternatives; women should consider welfare of unborn child.

Table 7. Opinions re anti-abortion arguments.

Arguments	Agree %	Neutral %	Disagree %	Total %
1 in 4 pregnancies aborted is too high	73	14	14	(101)
Abortions for lifestyle reasons are less acceptable than for health reasons	67	9	24	100
Consider all alternatives	94	2	3	(99)
Consider welfare of unborn child	75	8	18	(101)

The data clearly indicates that the strongest anti-abortion argument is that women should consider all of the alternatives before deciding whether to have an abortion or not. This strong preference is expressed in all segments including those who are strongly pro-abortion (91 per cent), those somewhat pro-abortion (97 per cent), and those who regard themselves as neutral (96 per cent).

Again, there is strong majority agreement in all segments for the view that one in four pregnancies resulting in abortion is too many (73 per cent),[20] and that the welfare of the unborn child should be a consideration wherever possible, before deciding to terminate a pregnancy (75 per cent).[21]

The weakest anti-abortion argument is that abortion for lifestyle reasons is less acceptable than abortion for health reasons, although 49 per cent of the strongly pro-abortion segment and 69 per cent of the moderately pro-abortion segment agree with this anti-abortion argument.

On the one hand, the strongest pro-abortion arguments are about a woman's right to choose and her empowerment to make a decision, which may be bad but is, in all the circumstances, justifiable. On the other hand, these results suggest that the strongest argument against abortion is that the real empowerment of women comes not from merely giving women right of access to abortion on demand, but instead comes from women being able to make a genuinely informed choice, after being informed of the alternatives available to them. Put another way, the overwhelming majority of the sample, including an overwhelming majority of more than 90 per cent of respondents in each segment, supports the fundamental proposition that any decision about whether to have an abortion should be preceded by a proper consideration of all the alternatives.

This means that the primary debate about abortion, as represented by the issue outlined in question 3 in this survey and in many other surveys, is in fact a debate about women's rights. The pro-abortion version is to argue in favour of women's right of access to abortion. The anti-abortion version, which has strongest support in the community, is to argue in favour of empowering women with information about all of the alternatives so that women can make a properly informed choice between alternatives, that is, a woman's right to all relevant information. When presented in these terms, the anti-abortion argument to buttress the empowerment of women with knowledge of alternative choices (94 per cent support) is more strongly supported than the pro-abortion argument that women should be able to take control of their own lives by having access to abortion on demand (75 per cent support). Australians are in favour of the right of a woman to choose an abortion, but would prefer that, in practice, that right not be exercised without a full consideration of all the alternatives.

It is worth noting also that while the abortion debate in academic, legal and polemical circles will revolve around whether or not the foetus is a person, this argument turns out to be the weakest pro-abortion argument. Only 42 per cent of the community agrees with the proposition that the foetus is not a person. Looking at the attitudes of the subgroups is also instructive.

Table 8. Belief that the foetus is not a person.				
Subgroups	Agree %	Neutral %	Disagree %	Total %
Strongly pro-abortion	61	18	21	100
Somewhat pro-abortion	48	18	34	100
Neutral	29	21	50	100
Somewhat anti-abortion	21	13	66	100
Strongly anti-abortion	18	7	75	100

It would appear that the only group among whom there is majority support for the proposition that the foetus is not a person, is the group who describe themselves as strongly pro-abortion. Thereafter support for that proposition falls away sharply. Again, it needs to be said that herein lies one reason, perhaps the major reason, for the deep ambivalence within the Australian community about the practice of abortion and why it is that so many Australians are unable to give abortion moral approval, even if they are prepared to tolerate it legally.

2.8 In what circumstances should abortion be lawful?[22]

In light of earlier questions about a woman's right to freely choose abortion, it would seem likely that the Australian community would support the complete decriminalisation of abortion, so that there would be no circumstances in which an abortion carried out by the medical profession and without negligence would be unlawful. It is here that the research further reinforces the complexity of Australian views on abortion and a need for more careful and nuanced assessments of what Australians want when it comes to social policy on abortion. For, despite the fact that earlier and simpler questions found that between 62 and 69 per cent of people think women should have unrestricted access to abortion whatever the circumstances, when more detail is sought as to what in fact should be legally allowed, that initial opinion becomes much more qualified.

Table 9. Support for legal abortion in given circumstances.

Circumstances	Strongly pro-abortion % (n=444)	Somewhat pro-abortion % (n=303)	Neutral % (n=51)	Somewhat anti-abortion % (n=178)	Strongly anti-abortion % (n=225)	Total Sample % (n=1201)
Severe disabilities	91	90	77	89	66	85
Mild disabilities	79	64	54	43	29	60
Late term	48	30	24	25	16	33
Financial hardship	62	44	15	19	7	39
Change of lifestyle	49	35	14	6	5	29
Avoid cost in non-hardship cases	47	26	10	6	5	26
Woman has received no counselling on alternatives	46	23	9	14	7	27
Effect on career	49	26	12	6	5	27
Under pressure from others	33	15	14	7	4	18
A form of contraception	32	11	15	2	5	16
Choosing the child's sex	18	9	6	1	1	9
Repeated abortions	39	20	5	6	3	21
Healthy foetus, no abnormal health risks to mother	56	35	23	11	5	33

Clearly there is significant support for legal abortion in cases of foetal abnormality. And where those abnormalities are severe, there is even strong support for legal abortion among those who would ordinarily regard themselves as strongly opposed to abortion (66 per cent). Beyond those cases, though, and when specific abortion scenarios are mentioned, the level of support for legal access to abortion tends to diminish rapidly. There is some sympathy for abortion in cases of real financial hardship (39 per cent), but only minority support for abortion being legal (i.e., unrestricted right of access) under a range of other *'soft'* scenarios. This result would suggest that the attitudes measured in question 3, relating to the broad issue of women having unrestricted right of access to abortion, no matter what the circumstances, is tempered significantly when specific abortion scenarios are raised.

At first blush, the result from question 3 and the result from question 14 seem to be contradictory. Question 3 established the fact that a significant majority of respondents support a woman's right to unrestricted access to abortion, no matter what the circumstance. However, when presented with a range of possible scenarios in question 14, many of the same respondents have said that they do not support access to abortion in cases where there are no obvious foetal abnormalities or likely financial hardship caused by the child being born.

How, then, are we to understand what the community is really saying? Can these seemingly contradictory attitudes be reconciled? Two possible explanations suggest themselves as a means of reconciling those contradictory attitudes. Question 3 and question 14 are measuring different attitudes. Question 3 is measuring attitudes to women's rights. Question 14 is measuring attitudes to abortion. On this account, the general public would support a tightening of abortion laws provided that women's rights were not restricted in the process. However, when the matter of tightening up abortion laws was further tested in stage 2 (focus groups) this part of the conclusion was found to be unsustainable. This finding will be developed later.

The pro-abortion attitude measured in question 3 is held by respondents who have not considered the various circumstances under which some women might exercise their legal right to have an abortion, such as those in question 14. When presented with those types of scenarios (perhaps for the first time) many respondents feel that exercising the right to an abortion should not be automatic in all cases.

2.9 In what circumstances can abortion be said to be moral?[23]

Not everything that is legally permitted is morally acceptable to a majority of citizens. From the fact that adultery is not punishable by law, it does not follow that people would regard it as morally acceptable. To further probe the ambivalence already found among Australians, the research sample was then asked what their response would be from a personal, moral point of view to the same scenarios that were presented to them when asked to give a view on what should be legally permissible. The question asked was this:

> *Q. 15: We will go over those circumstances once more, but this time I would like to ask, regardless of what the law allows women to do or not do in each situation, how you feel personally from a moral point of view. Do you feel that abortion is morally right or wrong in each of these situations?*

Table 10. Opinions on morality of abortion.

Varying situations	Strongly pro-abortion % (n=444)	Somewhat pro-abortion % (n=303)	Neutral % (n=51)	Somewhat anti-abortion % (n=178)	Strongly anti-abortion % (n=225)	Total Sample % (n=1201)
Severe disabilities	79	71	55	65	41	67
Mild disabilities	67	47	41	32	21	47
Late term	36	21	18	12	9	23
Financial hardship	43	25	11	8	4	24
Change of lifestyle	31	11	6	1	1	15
Avoid cost in non-hardship cases	26	10	8	2	2	13
No counselling on alternatives	26	12	7	5	1	14
Effect on career	28	10	12	1	1	14
Under pressure from others	18	7	4	1	1	9
A form of contraception	17	4	2	0	1	8
Choosing the child's sex	15	5	4	0	1	7
Repeated abortions	20	8	2	1	1	10
Healthy foetus, no abnormal health risks to mother	29	10	6	3	2	15

Moral approval is clearly given to only one of the abortion scenarios presented. The only group not supportive of abortion for a severe disability is the strongly anti-abortion group. Even here, a strong minority (41 per cent) believe that abortion would be morally justified. Even where mild disabilities are discovered in the foetus, the majority of Australians do not support abortion on moral grounds. The exception here is the strongly pro-abortion group (67 per cent). So the only abortion scenario, which is perceived as morally justifiable by a majority of the sample, is in the case of severe physical foetal abnormalities. Thereafter, moral support for abortion rapidly falls away. In the absence of physical abnormalities in the foetus, even in the most strongly pro-abortion segment, only a minority of this segment believes that abortion is morally justifiable. Put another way, only a small minority of the general public finds abortion to be morally justifiable (with the exception of cases of severe physical, foetal abnormality). The response to this question lends further support to our earlier conclusion that either:

- the attitude measured in question 3 is really about women's rights, not about abortion per se, whereas question 15 is directly measuring attitudes towards abortion; or

- questions 3 and 15 are measuring two facets of the same attitude, namely a support *in principle* for a woman's right to choose, but a preference on moral grounds that women *in practice* either do not choose abortion, or only choose abortion after consideration of all the alternatives.

2.10 Public expectations in abortion provision[24]

Having established an overall picture of abortion attitudes in Australia, their complexity and subtlety, the research then moved into an inquiry as to how much people know about the abortion issue; whether they consider there is need for more public discussion on the issue or whether they considered it to be a settled question, and whether they considered it to be a debate for women only as some Australian women politicians had suggested.

The first issue to be considered was the extent to which people were aware of any risks associated with this surgical procedure at either the physical or the psychological level.

Q. 16: Are you aware of any health risks to women associated with abortions such as clinical depression, increased risk of infertility, breast cancer, or infection?

Table 11. Awareness of health risks.

Degree of awareness	Strongly pro-abortion % (n=444)	Somewhat pro-abortion % (n=303)	Neutral % (n=51)	Somewhat anti-abortion % (n=178)	Strongly anti-abortion % (n=225)	Total Sample % (n=1201)
Yes, aware	54	39	42	36	46	45
Partly aware	22	33	22	31	21	26
Not aware of any risk	25	28	36	33	33	29

Only a minority (45 per cent) of the total sample indicated that they were aware of the health risks associated with abortion, with a majority (55 per cent) indicating that they were not aware or only partly aware of the associated health risks. What was not tested was whether those who claimed awareness of health risks were in fact really in possession of the facts.

Q. 17: Do you think that health professionals should advise women of any health risks before choosing an abortion, as is done with other medical procedures?

Table 12. Opinions on health professional giving advice on risks.

Opinion	Strongly pro-abortion % (n=444)	Somewhat pro-abortion % (n=303)	Neutral % (n=51)	Somewhat anti-abortion % (n=178)	Strongly anti-abortion % (n=225)	Total Sample % (n=1201)
Yes	98	99	97	99	97	98
No	2	1	3	1	2	2

There is almost universal agreement in the sample (98 per cent agree) that health professionals should advise women of the health risks associated with abortion, as is done with other medical procedures. Especially noteworthy is that this view is evenly expressed across all segments of abortion opinion, from strongly pro-abortion to strongly anti-abortion.

Q. 18: Do you think that a woman contemplating an abortion should first be given counselling about the risks and the alternatives, or do you think she should be offered voluntary access to this information if she wants it, or is providing access to such information not necessary?

Table 13. Opinions on counselling access.

Opinions on access to counselling	Strongly pro-abortion % (n=444)	Somewhat pro-abortion % (n=303)	Neutral % (n=51)	Somewhat anti-abortion % (n=178)	Strongly anti-abortion % (n=225)	Total Sample % (n=1201)
Should have counselling	72	74	88	85	90	78
Should have voluntary access to information	27	25	9	15	10	21
Provision of information not necessary	2	0	0	0	0	1
Don't know	0	1	3	0	0	1

Again we see strong community support (78 per cent of the total sample, and more than 70 per cent in each attitude segment) for a process in which women contemplating an abortion should first be given counselling about the risks and the alternatives. It is interesting to note that the community wants women to receive this counselling rather than adopting a process by which information is merely made available on a voluntary access basis (21 per cent). There seems to be little or no support for the idea that information provision is unnecessary (1 per cent).

Q. 19: Do you think such information counselling should be given by someone independent of the abortion provider?

Table 14. Provision of counselling by independent provider.

Opinion	Strongly pro-abortion % (n=444)	Somewhat pro-abortion % (n=303)	Neutral % (n=51)	Somewhat anti-abortion % (n=178)	Strongly anti-abortion % (n=225)	Total Sample % (n=1201)
Yes	85	82	83	89	91	86
No	11	9	4	6	6	9
Don't know	4	9	13	5	3	6

The independence of the counselling from the abortion provider is strongly supported with a substantial majority of respondents in the sample (86 per cent) believing that such information counselling should be given by someone independent of the abortion provider. Again, this view is uniformly expressed across all attitude segments (more than 80 per cent).

Taken together, these results indicate a strong community preference for social policy which includes:

- greater community education on the health risks associated with abortion; and

- women, who are contemplating an abortion, receiving counselling about the risks and alternatives from a health professional who is independent of the abortion provider, before making the decision to have an abortion.

If the community believes that the abortion decision should only be taken after a full and thorough consideration of all the relevant issues, what issues are considered to be relevant? To elicit a sense for where the community stands on this the following question was then put:

Q. 20: Which of the following things do you think should or should not be taken into consideration when deciding whether to have an abortion or not?

Table 15. Support for considerations in decision-making re abortion.

Factors to consider in abortion decision	Strongly pro-abortion % (n=444)	Somewhat pro-abortion % (n=303)	Neutral % (n=51)	Somewhat anti-abortion % (n=178)	Strongly anti-abortion % (n=225)	Total Sample % (n=1201)
Moral issues	57	71	90	80	85	71
Woman's health	96	97	99	100	91	96
Religious considerations	43	50	56	61	68	53
Woman's personal circumstances	84	83	72	76	64	78
Consequences for the unborn child	70	83	91	92	85	80

From the point of view of the health and general physical and social well-being of the woman, the dominant issues to be taken into consideration are her health (96 per cent) and her personal circumstances (78 per cent). This is balanced by a need to consider the consequences for the unborn child

(80 per cent), moral issues (71 per cent), and religious considerations (51 per cent). Concern for the unborn child is expressed not only by those opposed to abortion. Seventy per cent of the strongly pro-abortion segment also regard this as a critical issue to be considered. This again underscores the deeply ambivalent feelings of Australians to abortion, not wanting to impose on the woman, but expecting her to give deep and serious consideration to moral issues and the welfare of the unborn child.

So while there may be majority public support, as measured in question 3, to uphold a right of unrestricted access to abortion on demand, the majority of the sample, including a majority of pro-women's rights respondents, do not believe that this right of access should be exercised by women without proper consideration of the risks, the alternatives, the consequences and the morality of exercising that right in different circumstances.

That being the case there is also need to discover the kinds of persons that the community regards as best placed to offer the support and counselling that the community believes is needed. The sample was asked to identify the kinds of persons to whom the provision of advice is best entrusted.

> Q. 21: *If a woman is pregnant and is not sure whether to have the child or to have an abortion, who, if anyone do you think she should talk to in order to get the best advice?* [PROBE TO 3 RESPONSES]

Table 16. People to advise in decision-making.

Unprompted responses	Strongly pro-abortion % (n=444)	Somewhat pro-abortion % (n=303)	Neutral % (n=51)	Somewhat anti-abortion % (n=178)	Strongly anti-abortion % (n=225)	Total Sample % (n=1201)
Health professionals (excluding abortion clinics)	64	66	55	69	59	64
Family/ friends	54	59	30	40	52	52
Counselling services (including psych. counselling)	43	43	39	51	36	43
Religious representatives	3	5	5	13	18	8
Anyone woman chooses	4	3	2	1	1	3
Abortion clinics	2	3	2	2	1	2
Don't know	4	5	11	5	7	5

The percentages in each column in the above table add up to more than 100 per cent because each respondent was allowed to provide up to three responses to this question. On average, respondents gave 1.7 responses each to this question, suggesting that most respondents believe that a woman contemplating an abortion should seek advice from more than one source, which in turn assumes that respondents are unsure of which is the proper or best source.

In particular, respondents felt that advice should be sought from health professionals, family/friends, and professional counselling services. Only 2 per cent of the sample felt that a woman thinking about an abortion should seek advice from an abortion clinic before making a decision. Given that family and friends (52 per cent) and counselling services (43 per cent) are two of the three clearly preferred sources from which a woman could seek advice, how visible are those counselling services to the women who need them and the family and friends who might be expected to refer them to those services? We now sought to get a measure of community awareness of the organisations that could provide help.

Table 17. Named support services.

Groups mentioned (Unprompted responses)	Strongly pro-abortion % (n=444)	Somewhat pro-abortion % (n=303)	Neutral % (n=51)	Somewhat anti-abortion % (n=178)	Strongly anti-abortion % (n=225)	Total Sample % (n=1201)
No organisations named	55	59	62	58	59	58
Health organisations	19	26	15	24	20	22
Govt depts and agencies	20	14	10	13	12	16
Health professionals	8	7	17	6	6	8
Women's associations	8	4	6	9	6	7
Religious organisations	4	5	2	3	8	5
Helplines	3	3	3	2	4	3
Non-govt, not-for-profit organisations (e.g., Red Cross)	2	1	8	0	3	2

Q. 22: Can you name any of the organisations or the types of organisations in Australia which offer support services to women during pregnancy and after the child is born? [PROBE TO 4 RESPONSES]

These results show that a majority of the total sample (58 per cent), and a majority in each attitude segment could not name a single organisation or even type of organisation, which provides assistance and support services to women during pregnancy and after the child is born. This represents almost 60 per cent of the respondents in the sample. It suggests a very significant problem for women with an unexpected pregnancy and who may be considering abortion.

The problem is that, in the previous question, 52 per cent of the sample said that a pregnant woman should seek advice from family/friends about any decision to have an abortion. How can family members/friends offer informed advice about choices if nearly 60 per cent of them have no idea which organisations offer support services to pregnant women? Moreover, people wrongly identified some places as providing abortion counselling services: government departments and agencies (16 per cent), women's associations (7 per cent) and NGOs (2 per cent).

This inability to recognise places where a woman could receive counselling on alternatives to abortion as well as the risks of abortion is susceptible to two explanations. Either such help exists but has a very low profile in the community, or such help is not readily available, which would explain why people have not heard of it.

All of this suggests that there is either a need to raise community awareness of the existence of those support services so that family/friends of pregnant women can assist them to make informed decisions based on knowledge of the support services available, or that there needs to be greater provision of these services in the community.

2.11 Public debate on abortion – is it necessary?[25]

In 2004–2005, attempts to revisit the abortion issue as a public-policy issue worthy of more public debate in

Australia met strong resistance from those who believed that the issue was a settled issue. On this account renewed public debate was seen as nothing more than an attempt by 'conservative males' to turn back the clock on women's rights. 'Women don't want a debate on abortion', declared the Liberal Senator Jeannie Ferris on ABC radio. 'We don't need this debate, we don't want this debate … why have the debate? There is no mood for this debate. There is no intention by any Australians to reopen this debate in an obvious way.'[26]

Ferris encapsulated here the defensive response of the political activist and partisan. As she saw it, her generation of women had won a debate, was very satisfied with the terms of their victory, wanted no public debate which might overturn the status quo, and especially wanted no men involved in what she saw as an essentially women's issue. But were Ferris and the political elites that she represented right to assume that the community shared her views? Specific questions on these issues were put to the research cohort.

Q. 23: Should there be more public discussion about abortion issues, or not?

Table 18: More public discussion about abortion issues.

Response	Strongly pro-abortion % (n=444)	Somewhat pro-abortion % (n=303)	Neutral % (n=51)	Somewhat anti-abortion % (n=178)	Strongly anti-abortion % (n=225)	Strongly anti-abortion % (n=225)
Yes	64	66	67	82	84	71
No	33	27	12	14	14	24
Undecided	4	8	22	4	2	5

Q. 24: Should men have an equal right to publicly comment on the topic of abortion?

Table 19. Equal right for men to comment publicly.

Response	Strongly pro- abortion % (n=444)	Somewhat pro- abortion % (n=303)	Neutral % (n=51)	Somewhat anti- abortion % (n=178)	Strongly anti- abortion % (n=225)	Total Sample % (n=1201)
Yes	65	79	75	84	85	76
No	31	17	25	10	14	21
Undecided	3	4	0	5	2	3

Q. 25: Should there be a formal public enquiry on the facts of abortion in Australia?

Table 20. Formal public enquiry on abortion facts.

Response	Strongly pro- abortion % (n=444)	Somewhat pro- abortion % (n=303)	Neutral % (n=51)	Somewhat anti- abortion % (n=178)	Strongly anti- abortion % (n=225)	Total Sample % (n=1201)
Yes	49	55	70	77	78	61
No	47	37	15	14	16	32
Undecided	4	8	15	9	6	7

Q 26: And would you describe yourself as very well informed, moderately well informed, or not very well informed on the topic of abortion?

Table 21. Degree of being informed on the abortion topic.

Degree of being informed	Strongly pro- abortion % (n=444)	Somewhat pro- abortion % (n=303)	Neutral % (n=51)	Somewhat anti- abortion % (n=178)	Strongly anti- abortion % (n=225)	Total Sample % (n=1201)
Very well informed	29	17	19	13	25	22
Moderately informed	54	54	38	50	54	53
Not very well informed	17	29	38	36	20	24
Can't say	1	0	4	0	1	1

Contrary to the position adopted by most of the female and a good number of the male members of parliament, the Australian community not only believes that there should be more public discussion about abortion issues (71 per cent), including the holding of a formal public enquiry (61 per cent), but that men and women equally have the right to participate in the abortion debate (76 per cent). This clear majority opinion is expressed across all attitude segments except in the case of a public inquiry where 49 per cent of those strongly pro-abortion give their support.

This support for public discussion is matched by the public's self-assessment that only 22 per cent regard themselves as well informed on the topic of abortion. Far from abortion being a settled issue, the Australian community seems to be conscious that it is not well informed and accordingly would welcome more public discussion and a formal public enquiry.

2.12 First stage conclusion

The first stage of the research project provided sound benchmarks for further investigations of the beliefs, attitudes, expectations, and level of knowledge of Australians on abortion and set the stage for a qualitative, focus group study of public attitudes to abortion. A qualitative study was necessary to ensure that interpretations of the first stage were soundly based.

2.13 Second stage (qualitative)[27]

This second stage of the research project was carried out by the Sexton Marketing Group and reported back to the researchers on 10 March 2005.

The main research objectives were to:

• gauge public reaction to the incidence of abortions in Australia,

• determine whether abortion is perceived as an important social issue in Australia,

- better understand attitudes towards having access to abortion on demand,

- determine whether the public believes it is desirable to reduce the number of abortions, and if so what would be the best methods to achieve this.

A total of six focus-group discussions were conducted in February 2005, with the following composition.

Table 22. Composition of focus groups.		
Venue	'Soft' supporters of abortion on demand Aged 18-65	'Soft' opposers of abortion on demand Aged 18-65
Brisbane	mixed gender	males
Sydney	males	females
Melbourne	females	mixed gender

The group participants were selected at random by independent, focus-group recruiting agencies, using a screening question 'What is your attitude towards the idea that women in Australia should have unrestricted right of access to abortion on demand, no matter what the circumstances? Do you strongly agree, somewhat agree, neither agree nor disagree, somewhat disagree, or strongly disagree with that view?' Group participants were those people who 'somewhat agreed' or 'neither agreed nor disagreed' or 'somewhat disagreed'. They were then recruited into specific group sessions based on attitudinal similarities and various gender combinations. The focus-group results across the three locations (Brisbane, Sydney and Melbourne) were very similar. There were no significant geographic differences evident in the findings. This qualitative research shed further light upon the findings of stage 1 and assisted us in refining our interpretation of that data.

The groups' findings were revealing about the way the public reacts to the incidence of abortion in Australia. Participants did not know that the incidence of abortion was so high. This was particularly the case when that rate was expressed in terms of a ratio of abortions to pregnancies. They expressed quite strong emotional reaction to this statistic, expressing concern, embarrassment, surprise, revulsion and even shock at this figure.

At the very least, group participants almost universally felt uncomfortable with this incidence figure. In some cases, it sat uncomfortably with them from a moral perspective ('that's one in four unborn Australian children who never see the light of day'). In other cases, it sat uncomfortably with them from a broader social perspective, representing some kind of 'failure' by Australians to manage the issue, and a cause for national 'shame' or at least 'concern'.

Regardless of attitude towards abortion on demand, the vast majority of group participants, across all focus groups, agreed that one in four pregnancies in Australia being terminated through medically induced abortion each year is too many. They were discomforted by this fact and believed that something should be done to try to reduce the number of abortions. This is a very important research finding. Australians might be divided in terms of their attitudes towards abortion on demand, but they are united in their view that one in four pregnancies being aborted in Australia is too many and that it would be a good thing if the number could be reduced.

What, then, did members of the focus group think should be done to achieve a reduction in the number of abortions? Definitely not by making abortion laws more restrictive. Such a strategy was not acceptable to the focus groups. This was so in spite of the strong expressions of discomfort with the incidence of abortion or its morality ('that's one in four unborn Australian children who never see the light of day'), and even though it sat uncomfortably with them from a broader social perspective, representing some kind of 'failure' by Australians to manage the issue and a cause for national 'shame' or at least 'concern'.

So, regardless of their views on abortion, group participants seemed to be committed to the idea of upholding the rights of the individual in a democratic society, including the legal right of women to choose in relation to abortion. Even those opposed to abortion felt uncomfortable with the idea of using laws to restrict a woman's right to choose. They would prefer other means of reducing the abortion rate. It is a clear and important finding of this research that there is very little public support, within the segment of the population who hold 'soft' attitudes towards abortion, to use the law as an instrument to reduce abortions if it means restricting women's right of access.

2.13.1 The focus group discussions revealed the reasons behind this view

People believe that the law is a relatively blunt instrument, which is unlikely to take into account the complexities and subtleties of each individual case where abortion is under consideration. The group participants felt uncomfortable that some women might suffer hardship, disadvantage, or psychological damage if a blanket law prevented them from having access to abortion.

There is a fear that a restriction on legal abortion will lead to an increase in 'backyard abortions', but more importantly a fear that it will result in a rise in social alienation of women who have an abortion. This concern about discriminating against some people in the Australian community on moral/ judgmental grounds was a wide-felt concern in the focus groups. In their view, Australians are a tolerant people, largely non-judgmental and fundamentally egalitarian. They believe that the rights of the individual represent one of the cornerstones of Australian democratic society.

Hence, if legal restrictions are not the answer, what social policies could be introduced to facilitate a reduction in the number of abortions while retaining the right to legal access to abortion if that is what a woman chooses? The greater proportion of the groups' discussions focused on the importance of making considered and informed decisions and acting responsibly in relation to exercising the right of choice of abortion. Regardless of their views on women's rights, most group participants held an aversion to the termination of the life of an unborn child, because their deep-seated belief is that life is precious and should be protected. Therefore, group participants felt that there is a responsibility to avoid unwanted pregnancies in the first place, but also to ensure that any pregnancy should not be terminated without the decision to do so being an informed decision.

2.13.2 What could this mean in practice?

Firstly, the focus groups believed that an essential part of the strategy should be to reduce the numbers of unwanted pregnancies among teenage girls and young women. While some members were concerned that greater sexual awareness may encourage experimentation and even promiscuity among teenagers, there was clear majority support for a school-based sex-education program which should include the issue of pregnancy and its consequences as well as the importance of acting responsibly when it comes to decisions about sexual activity. There was an acknowledgement that parents are the first educators of their children and have particular responsibilities to their children in sex education. However, countervailing circumstances included the reality that in many homes conversations about sex are difficult to manage because child or parents or both find it embarrassing or even taboo, because parents themselves may lack the knowledge or communication skills, or because in some situations the parents might not provide the best role models for their own children.

For older women (those who have left school), the prevailing view was that, if at all possible, precautions should be taken not to get pregnant in the first place, if a pregnancy is not wanted.

Group participants had a critical view of women who engaged in sex that led to unwanted pregnancies, and then used abortion as a first option to 'fix the problem'. They felt that this was irresponsible behaviour, especially if it involved multiple sex partners — partly because of the physical risk of STIs, partly because of the longer term consequences to the woman (e.g., increased chance of infertility), partly because of the cost to the health system, and partly because of the 'trivialisation' of the fate of the developing foetus.

A clear outcome from these focus-group discussions was the belief that part of the solution to too many abortions in Australia is to reduce the number of unwanted pregnancies via education strategies that encourage responsible action, and for those who engage in sexual activity to use contraception.

2.13.3 Informed decision making once pregnancy established

Once the discussion moved to the topic of women who are already pregnant but who are contemplating an abortion, group participants almost universally held the view that abortion should not be the automatic option of first choice, and that any decision about abortion should be taken in the context of a considered judgment about alternatives to abortion, as well as consideration of the risks and the consequences involved.

There were few abortion scenarios which did not fit with this view that alternatives should be considered first. The only real exception was if the pregnancy was immediately life threatening to the mother and to a lesser extent if it was established beyond doubt that the foetus had severe abnormalities. In these cases group participants held that that there were fewer moral issues surrounding abortion in these circumstances than in other cases.

At the other extreme, there was almost universal rejection of the idea of using abortion as a means of gender selection of children, or using abortion out of convenience as an alternative to contraception. Group participants felt that this type of behaviour was irresponsible and immoral, and that some form of counselling should be required in these cases. This view was held by most group participants, regardless of attitudes to abortion.

For most other abortion scenarios not involving serious health risks to the mother or serious foetal abnormality, but including teenage pregnancies, mild foetal abnormalities, pressure from family or partners to have an abortion, financial hardship, serious interruption to critical developmental periods in the woman's or teenage girl's life, the prevailing view in the focus groups was to uphold the woman's right to choose. However, participants also held that before a decision was made to have an abortion the woman needed to ensure that she had adequately considered all other alternatives and that she understood the risks and consequences of abortion.

There was a great deal of discussion about the complex, individual circumstances which can surround each woman's case, and how difficult it is to apply a simple rule which states that women should not choose abortion in specific categories of circumstance. No matter what the circumstance, group participants could not agree that abortion should never be the option chosen. However, they did agree that, in virtually every scenario, abortion should not be chosen unless the alternatives have been given serious consideration.

The common view in the focus groups was, if the alternatives, risks and consequences have been taken into account, it is likely that some women will decide not to have an abortion in circumstances where, without due consideration, they might well have chosen otherwise. Participants also held that even if abortion is chosen after due consideration, 'at least it has been an informed decision'.

2.13.4 Where does the responsibility for ensuring informed choices lie?

Focus-group participants believed that there are responsibilities on both the medical profession and the pregnant woman herself. On the one hand, it is the responsibility of the health professions to encourage women who are contemplating an abortion to go through a process of serious consideration of alternatives. On the other hand, it is the responsibility of the woman to undertake a process of serious consideration of risks and alternatives.

Therefore, the support of women's rights is balanced by a view that, with rights, come responsibilities. The responsibilities however, include the responsibility of society to encourage women themselves to take appropriate action to avoid unwanted pregnancy in the first place, and thereafter to encourage women who are pregnant and contemplating an abortion to consider the alternatives before making any decision.

2.13.5 What of late-term abortions?[28]

An important point to note about the findings of this research study is that the results need to be interpreted as a collective; and individual findings, such as focus-group reaction to only one aspect of the abortion issue, should not be taken out of context and selectively used to support a particular point of view.

An example is the finding that the focus-group participants were generally concerned about late-term abortions being available on demand, with some support for restrictions being imposed on late-term abortions. Out of context, this result might be interpreted as public support for changing the law to ban late-term abortions. However, in the broader context of public consideration of the complexity of this issue, this conclusion would be unwarranted. In the broader context, group participants felt that later term abortions may be warranted if, for example, the pregnancy posed a serious risk to the mother's health, or if the unborn child was so severely disabled that it would lead an extremely poor quality of life. Some group participants felt that there may be other compelling individual circumstances in which late-term abortions may be warranted.

Group participants favoured the idea of finding ways to reduce the number of late-term abortions without imposing a blanket ban on them. Their concern about a ban is that particular women in particular circumstances might be disadvantaged by such a ban, and they felt uncomfortable about the idea of some women being selectively discriminated against in these circumstances.

2.13.6 Fourfold strategy

This fourfold strategy for reducing the number of abortions is represented in the schematic diagram below. Essentially it is a strategy spontaneously suggested and universally endorsed by the focus-group participants and strongly supported by them as a way of balancing women's rights, on the one hand, and the moral issue of choosing abortion on the other. The strategy involves women being assisted by society to take greater responsibility for avoiding unwanted pregnancies, and for considering all of the alternatives to abortion before exercising the right to choose an abortion.

Table 23. Fourfold strategy for reducing number of abortions		
Issue	**Community responsibility**	**Individual women's responsibility**
Reduce unwanted pregnancies	Sex education, contraceptives available	Take action to avoid unwanted pregnancy
Abortion as a choice of last resort	Counselling offered on alternatives to abortion and the risks and consequences of abortion	Access counselling services so that any decision about abortion is an informed decision

In the next chapter we will look at the way in which we further refined our understanding of Australian attitude to abortion and related issues based upon these first two stages of our research project.

Chapter 3

Analysis of new data:
sex education, counselling, RU-486
and stem cell research

John Fleming

3.1 Stage 3

3.1.1 Sex education as a strategy to reduce abortions

One of the key strategies to reduce the number of unwanted pregnancies identified in the second stage of the report was the use of sex education in schools. As we see in chapter four of this book, there is little evidence to support the efficacy of existing sex-education programs as a means of reducing unwanted pregnancies. However, at first blush the community appeared to think differently. What we needed to discover, in detail, was the level of knowledge in the community about the nature and content of sex-education programs; who has been responsible for the design of the programs; whether the content of the programs and style of teaching reflect parental expectations; and the extent of parental access to the development and implementation of these programs.

The third stage of the research dealt with these questions and many others besides. In May 2006 The Sexton Marketing Group, using the same research techniques described in the first-stage quantitative study, examined the depth and reach of Australians' knowledge where sex education is concerned. The research found that 92 per cent of Australians support sex education in schools.[1] This level of support should be compared to the levels of support that the community has for other strategies to reduce the number of abortions in Australia.

Q.7: I will list some possible ideas to reduce the number of abortions in Australia, and I would like you to tell me, for each one, if you strongly oppose, somewhat oppose, or are neutral, or somewhat support, or strongly support each idea as a way of reducing the number of abortions in Australia.

Table 1. Support for strategies to reduce abortions.	
Strategy	**Support %**
Reduction of poverty	81
Greater restrictions on sexually explicit media content	58
Greater respect for women who decide to have a child	88
Access to voluntary counselling about alternatives	94
Compulsory counselling about alternatives	64
Greater financial incentives to have children	49
Counselling about the health risks of abortion	91
Greater effort to support pregnant woman by family agencies	86
Better information for women about their fertility	94
Greater communication between women and their partners	89
Restriction of legal access to abortion in some circumstances	40

It needs to be understood, then, that Australians are not saying that they would rely on only one strategy. On the contrary the evidence is that the public supports a raft of strategies to reduce abortions, among which sex education in schools is one of the most strongly supported.

Of the 92 per cent support for sex education in schools, 84 per cent 'strongly' support and 8 per cent 'somewhat' support this strategy with 74 per cent believing sex education should be compulsory. When asked, *Do you, or would you, support a child of your own receiving sex education at school as part of the curriculum, or not?* (Q.9), 95 per cent said that they would.

Most (57 per cent) believe that sex education is most appropriate at the onset of puberty (11–13 years of age), with 31 per cent holding that it should occur earlier.

In question 11 respondents were then asked:

Would you prefer to have a sex-education curriculum developed at a national level for all schools in Australia, or at a state level, or at an individual-school level?

Sixty-six per cent supported the idea of a national sex-education curriculum (standard and set at a national level) as opposed to individual state-based curricula (16 per cent) or individual-school curricula (11 per cent).

There is strong support for a multi-faceted input into the development of an appropriate curriculum, including input from:

Table 2. Components of multi-faceted input into curriculum.	
Components	**%**
The Federal Government	71
State governments	88
Independent schools	79
Teachers	80

Parents	80
Major church groups	41
Sex-education experts	92
The medical profession	95
Successful curricula developed in other countries	87

3.1.2 Sex education: content and delivery[2]

Having established that there is a strong preference for sex-education programs to be taught in schools, programs into which there has been input from the broader community including parents, we then asked a series of questions about what the program content should be and who should teach it. A commonly expressed division of opinion within the community concerns the appropriateness of teaching 'safe sex' practices and the appropriateness of encouraging sexual abstinence as the primary strategy. Respondents were asked:

> *Q. 13: As a broad principle, do you think a sex-education program in schools should be more about encouraging teens not to engage in sexual intercourse at least until they reach adulthood, or do you think such programs should be about what to do to avoid sexually transmitted diseases and unwanted pregnancies if they have sexual intercourse?*

Table 3. Support for components of sex education program.

Components	% Support
Safe-sex practices	53
Sexual abstinence	21
Both	23

When given a forced choice between the two positions, 66 per cent of respondents said they would prefer a curriculum that educates about safe-sex practices, with 28 per cent preferring a curriculum emphasising sexual restraint until later years.

This result probably reflects parental acknowledgment that teaching abstinence may be a useful short-term objective, but for the longer term teaching safe-sex practices is probably of more utility (given that this is likely to be the only formal education which their child will ever receive on this topic both before and during adulthood).

The interpretation of these results needs to take into account a later question about community attitudes to the sexual behaviour of young people. When taken together it becomes clear that parents do not support sexual promiscuity. When asked if they would prefer that their child abstained from sexual activity until meeting a permanent partner, 50 per cent indicated that they would prefer this, with 44 per cent 'not objecting' to their child having more than one relationship providing that they engage in safe-sex practices before settling into a permanent relationship. This was established by describing two different scenarios for respondents to consider.

> *Q. 21*: Parent Smith and Parent Jones have two quite different views about their own children.
>
> Parent Smith says: '*Ultimately it is my son's or daughter's choice, but I would prefer that they waited until they meet the person they want a permanent relationship with before they enter into a sexual relationship.*'
>
> Parent Jones says: '*I don't object to my son or daughter having more than one sexual relationship as long as they practice safe sex before settling into a permanent relationship.*'
>
> Which of those two opinions more closely reflects your own opinion — the first, Parent Smith, or the second one, Parent Jones? [Is that strongly/ somewhat agree with?]

Response	Support %	Oppose %	Neutral %	Total %
Table 4. Parental attitudes to sexual activity of children.				
Strongly agree with Parent Smith	41	34	24	36
Somewhat agree with Parent Smith	15	14	13	14
Neutral/agree equally with both	5	1	6	5
Somewhat agree with Parent Jones	15	20	16	16
Strongly agree with Parent Jones	22	32	39	28
Can't say	2	-	3	2
TOTAL	100	(101)	(101)	(101)

Moreover, when asked (Q. 22), *As a broad principle, should sex-education programs in schools reflect the values and ideals which are taught by parents in the family home, or should such programs be developed purely as facts about sex without any reference to family values?* 57 per cent said that they believed that sex-education program content should reflect family values and ideals, with 35 per cent believing that such programs should be value-neutral (i.e., purely factual without any reference to family values).

This strong insistence on the role of the family in sex education was further underscored when respondents were asked:

> *Q. 20a: Compared with the school, do you think parents should play no role, or a secondary role to the school, or an equal role, or a primary role in the sex education of their own children?*

Eighty-four per cent of Australians believe that parents should play at least an equal role (39 per cent) or a primary role (45 per cent) in the sex education of their own children, relative to the role played by schools, compared with 13 per cent who believe that parents should play a minor role (11 per cent) or no role (2 per cent). But when asked (question 20b), *Do you think that parents have too much say, or enough say, or not enough say in what should or should not be included in sex-education programs in schools?* it was clear that 35 per cent thought that parents do not have enough say and a further 31 per cent did not know what level of influence parents have on sex-education curricula in schools. Only 28 per cent thought parents had enough say with a further 6 per cent believing parents had too much say.

Given the strong community preference for parental involvement in the development of sex-education programs we next looked at what, in fact, parents know about the content of existing programs and the degree to which they would feel able to be heard when voicing their concerns. When questioned (Q.7), *How familiar are you with the content of sex-education programs currently being run in schools? Would you say very familiar, somewhat familiar, not very familiar, or not at all familiar?* a total of 74 per cent indicated that they are not familiar with the content of sex-education programs. Eighteen per cent said they are not very familiar, and 56 per cent said they are not at all familiar with the content of sex-education programs currently being run in schools.

Respondents were next asked:

Q. 18: Based on what you know about the content, do you approve of all of the content, or only some of the content or none of the content?

Given the lack of familiarity with the content of programs, it is perhaps not surprising that only 28 per cent could say they approved of the full content of sex-education programs, with a further 18 per cent saying they could approve of some of the content, and 54 per cent could not indicate approval or disapproval due to their lack of knowledge of the content. Ignorance of the content of sex-education programs was matched by a complete lack of knowledge (89 per cent) as to who had actually developed the sex-education curricula currently being used in Australian schools. And all of this despite the fact that 95 per cent of Australians believe that parents should have some form of access to the sex-education materials.

We also wanted to find out who Australians believe should be teaching sex-education programs in our schools: a generalist teacher or someone specifically trained and qualified in this area with a specialised knowledge. Respondents were also asked:

> Q. 15: *Who do you think should run a sex-education program in schools? Should it be the school's teachers, or trained educators who do the rounds visiting each school?*

Eighty per cent of Australians believe that trained educators should visit schools to conduct the programs, with only 15 per cent nominating the school's own teachers as the preferred educators. It is not known whether this reflects dissatisfaction with the current standard of sex education in schools or reflects the importance that Australians attach to this subject in the current climate. What is known is that Australians are by no means confident that education authorities would listen to or take action to meet their concerns about sex-education courses if they were to speak out on them. Respondents were asked:

> Q. 20c: *From what you have seen or heard, when parents speak out about the content of sex-education programs in schools, do the education authorities who run those programs tend to listen and act upon parents' wishes or not?*

While 17 per cent believe that the education authorities listen and act on parents' wishes, 32 per cent believe that the authorities tend not to listen or act on their wishes. More than half (51 per cent) are unsure of the response by education authorities to parental wishes.

So, our research has established that the Australian community:

- is strongly supportive of sex-education programs in Australian schools;
- believes such programs to be a necessary strategy to reduce the number of unwanted pregnancies and with it the number of abortions in Australia;
- expects sex-education programs to reflect family values;
- expects that parents be involved in the development of the materials;
- is largely ignorant of the content of sex-education programs and the identity of their authors; and
- lacks confidence that education authorities would take their concerns about sex education seriously.

Having asked a wide range of questions about the community's knowledge of and attitudes to sex education in schools, we then revisited the question of sex education as an effective strategy to reduce the numbers of unwanted pregnancies:

Q.22b: Do you think sex education in schools has the effect of decreasing unwanted teenage pregnancies, or increasing unwanted teenage pregnancies, or has little or no effect on teenage pregnancy rates?

While 92 per cent of the respondents said at the beginning of the stage 3 questionnaire that they favoured sex education as a strategy to reduce the numbers of unwanted pregnancies and therefore the numbers of abortions, and having answered a raft of other questions on the subject dealing with their knowledge of such programs, now only 53 per cent of respondents were prepared to say that they actually believed that sex education in schools decreases unwanted pregnancies. Of the rest, 4 per cent believe that sex education in schools increases unwanted pregnancies and 43 per cent believe that such programs either have no effect (30 per cent) or do not know what effect they have (13 per cent).

3.1.3 Public education programs for women past school age

Even more tellingly, respondents did not know that school-aged girls who were receiving sex education did not represent the majority of women who had abortions.

> *Q. 23: On the broader topic of abortion now, were you aware that most abortions conducted in Australia involve women over 18 who have left school, and not teenage girls?*

Since 63 per cent of the sample did not know this, it is not unreasonable to conclude that sex education has a limited impact in preventing unwanted pregnancies. That being the case, what strategies could be put in place to reach those women at risk of an unplanned pregnancy and who are no longer at school? We tested the degree of public support there might be for the expenditure of public funds on public education campaigns by asking the following:

> *Q. 24:One strategy to reduce abortions among adult women is to run a public education campaign on how to avoid unplanned pregnancies. Do you agree or disagree with public funds being spent on such a campaign if the aim is to reduce unplanned pregnancies and to reduce the number of abortions? [Is that strongly or somewhat agree / disagree?]*

Seventy-nine per cent of Australians agree (60 per cent strongly agree, 19 per cent somewhat agree) with the expenditure of public funds on a public education campaign on how to avoid unplanned pregnancies, as part of a strategy to reduce the number of abortions. A total of 14 per cent of Australians would disagree (8 per cent strongly disagree, 6 per cent somewhat disagree) with such a use of public funds.

Q. 25: Which of the following ideas do you think should form part of such a campaign, if the campaign was run by the federal government?

Table 5. Campaign Strategies.	
Strategy	**% Support**
An information website	85
A free booklet or CD / DVD available on request	88
A booklet distributed to every household	46
Information available from local GPs	95
An information counselling hotline	91
Free seminars	71

All of the above suggestions received strong support except the delivery of a booklet to every household, perhaps indicating either that the seeming imposition of information and advice on people is unwelcome or that people are aware that such a scattergun attempt at communication is likely to be ineffective.

3.1.4 Counselling women on risks and alternatives[3]

The second main strategy endorsed by Australians to reduce abortion numbers by non-coercive means was the provision of counselling services to provide women with information about the risks of having an abortion and knowledge about the alternatives to abortion.[4] In stage 3 we decided to identify the kinds of public initiatives which would meet community expectations where counselling is concerned, including the kinds of things that such counselling should be designed to cover. The following question was put to respondents:

> *Q. 26: One of the ideas suggested for women who are pregnant and thinking about having an abortion is to make counselling available to these women about alternatives to abortion and also about the risks of having an abortion, so that any decision they make is a fully informed decision – do you agree or disagree with the idea of making these sorts of counselling services available? [Is that strongly or somewhat agree / disagree?]*

We found that 95 per cent support (80 per cent strongly, 15 per cent somewhat) the idea of making counselling available to pregnant women about the alternatives to abortion and about the risks involved in having an abortion. When it came to the right of women to be informed as to any risks associated with the abortion procedure, there was near unanimous support, no doubt based upon the right of women to give or withhold consent to undergo such a procedure based upon all relevant knowledge. So, in answer to Q. 27, *Should a pregnant woman thinking about an abortion be advised of the health risks involved, as is done for any other surgical procedure?* 99 per cent of Australians believe that women thinking about having an abortion should be advised of the health risks involved, as is done for other surgical procedures.

Given the (virtually) unanimous support for information on health risks to be provided to women thinking of having an abortion, we needed the community to confront question 28 as to who they thought would be best placed to provide this advice:

> *Q. 28: Who do you think should provide this advice on the health risks – should it be her local GP, or a health counsellor referred to by the GP, or should it be the doctor in the abortion clinic?*

While 44 per cent believe that any or all of these should provide advice on the health risks to the women concerned, a further 36 per cent believe that this advice on the health risks should come from the local GP, 8 per cent believe it should come from a health counsellor referred to by the GP, and 11 per cent believe the abortion clinic should provide the advice. This strong confidence in general practitioners to provide advice on risks formed the background to community expectations that GPs are the best gatekeepers for referral for abortion.

Next, question 29 was put to the respondents:

> Q. 29: *Under the current law, a pregnant woman can go directly to an abortion clinic, without consulting anyone first, ask for an abortion, and have the abortion that day, without any questions asked about the reasons or the circumstances. Is this acceptable in your view, or do you think that a woman thinking about an abortion should first be required to get a referral to an abortion clinic by her local GP?*

In reply, 66 per cent of Australians believe that a woman thinking about an abortion should be required to obtain a referral from her local GP to an abortion clinic. Only 29 per cent find the current situation acceptable, namely that a woman can go directly to a clinic without any prior consultation.

Such is the seriousness of the need to make an informed decision and without undue pressure from others or from circumstances that 74 per cent of Australians believe that there should be a compulsory 'cooling off' period to give a woman who has requested an abortion time to consider her decision more fully (Q. 30a.). A total of 21 per cent support women having same day access to the abortion procedure with no cooling-off period.[5] When asked Q. 30b: *If there was going to be a cooling-off period, how long do you think that should be? Would you say 2 days, 7 days, 14 days, or some other length of time?* 40 per cent believe that a seven-day cooling-off period is appropriate, 24 per cent believe two days is sufficient, while 19 per cent believe that a cooling-off period of longer than seven days is appropriate. That is to say, 59 per cent of Australians would endorse a 'cooling off' period of at least seven days.

The degree of strength with which Australians believe that while women have a right to choose abortion, at the same time they have an obligation to make that an informed choice, is reinforced by the belief of 89 per cent of Australians that GPs should be required by law to disclose the health risks of abortions to patients. When asked Q. 32: *Which of the following pieces of information do you think it should be compulsory for the doctor to give to the patient who is considering an abortion?* respondents were virtually unanimous in thinking that anything that would impact on that woman's health should be revealed to the patient by the GP. A majority of respondents (53 per cent) believed that it should be compulsory also to show the stage of development of the foetus by models, pictures, or via an ultrasound.

Q. 32: Which of the following pieces of information do you think it should be compulsory for the doctor to give to the patient who is considering an abortion?

Table 6. Support for information given prior to abortion.	
Information	**% Support**
Explaining the health complications which can occur during surgical abortion procedures	96
Explaining the mental-health risks	93
Showing the risks of infertility	94
Showing the stage of development of the foetus with models/diagrams	53

Respondents also believed (Q. 33a.) that while counsellors should discuss abortion as one option while presenting and discussing all of the alternatives to abortion (77 per cent), counsellors should not try in any way to influence the woman's decision (80 per cent). It is the woman who should make the final decision (Q. 33b). But 85 per cent of Australians also believe that there should be a 'legal requirement on the GP to inform the patient that counselling is available on the alternatives to abortion' (Q. 34).

By far the greatest concern is for women to have access to counselling if they are considering abortion for reasons not related to the health of either the mother or her foetus:

> *Q. 35: Often the reasons for a woman wanting an abortion relate to financial or career pressures, social or family pressures, not knowing how to balance the demands of a new baby with other demands, feeling isolated with no one there to help, being afraid of what the future holds, and so on. Often these women would prefer not to have an abortion, but don't know what else to do. Do you support the idea of women in these sorts of situations having access to counselling about alternatives to abortion, or not?*

In these circumstances, 96 per cent believe that women in such situations should have access to counselling about the alternatives to abortion.

The research has revealed a high level of confidence in Australia's general practitioners as well as high expectations of the way in which they would like GPs to manage patients requesting an abortion. Apart from the expectations already described above, Australians not only see great importance in GPs as providers of information in relation to the risks associated with the abortion procedure and its aftermath, but also as strong agents of influence to get their patients to consider all alternatives before exercising their legal right to have an abortion. On this latter issue, Australians so strongly believe in the provision of counselling for alternatives that they want such counselling to be compulsory, not optional. Indeed, in response to Q. 38: *Should it be compulsory for women wanting an abortion to go through such a counselling service to ensure that they are aware of the alternatives available to them?*

62 per cent opted for compulsion and 33 per cent for not making it compulsory.

Where alternatives to abortion are concerned, the majority of Australians (55 per cent) believe that this is best dealt with by specialist counselling groups, and 24 per cent think the GP is best placed. However only 11 per cent believe an abortion clinic is best equipped to offer such counselling. Importantly, 61 per cent of Australians 'think GPs should actually recommend that such patients use counselling services in order to ensure that any decision they make is a fully informed one,' with a further 36 per cent thinking 'the GP should just make them aware of the services'.

3.1.5 Who should counsel and on what?[6]

There being a strong consensus among Australians for the provision of counselling for alternatives to abortion, the research next sought to discover community expectations of what range of topics should be covered and who should provide the counselling services. It has already been established that the counselling should be non-directive, that the patient be free to make her own decision at the end of the process, and that counsellors should not attempt to impose their own views on patients.

In our research we first sought an opinion of the kinds of topics that should be raised in the counselling sessions. A raft of topics was suggested, and community support gauged.

Q. 39: If such a counselling service was available, which of the following counselling topics do you think would help women to consider alternatives to abortion?

Table 7. Opinions re helpful counselling topics.			
Counselling discussion areas	Yes %	No %	Don't Know %
Options for continuing education or training, or returning to work after childbirth	85	9	6
Involving the woman's partner or family in supporting her during the pregnancy and after childbirth	88	7	5
Household budgeting and financial support available when the baby is born	90	7	3
Ways to balance career and parenthood	92	6	3
A network of other pregnant women and mothers with young babies who thought about abortion but decided against it	83	13	4
Support agencies and groups in the community who will reduce any sense of loneliness, isolation, or helplessness during the pregnancy	94	3	3
Understanding how to handle rejection from family and friends	92	5	3
Analysis of why the woman considered an abortion, and exploring the alternatives which might provide a satisfactory solution to her needs	89	6	5

Here we can see strong, even overwhelming, community support for each of the above topics to be included in the counselling services provided by those accredited to provide such services. But who should be accredited to receive public funding to provide these services? We put that question to the respondents.

Q. 40: *Which of the following groups in the community do you believe are well equipped to offer this type of comprehensive counselling service on alternatives to abortion, and to be able to put pregnant women in direct contact with the relevant support agencies for women who are pregnant or who have new born children?*

Table 8. Groups best equipped to assist.			
Groups	Yes %	No %	Can't say %
Local GP	68	27	6
Other health professionals such as psychologists or social workers	85	11	5
Federal and state governments	41	50	9
Specialist counsellors set up specifically to counsel on alternatives to abortion	89	8	2
Professional counselling agencies such as Centacare and Anglicare which are affiliated with major churches in Australia	64	30	6
Abortion clinic	68	27	5

While all of the above groups received approval from the community, that approval is not unconditional. As can be seen from earlier questions, there is an expectation that providers of these services should be professional, non-directive, respect the right of the woman to make her own decisions, and be independent, especially from abortion providers.

3.1.6 Who should be present at counselling sessions?[7]

Apart from the woman being counselled, we thought it would be interesting to test what the community thinks about the partner and family members being part of the counselling process. A clear and substantial majority of Australians (70 per cent) believe that the counselling process for a pregnant woman *should* also include her partner, with only 9 per cent indicating that the partner should not be included and 20 per cent saying that inclusion or exclusion of the partner depends upon the circumstances. However, a clear and substantial majority of Australians (79 per cent) also believe that the partner should have no independent right of access to the counselling sessions, and that the woman's *consent* would be required for him to be able to be present.

Where members of the family are concerned only 33 per cent think that family members *should* be at the counselling, but 89 per cent believe that it is up to the woman to decide whether or not to include other family members.

Anecdotally, there have been reports of women who have felt pressured into having an abortion. That there is something in this is supported by the fact that at least 23 per cent of the respondents said they were aware of someone who had been pressured into an abortion against her wishes. In situations like this, 67 per cent of the survey respondents believe that those people who place pressure upon a woman to have an abortion against her wishes *should* receive counselling about the alternatives. Twenty-four per cent do not believe that these people should be counselled.

3.1.7 Underage girls and abortion without parental consent[8]

One of the most controversial aspects of the contemporary practice of medicine is the legal provision made by Australian parliaments for underage girls to be able to seek and receive medical assistance without parental knowledge and consent.

Abortion is a particular instance of the medical assistance that may legally be provided under these conditions. We thought it might be useful to test how far the community accepts the provision of abortion to underage girls without parental consent.

> *Q. 43: Under the present law, an underage girl can ask for and receive an abortion without any parental consent and without parents even knowing that it has happened. Do you agree that this is reasonable, or do you think abortion should only be available to girls under 16 with parental consent?*

Table 9. Availability of abortion to under-aged.	
Response	**Support** %
Available without parental consent	28
Available only with parental consent	63
Can't say	9
TOTAL	100

There is a clear community preference, to put it no more strongly, that the community wants parents to have the final say in the matter of abortion where their under-age children are concerned.

It is interesting to note, however, that a bare majority of Australians (51 per cent) would support a parental decision to put a daughter under sixteen years of age on the contraceptive pill to avoid an unwanted pregnancy. One quarter of the population would prefer the parents to take more responsibility over the social life of their teenage children and their contact with members of the opposite sex, with another 22 per cent believing that any response they would give would depend on the situation.

3.1.8 Who should fund abortion and on what conditions?[9]

In response to Q. 45: *In your view, should all abortions be funded by Medicare as they are now, or should some types of abortions not receive Medicare funding?* 62 per cent said that they believed all abortions should be funded by Medicare, while 29 per cent said that some abortions should not be funded by Medicare. It is interesting to note that there was significant difference in the degree of support for Medicare funding of abortion between those who support abortion (59 per cent), and those who either oppose abortion (67 per cent) or are more neutral in their attitudes to abortion (68 per cent).

Moreover, access to Medicare funding of abortion ought to be, in the view of a significant majority (65 per cent), conditional upon the woman first receiving counselling about the alternatives. However, 30 per cent do not support this pre-condition for Medicare funding.

3.1.9 Effectiveness of financial strategies to reduce abortion numbers[10]

This part of the research now addressed community attitudes about the effectives of particular financial measures, which could be taken to reduce the number of abortions by non-coercive means in line with community expectations as to what Australian public policy should be.

First, we established that 67 per cent of the community think that the provision of counselling services about abortion and about alternatives to abortion would reduce the number of abortions in Australia. Twenty per cent believe it would not reduce abortions, with 13 per cent unsure.

Next, a broad financial question was put to respondents:

Q. 48: The theme in this survey has been how to reduce the abortion rate in Australia. Do you think that financial incentives, that is, making it more financially attractive to women to have their baby rather than have an abortion, might work?

Forty-seven per cent believe that financial incentives to encourage pregnant women to go full-term and give birth to their child might work as a strategy to reduce the number of abortions, but 40 per cent do not believe this would be an effective strategy, and 13 per cent are unsure. However, when a number of financial initiatives were put, there was greater confidence in particular strategies that did not just involve giving people more money.

Q.49: I will list some possible financial strategies and ask if these are likely to work to reduce the abortion rate.

Table 10. Support for financial strategies.

Financial Strategies	Yes %	No %	Don't know %
Raising public awareness of the full range of financial payments and benefits to which parents are entitled	62	35	3
Increasing the amount of those benefits	42	50	9
Encouraging employers to adopt more generous parental leave entitlements	70	26	4
Making it a legal guarantee that employers must reinstate an employee at the same pay level after maternity or paternity leave is finished	75	21	3
Encouraging employers to offer flexible working hours and part-time work to employees with young babies	86	12	2
Allowing a parent to bring their baby to work to be cared for in an on-site baby crèche	76	20	4
Granting special concessions to parents with young babies for the first 12 months, such as discounted public transport, goods and services	71	26	3
Giving new parents access to a strong community network of support including help with the baby, social outings, making friends with other new parents, and childcare services	86	12	2
Making it easier for women to return to work or complete their education and training	90	8	2
A fund contributed to by both employers and employees to fund substantial maternity and paternity leave such as up to 12 months on full or part pay	67	27	7
More childcare places and more funding for childcare	86	12	1

3.1.10 Observations from stage 3[11]

The evidence in the research suggested broad community support for a wide range of social-policy initiatives that ought to be taken at federal and state government levels. It is clear that Australians support a woman's right to have a legal abortion if that is what she chooses. But, equally, Australians are deeply disquieted about the morality of abortion and about the incidence of abortion in Australia. They want the numbers of abortions reduced while still preserving women's legal right of access to abortion.

The deep ambivalence about abortion suggests that Australians have accepted the essential messages of both sides to the abortion debate. Australians are both pro-choice and pro-life. They support a woman's right to choose an abortion but would prefer that, in practice, this right was not acted upon, that abortion in Australia was, comparatively speaking, a rare event. That being the case, Australians are open to a wide range of initiatives which they hope or believe would assist women facing pregnancy in personally distressing circumstances to make choices other than abortion.

The survey shows strong public support for, and confidence in, the introduction of counselling services for pregnant women (who are thinking of an abortion) about the alternatives to abortion.

The majority believe that this is a good strategy and that it will work to reduce the number of abortions, by giving women the information they need to make an informed decision without denying them right of access (under the current law) to abortion services.

There is also strong support for sex education in schools, but less confidence that it will work as a strategy to further reduce unplanned pregnancies. This is because sex education is already in place in most schools, whereas the counselling services proposed are a new service. The only way in which current sex-education programs can have a greater impact on the number of unplanned pregnancies is to review and overhaul the content of these programs to place greater emphasis upon encouraging behaviours which reduce unplanned pregnancies.

The general public believes that there should be a national approach to this, and that there should be consistency between what parents teach in the home and what is taught in such programs in schools.

In terms of financial support, a majority do not believe that increasing direct financial support to pregnant women will reduce the number of abortions, but a majority believes that independent financial support will help to achieve that outcome, in particular:

- more childcare places,
- greater workplace flexibility,
- greater opportunity to return to work, training or education for mothers with young children,
- a more active community support network for pregnant women and mothers with young children.

3.1.11 Federal Government initiatives

Some time after the completion of stage 3 of the research project there were suggestions that the federal government might announce a number of new initiatives in social policy to address the problems already identified by our research. Indeed, on 2 March 2006 such an announcement was made and read thus:

> The Government has decided to introduce a new Medicare payment for pregnancy-support counselling by general practitioners and, on referral, by other health professionals. This will provide additional support and information to women who are anxious about their pregnancy. Women who have had a pregnancy in the preceding 12 months will also benefit by being able to access pregnancy-support counselling under Medicare.

The Government will also fund a National Pregnancy Support Telephone Helpline, which will provide professional and non-directive advice 24 hours a day, seven days a week. The Helpline will provide assistance to women, their partners, and family members who wish to explore pregnancy options. The Helpline will provide information on a full range of services and organisations available to support pregnant women. It will be for women seeking assistance to decide which particular organisation or service they wish to get further advice from. The Helpline operator will be decided in an open tender process with an advisory committee, comprising key professional organisations.

Counselling provided through Medicare and the Helpline will include advice on all options available, including adoption. Counselling will be provided by professionals with no financial links to abortion providers. Sufficient information will be provided to identify the broad philosophy within which any organisation or service provider operates.

On both sides of the recent RU486 debate, there was a clear consensus that Australia's abortion rate is far too high. The Government does not support changing the abortion law nor does it support restricting Medicare funding for abortion. Nevertheless, the Government wants to give more support to women who are or have been uncertain about continuing a pregnancy.

These new measures are expected to cost $51 million over four years. The Helpline is expected to cost $15.5 million over four years. Medicare-funded counselling is expected to cost $35.6 million over four years. The MBS item will commence on 1 November 2006 and the Hotline will commence within nine months.

These new measures will improve the availability of timely, confidential, professional pregnancy counselling for Australian women and their partners, including those in rural and remote areas. They will be implemented in consultation with professional groups. Training programs will be developed to support GPs, other health professionals and phone counsellors with pregnancy counselling skills.[12]

In the month *before* this announcement was made, we decided to see what kind of support there might be for these kinds of initiatives and also to gain some purchase on community attitudes to the making available for use in Australia of the abortion drug RU-486 and to embryonic stem cell research.

3.2 Stage 4

For the fourth and final stage of our research, we again engaged The Sexton Marketing Group to conduct a 1200-sample national poll to identify public expectations regarding the process and outcomes for the new pregnancy-counselling services, as well as attitudes on the related topics of RU-486 and embryonic stem cell research. Again, participation in the survey was voluntary. To avoid any selection bias towards adults interested in the topic of abortion, the survey was introduced as a survey on social issues, without specific mention of the topic of abortion. After agreement to participate, respondents were then given the option to decline to participate if they did not want to be interviewed on the specific topic of abortion. A total of four respondents declined to participate in the survey when informed that the survey included questions on abortion.

3.2.1 Public reaction to federal abortion initiatives[13]

In the first place we were able to reconfirm earlier findings that Australians support measures to reduce the abortion rate. Although 83 per cent of respondents support women's right to choose an abortion, 88 per cent agree that it would be a good thing if the current 1-in-4 abortion rate could be reduced whilst maintaining the right to choose. We confirmed a number of other findings as well, such as support for sex education in schools as a strategy for reducing unwanted pregnancies and therefore the incidence of abortion (95 per cent).

Next we looked at what support there might be for new government-funded counselling services and an information helpline to give women greater choice where an unwanted pregnancy is concerned.

Q. 5: Which of the following initiatives do you support or oppose as part of a strategy to reduce the number of abortions in Australia? For each one that I read out, please indicate if you strongly support, somewhat support, somewhat oppose, or strongly oppose each one.

Table 11. Support for initiatives to reduce abortion.

Initiatives	Strongly support %	Somewhat support %	Neutral %	Somewhat oppose %	Strongly oppose %	Can't say %
Sex education in schools	85	10	2	1	2	0
Publicly available information on avoiding unwanted pregnancies	86	11	1	1	1	0
Ensuring access to voluntary counselling about the alternatives to abortion	89	9	1	1	0	0
An information help-line so that pregnant women can access information re choices available	89	9	1	1	0	0
Information and counselling available to pregnant women under pressure to have an abortion due to financial, family, or career reasons	87	10	1	2	0	0
Help to manage pressures without resorting to an abortion	83	13	1	2	1	0

The results showed an overwhelming support for federal government initiatives to introduce the counselling services (98 per cent) and the helpline (98 per cent). In each case, 89 per cent of the community said they strongly supported these initiatives. But to further test the level of support for these initiatives, we also looked at the political implications of implementing or not implementing the new policy.

Q. 37: Would any of the following issues have the potential to shift your vote at the next federal election:

Table 12. Issues with potential to change voting.

Issues	Yes %	No %
The level of funding which different parties or candidates commit to pregnancy support services	27	73
The stance that different parties or candidates take on the abortion pill RU-486 and whether it should be legalised or not	35	65
The stance that different parties or candidates take on the issue of embryonic stem cell research	41	59
The stance that different parties or candidates take on the legalisation of cloning of human embryos for research	48	52

When we looked only at the 'soft' supporters of political parties we found that 35 per cent of this cohort, 37 per cent of 'soft' ALP voters, 34 per cent of 'soft' Coalition voters, and 49 per cent of 'soft' minor party and independent voters would potentially shift their vote away from their currently preferred party or candidate if the party or candidate did not support these new initiatives.

It would seem, then, that the primary motivations for supporting these social-policy initiatives where abortion is concerned are the almost universal public support for

a) women's rights to have access to information about the abortion procedure, the risks and alternatives (98 per cent); b) women's right to have access to help to keep the baby if that is their choice (95 per cent); and c) identifying and helping women to deal with pressure or coercion to have an abortion against their will (95 per cent).

There are, then, three principles, which underlie this strong public support for the new initiatives:

- the right of women to be well-informed by persons independent of the abortion provider;
- the right to have access to real choice;
- the right to be free from external pressure or coercion forcing women to act against their will.

We then looked more closely and more specifically at each of the government initiatives as we understood them to be prior to any official announcement of them, and with as much content around them as we could supply

Q. 6a: In order to help women who are thinking about having an abortion make a fully informed decision about what is best to do in their situation, the federal government is funding two new initiatives, namely a telephone information helpline as well as counselling services which pregnant women can access for free, just by asking their doctors. Do you support or oppose the introduction of a telephone helpline for pregnant women? [Is that strongly support / oppose or somewhat support / oppose?]

Table 13. Support for telephone hotline.

Telephone Hotline	Support %
Strongly support	82
Somewhat support	13
Neutral/ Neither support nor oppose	1
Somewhat oppose	2
Strongly oppose	1
TOTAL	(99)

Support levels for the introduction of a government-funded, telephone helpline service for pregnant women thinking about an abortion are very high (82 per cent strongly support, 95 per cent total support) indicating that this initiative would be very much in line with the current thinking of the Australian community.

Q. 6b: Do you support or oppose the initiative to make a free counselling service available to pregnant women who are thinking about an abortion so that they can also receive information about the other options available to them? [Is that strongly support / oppose or somewhat support / oppose?]

Table 14. Support for free counselling service.	
Free Counselling Service	**Support %**
Strongly support	85
Somewhat support	12
Neutral / neither support nor oppose	1
Somewhat oppose	1
Strongly oppose	1
TOTAL	100

This question shows that there is an even higher level of support (85 per cent strongly support, 97 per cent total support) for making a free counselling service available to pregnant women who are thinking about an abortion so that they can also receive information about the other options available to them. But we needed also to know what would be the essential purposes for the new counselling services that would justify them being provided.

Q. 7: These two new services, namely the information help-line and the counselling service, could have various purposes or objectives, which I will read out to you. Please tell me, 'Yes' or 'No', if you believe that each one should be one of the reasons for setting up these new services:

Table 15. Support for objectives of service.			
Objectives for s````ervices	Yes %	No %	Can't say %
For women thinking about an abortion, to give them more information about abortion procedure and risks involved	98	2	0
To give pregnant women more information about the stages of pregnancy, giving childbirth, and raising children	95	4	1
To help women understand better the reasons why they are thinking about an abortion, and the alternative courses of action that they can take	95	3	1
To help women who would prefer to have their baby, but who feel that they are being pressured into having an abortion by others or by their circumstances	95	4	1
To identify if a woman is being forced against her will to have an abortion and to help her deal with this issue	95	4	1

The results for question 7 show that there is a high level of community support for all of the listed possible objectives of the new counselling service and the telephone helpline service. This provides further evidence of strong community support for the services to provide:

- information about the abortion procedure and the risks involved (98 per cent support),
- information about the stages of pregnancy, giving birth, and raising children (95 per cent support),

- help so women may better understand the reasons why they are thinking about an abortion, and what are the alternative courses of action that they can take (95 per cent support),

- help to women who would prefer to have their baby but who feel that they are being pressured into having an abortion (95 per cent support),

- identification of those cases where the woman is being forced by someone else against her will to have an abortion and help given her on ways of dealing with this (95 per cent support).

The community went even further in its views on the provision of information about the abortion procedure and any risks associated with it, as shown in responses to the following question:

> *Q. 9: Before a woman makes a decision about whether to have an abortion or not, do you think she should be advised what is involved in the abortion procedure and the potential physical and mental health risks for her?*

An overwhelming 97 per cent of the sample said that they believe that such a woman should be so advised. Given a choice of alternative sources of advice on the abortion procedure and the risks involved, 49 per cent of the sample believe that this advice should be provided by GPs, 19 per cent believe the advice would be best provided by a government funded counsellor, 7 per cent believe the information hotline would be the best source of this advice, and 7 per cent believe abortion clinics would be the best source of this advice. A total of 18 per cent are uncommitted in their choice.

So there is clear support in the community for this advice coming from GPs and the new services (a total of 75 per cent support) rather than from abortion clinics (7 per cent). Even removing GPs from the equation, there is still stronger support for the advice to come from the new services (26 per cent) compared with abortion clinics (7 per cent). If the 15 per cent who answered 'any of these' are included, 41 per cent of the sample believes that the new services could or should provide this advice, compared with 22 per cent who believe abortion clinics could or should provide the advice.

One possible conclusion that could be reached is that women would only have access to abortion providers upon reference from a GP who would counsel on the nature of the procedure and its risks. This is similar to the situation that obtains in South Australian law where a woman may have an abortion after her case has been independently reviewed by two medical practitioners.

We next considered questions about who should provide the counselling services on alternatives to abortion. In whom does the community put its trust here? We explored these and a variety of related questions.

Q. 11: If a woman wanted advice on the alternatives to having an abortion, which included adoption, or keeping the baby herself, do you think this advice on the alternatives would best come from the abortion clinic or from a counselling service independent of the abortion provider?

Table 16. Best advice: abortion clinic or independent counselling?	
Responses	**Support %**
Abortion clinic	11
Independent counselling service	77
Either	9
Neither	2
Can't say	1
TOTAL	100

Here we see a strong preference (77 per cent) for counselling on the alternatives to having an abortion, including adoption and keeping the baby, to be provided by an independent counselling service rather than from an abortion clinic (11 per cent).

Q. 12: Do you think it would be better for a woman thinking about an abortion to receive advice on abortion itself from her GP and then receive advice on other options from a specialist pregnancy counselling service, or do you think that the counselling service should counsel her on both abortion and the alternatives?

Table 17. Integration or separation of counselling on abortion procedure and alternatives.	
Counselling options	Support %
GP counsels on abortion; specialist counsellor on alternatives	44
Specialist counselling service counsels on both abortion and the alternatives	39
No preference / either	16
Neither	0
Can't say	1
TOTAL	100

The community is largely divided on whether advice on abortion and the alternatives should be integrated and provided by the one counsellor, or separated. In the latter case the GP would provide advice on the abortion procedure and its associated risks, while a separate counsellor would provide advice on the alternatives. These results suggest that both options, a fully integrated counselling service and separated counselling services, should be made available in the community.

The issue of community trust in the professionalism and objectivity of the services provided is clearly an important one that needed to be explored.

Q. 13: Assuming that a pregnant woman is referred by her GP to a government-funded counselling service to talk about her situation and all the options available to her, which of the following groups in the community would you trust to offer completely objective or non-directive counselling on both abortion and the alternatives?

Table 18. Trust in groups offering objective or non-directive counselling.

Groups	Yes %	No %	Don't know %
The federal health department	58	31	11
Individual state govt health depts	63	26	11
GPs	83	13	4
Psychologists	72	19	9
Centacare and Anglicare family counselling/support services	61	31	8
Abortion clinics	52	42	7
The Family Planning Association	78	15	6
Social workers	73	20	7
Independent pregnancy-support groups	74	17	9
Private counsellors not affiliated with any larger groups	74	18	9

The results for this question show that there is a relatively low level of trust of abortion clinics (52 per cent) to offer completely objective or nondirective counselling on both abortion and the alternatives. This contrasts with the much higher levels of community trust placed in:

- The Family Planning Association (80 per cent);
- GPs (80 per cent);
- social workers (75 per cent);
- independent pregnancy support groups (73 per cent);
- private counsellors not affiliated with any larger groups (73 per cent);
- psychologists (71 per cent);
- Centacare and Anglicare (61 per cent).

Q. 14: I will read out those groups again, but this time please tell me if you have confidence that their counsellors are professionally trained and competent to handle this type of counselling?

Table 19. Confidence in training and competence of groups.

Groups	Yes %	No %	Don't know %
The federal health department	60	28	11
The individual state government health depts	63	26	10
GPs	79	16	5
Psychologists	73	19	8
Centacare and Anglicare family counselling/ support services	63	26	11
Abortion clinics	62	30	8
The Family Planning Association	78	13	8
Social workers	69	24	7
Independent pregnancy-support groups	69	19	12
Private counsellors not affiliated with any larger groups	67	22	12

The results from this question reveal some concern in the community about the professionalism and objectivity of counsellors in general. The perceived professionalism of various types of counsellors is moderate but not strong in the community, with an average of around 20 per cent of the community believing that there are likely to be issues of professionalism. This is an issue which, beyond the provision of counselling in the area of abortion, needs to be more fully explored so that the gap between community expectations and the practice of counselling as a trustworthy, professional, and objective endeavour can be significantly lessened. This is outside of the scope of the present study, but it is important to know which counselling services are more trusted than others where counselling for alternatives to abortion is concerned, there being high levels of trust in the capacity of GPs to provide all necessary information about the abortion procedure.

Q. 15: Let's assume now that a woman has received all the information she needs from her GP about having an abortion, but she wants to talk to a counsellor about other choices, so she does not want the counsellor to talk about abortion, she just wants information on other choices. Which of the following counselling groups do you think would be well-equipped to give her advice on other choices?

Table 20. Groups best equipped to counsel re alternatives.			
Groups	Yes %	No %	Dont know %
The federal health department	60	32	8
The individual State Government health departments	64	29	7
GPs	79	18	4
Psychologists	68	25	6
Centacare and Anglicare family counselling/support services	72	21	7
Abortion clinics	53	42	5
The Family Planning Association	82	13	5
Social workers	74	21	5
Independent pregnancy-support groups	77	15	8
Private counsellors not affiliated with any larger groups	71	20	9

This result clearly shows that abortion clinics would be the least trusted provider of counselling services on the alternatives to abortion. This may be because of a perceived conflict of interest between clinics whose financial viability and success relies on the number of procedures that they perform, and the woman who will have different interests to be satisfied. So we thought it would be interesting to see if the levels of trust would increase if the counselling services were subject to very strict Federal Government supervision.

> *Q. 16: If the Federal Government put very strict rules and guidelines in place to make sure that the counselling was objective and impartial, no matter who provided it, which of the following groups do you think should be allowed to offer this counselling service to the community?*

Table 21. Opinions on groups allowed to offer counselling service.			
Groups	Yes %	No %	Don't know %
The federal health department	74	22	4
The individual state government health departments	77	20	3
GPs	89	10	1
Psychologists	79	18	3
Centacare and Anglicare family counselling/support services	77	19	4
Abortion clinics	68	29	4
The Family Planning Association	87	10	3
Social workers	79	17	4
Independent pregnancy-support groups	82	15	4
Private counsellors not affiliated with any larger groups	79	17	4

These results give real support to the idea that some form of accreditation by the Federal Government would significantly assist in building community confidence in the services provided by the various types of counsellors. However, even with accreditation, abortion clinics still receive the lowest rating by the community in terms of their suitability to offer the new services. The following table shows the levels to which community trust and confidence builds with counselling services for abortion being properly accredited.

Table 22. Levels of community trust re: accreditation.		
Federal Government accreditation	**Without**	**With**
The federal health department	60	74
The individual state government health departments	64	77
GPs	79	89
Psychologists	68	79
Centacare and Anglicare family counselling/support services	72	77
Abortion clinics	53	68
The Family Planning Association	82	87
Social workers	74	79
Independent pregnancy-support groups	77	82
Private counsellors not affiliated with any larger groups	71	79

Thus far the research has indicated the overwhelming support of Australians for procedures which govern the provision of abortion to safeguard the right of a woman to be aware of the nature of the procedure, to have revealed to her all of the risks associated with the procedure, and to have knowledge of and access to alternatives to the abortion choice.

We next moved to consider some further implications of freedom of choice and informed consent and the extent to which a counsellor should probe the circumstances in which the woman finds herself. These included situations where the woman feels oppressed by external pressures.

Q. 17: In some cases where a pregnant woman is thinking about having an abortion, she is under pressure to have the abortion from her partner, family, employer, or for reasons related to finances, career, or needing to complete her education. Do you think that the counselling process should try to help the woman to understand these pressures and discuss with her how best to deal with them, or do you think that counselling should not go that far?

Table 23. Counselling to cover area of external pressures.	
Response	**%**
Yes, should cover this	91
No, should not go that far	6
Don't know	3
TOTAL	100

An overwhelming majority (91 per cent) of survey respondents believe that the counselling process should extend to identifying external pressures on the woman to have an abortion, and to help the woman to understand these pressures, and to discuss with her how best to deal with them. Only 6 per cent believe that the counselling should not go that far.

Q. 18: As a general principle, if a counsellor is approached by a woman who is thinking of having an abortion but who tells the counsellor that she would really prefer to keep the baby if she could find a solution to the financial, social, or work pressures on her, do you believe that the counsellor should try to help the woman to find solutions to these pressures on her, or not?

Table 24. Counsellor should help find solutions.	
Response	**%**
Yes	96
No	3
Don't know	2
TOTAL	(101)

The results for question 18 show 96 per cent support for counsellors trying to help women to find solutions to the external pressures placed upon them to have an abortion, if the woman indicates that she would prefer to keep the baby. Put another way, there is a community expectation that counsellors will be active in trying to provide access to the practical assistance that meets a woman's expressed needs and which will assist her to keep her baby.

Q. 19: Do you think the counsellor should try to establish if having an abortion is the woman's personal choice or if she is being threatened or forced against her will by someone else to have an abortion?

Table 25. Counsellor to ascertain if abortion is by choice.	
Response	**% Support**
Yes	92
No	5
Don't know	2
TOTAL	(99)

Ninety-two per cent of survey respondents believing that the counsellor should try to establish if abortion is the woman's personal choice or if she is being threatened or forced against her will by someone else is further evidence of the community's support for free choice. Coercion either to have the child or not have the child is contrary to what the community wants or expects in terms of women's free choices. On the one hand, the community expects that abortion will be available if the woman chooses that even though the community is deeply disquieted about the number of abortions and the morality of abortion in most cases. On the other hand, Australians expect that the abortion choice should be free from duress.

With all these safeguards in place, would there be any impact on the abortion rate in Australia? And are Australians realistic in their expectations about that impact?

Q. 20: If these counselling services were able to introduce women thinking about an abortion, to a range of strategies and help to resolve the social and financial pressures, which have caused them to consider an abortion, do you think that this is likely to lower the abortion rate in Australia substantially or moderately or slightly or not at all?

Table 26. Belief that services will reduce abortion rate.	
Degree of Effectiveness	**% Support**
Substantially	14
Moderately	43
Slightly	32
Not at all	9
Can't say	3
TOTAL	(101)

The results here indicate that 89 per cent of survey respondents believe that these counselling services will reduce the abortion rate in Australia to at least some extent, provided that the services introduce women thinking about an abortion, to a range of strategies and help them to resolve the social and financial pressures which have caused them to consider an abortion.

A total of 14 per cent of the sample believes that the abortion rate will be substantially reduced as a result, and 57 per cent believe that the abortion rate will be substantially or moderately reduced. Seventy-two per cent of the sample believes that there will be a moderate or slight decrease in the abortion rate, which suggests that community expectations about the effect of the provision of these services are not exaggerated.

3.2.2 The introduction of RU-486 in Australia[14]

At about the same time when the Federal Government was giving consideration to abortion counselling services, the issue of the availability of the abortion drug RU-486 was also raised. This issue was extensively covered in the Australian media in the early months of 2006. The matter was raised in the context of a motion in the Parliament about whether the Health Minister should continue to have exclusive control over the importation of the drug or whether this should be passed to the Therapeutic Goods Administration.

The Federal Parliament passed the *Inquiry into Therapeutic Goods Amendment (Repeal of Ministerial Responsibility for Approval of RU-486) Bill 2005*, the purpose of which was to 'remove responsibility for approval for RU-486 from the Minister for Health and Ageing and to provide responsibility for approval of RU-486 to the Therapeutic Goods Administration'. The vote was 45 to 28 in the Senate and at the second reading in the House of Representatives on 16 February the vote was 95 to 50. No vote was taken on the final, third reading.

Missing from the discussion on RU-486 were the views of the community as a whole. The debate was dominated by the major 'pro-life' and 'pro-choice' protagonists in the Federal Parliament, and provided the occasion for highly emotionally charged speeches. While the Parliament was engaged in this debate, we undertook to find out where the community stood on the issue, the level of community knowledge, and to see what difference a better informed public makes to the expression of public opinion. So we began by asking questions about awareness.

> *Q. 21: Still on the topic of abortion, but just changing the subject slightly, have you heard of a pill which can be taken to induce an abortion in the early weeks, known as RU-486?*

Table 27. Awareness of RU-486.	
Response	**%**
Yes	72
No	28
TOTAL	100

The results in this survey show that 72 per cent have heard of the abortion pill RU-486.

Q. 22a: Would you say that your level of knowledge about RU-486 is very good or moderate or limited or very limited?

Table 28. Knowledge about RU-486.	
Level of knowledge	**%**
Very good	5
Moderate	19
Limited	26
Very limited	38
Can't say	11
TOTAL	(99)

So while there is a reasonably high recognition factor about the name of the drug, there is very little real knowledge about the drug itself. In fact, only 5 per cent of the sample believes that they have a very good knowledge of RU-486, with a further 19 per cent believing they have a moderate knowledge, leaving 76 per cent of the sample who indicate that they have little or no knowledge of the drug. This explains why it is relatively easy to influence public opinion on RU-486, because 76 per cent are susceptible to one-sided arguments in favour of or against RU-486 due to their limited knowledge of the drug.

Q. 22b: Based on what you know, do you think that RU-486 is the same as the 'morning-after pill' or is that something different?

Table 29. Comparison: RU-486 with 'morning after pill'.	
Response	**%**
Same	25
Different	42
Don't know	34
TOTAL	(101)

These results indicate significant confusion between RU-486 and the morning-after pill, with 59 per cent of the sample believing that they are either the same thing or unsure of whether they are the same or not. In fact RU-486 is used to procure an abortion on a woman who already has the embryo/foetus embedded in her uterus while the morning-after pill is used to either prevent ovulation or to prevent the fertilised ovum from implanting in the uterine wall.

Q. 23: RU-486 is currently not available in Australia but is available in some other Western countries. Based on what you have seen or read or heard, do you think RU-486 should be made available in Australia as an alternative to the surgical abortion procedure or not?

Table 30. Support for availability or RU-486 in Australia.	
Response	**%**
Yes	52
No	24
Unsure	24
TOTAL	100

The results of this survey show that 52 per cent believe that RU-486 should be made available in Australia as an alternative to the surgical abortion procedure, with 24 per cent opposing and 24 per cent undecided.

Q. 24: Please indicate whether you strongly agree, somewhat agree, somewhat disagree, or strongly disagree with the following opinions [see Table 31] in favour of introducing RU-486 into Australia:

Table 31. Support for opinions in favour of RU-486.

Opinions in favour of RU-486	Strongly agree %	Somewhat agree %	Neutral %	Somewhat disagree %	Strongly disagree %	Can't say %
A safe way to have an abortion	12	21	10	9	12	35
Gives women greater choice of way to have of abortion	37	29	5	5	8	16
Safer than surgical abortion	12	20	12	8	9	39
More convenient than surgical abortion	34	34	5	2	6	19
Lower cost than surgical abortion	22	29	8	2	4	36
Causes minimum disruption to the woman's routine	21	31	8	4	6	30
Allowed by other countries, so Australia should allow it	21	23	7	16	22	11
Right of Aust. women to have access to the latest drugs (e.g. RU-486)	38	28	6	7	11	9

The results revealing the following arguments in favour of introducing RU-486 are the strongest arguments in terms of influencing public opinion in favour of its introduction:

- RU-486 is more convenient than surgical abortion (68 per cent agree).

- It is the right of Australian women to have access to the latest drugs such as RU-486 (66 per cent agree).

- RU-486 gives women greater choice of abortion procedures (66 per cent agree).

- RU-486 causes minimal disruption to the woman's routine (52 per cent agree).

- RU-486 has a lower cost than surgical abortion (51 per cent agree).

All other arguments in favour of RU-486 seem to be unpersuasive and received less than 50 per cent support, including:

- RU-486 is a safe way to have an abortion (33 per cent agree).

- RU-486 is safer than surgical abortion (32 per cent agree).

- Many countries allow the use of RU-486 so Australia should allow it too (44 per cent agree).

So the arguments in favour of RU-486 that resonate most strongly with the community relate to women's rights and giving women greater choice, as well as arguments about convenience, minimal disruption and cost.

The arguments, which are least effective, are arguments about the safety of the procedure and the argument that if other countries have approved RU-486 then Australia should follow suit.

Q. 25: Now I will read out some opinions against making RU-486 legal in Australia and ask if you strongly agree, somewhat agree, somewhat disagree, or strongly disagree with each one:

Table 32. Support for opinions against RU-486.

Opinions against RU-486	Strong agree %	Somewhat agree %	Neutral %	Somewhat disagree %	Strongly disagree %	Can't say %
Not proven to be safe - ten women died in other countries.	20	18	9	18	13	22
Neither quick nor convenient - can cause protracted pain and discomfort over many days	16	21	10	15	7	31
Will increase unwanted pregnancies among those women who think that a pill will fix the problem.	28	26	5	15	17	10
Abortion often takes place in locations where the process is not overseen by a doctor.	30	32	5	11	8	14
Australia does not need to blindly follow the lead of other countries in terms of the adoption of every drug.	48	24	4	9	6	8
No need in Australia. Abortion available in high-standard clinics.	25	22	8	18	15	12
If the pill does not completely abort everything, a woman can become seriously infected and even die.	26	24	10	8	5	28
If taken without medical supervision, we will effectively go back to the days 'backyard abortions'.	25	22	5	15	19	13

In this question arguments against the introduction of RU-486 into Australia were presented. The arguments against RU-486, which received the strongest support or agreement from the survey sample, are:

- Australia does not need to blindly follow the lead of other countries in terms of the adoption of every drug (72 per cent agree).

- Instead of the abortion taking place in a surgery, it often takes place in the woman's home or other locations where the process is not overseen by a doctor (62 per cent agree).

- It will increase unwanted pregnancies (54 per cent agree).

- It may cause serious infection or death if the pill does not completely abort everything (50 per cent agree).

The arguments against RU-486 that did not receive majority support were:

- Ten women have died in other countries, so it is not proven to be safe (38 per cent agree).

- RU-486 can cause protracted pain and discomfort so it is neither quick nor convenient (37 per cent).

- We don't need RU-486 in Australia because women who want an abortion can get one in high-standard clinics (47 per cent agree).

- If some women obtain it and take it without medical supervision, we will effectively go back to the bad old days of 'backyard abortions' (47 per cent agree).

Overall, then, the results suggest that the strongest arguments against RU-486 relate to Australia not blindly following other countries; potential to increase unwanted pregnancies; lack of medical supervision of the abortion; and the resultant risk of serious infection or death.

Having put the arguments in favour of and those against the introduction of RU-486 into Australia, we then sought to find out what impact knowledge of these arguments had on overall attitudes. First we asked people where they thought the strength of the argument lay.

Q. 26: Do the arguments in favour or the arguments against RU-486 seem stronger overall to you?

Table 33. Perceived strength of arguments re: RU-486.	
Opinions	**%**
Arguments in favour	36
Arguments against	43
Can't say	21
TOTAL	100

Taking the arguments in favour and against the introduction of RU-486, 43 per cent of the sample believe that the arguments against RU-486 are stronger, 36 per cent believe the arguments in favour of RU-486 are stronger, and 21 per cent are unsure of which set of arguments is stronger. This would suggest that the arguments against RU-486 have a slightly stronger potential to influence public opinion than the arguments in favour of the drug's introduction into Australia. And now, in the light of these considerations we returned to the question of what people thought Australia's current policy should be in relation to RU-486.

Q. 27: Do you believe RU-486 should be introduced into Australia immediately, or delayed until the risks are better understood and a number of lawsuits over RU-486 in the US are resolved, or should RU-486 not be introduced at all?

Table 34. Opinions re introduction of RU-486.	
Opinions	**%**
Introduce now	17
Delay until more information available	59
Do not introduce at all	18
Can't say	6
TOTAL	100

This question shows that there is a majority support for delaying the introduction of RU486 until the risks are better understood and a number of lawsuits over RU-486 in the United States are resolved. A total of 59 per cent of the sample believe that this is better than introducing the drug immediately (only 17 per cent of the sample believe it should be introduced now). A total of 77 per cent believe that RU-486 should either be disallowed in Australia or that any decision about its introduction should be delayed until the risks are better understood and the lawsuits in the United States are resolved.

Here we see a case where informed public opinion can take a quite different conclusion from that of politicians influenced, as they frequently are, by those who can shout loudest. Indeed, this result is consistent with the total body of our research which suggests that Australians are concerned about the risks to women of surgical and medical interventions where abortion is concerned and are more risk averse than the politicians who make public policy in their name.

We were particularly interested to see what, if any, difference age and gender make to attitudes to the introduction to RU-486. It had occurred to us that younger women, the ones who would be most likely to have direct exposure to RU-486, may be more cautious about the drug than the older women who were most vociferous in the parliamentary debate. What we found was that prior to any exposure to the 'for' and 'against' arguments, the *strongest* level of support for RU-486 is among:

- females aged 25–34 and females aged 50–64 (59 per cent support in both groups), followed by:
- females 18–24 and males 50–64 (56 per cent support in both groups),
- males 35–49 (54 per cent),
- females 65+ (51 per cent).

The *weakest* level of support (i.e., support less than 50 per cent) came from

- males 18–24 (43 per cent),
- males 25–34 (45 per cent),
- females 35–49 (49 per cent),
- males 65+ (43 per cent).

However, after exposure to arguments both 'for' and 'against', the highest level of agreement that it is best to *delay* the decision or not introduce the drug at all is among:

- females 18–24 (89 per cent delay or oppose),
- females 25–34 (87 per cent delay or oppose),
- males 18–24 (85 per cent delay or oppose),
- males 25–34 (81 per cent delay or oppose),
- females 35–49 (81 per cent delay or oppose),
- females 65+ (77 per cent delay or oppose),
- males 65+ (73 per cent delay or oppose),
- females 50–64 (72 per cent delay or oppose),
- males 35–49 (72 per cent delay or oppose),
- males 50–64 (64 per cent delay or oppose).

This result shows that the groups who show the strongest support for the introduction of RU-486 (before any debate arguments are presented) are females of reproductive age (18–34) and males and females aged 50–64 whose adult children are of reproductive age. But after exposure to the 'for' and 'against' arguments, the groups most supportive of delaying the introduction of RU-486 or not introducing it at all are:

- females 18–24,
- females 25–34,
- males 18–34,
- females 35–49.

Those most affected by a properly informed debate in which both the pros and cons of RU-486 are aired, are the very same segments most supportive of its introduction before such a debate. They shift dramatically in numbers to be most in favour of delaying the drug's introduction.

The conclusion to be drawn then is that those age groups most likely to use RU-486 are the strongest advocates of introducing it, if the debate focuses on their rights. But, these same segments are the strongest advocates of *delaying* the introduction of RU-486 if the debate shifts to include reference to the risks to their own health from taking RU-486. Put another way: 'I've got a right to choose RU-486, but I've also got a right to be protected from any drug which could have serious side effects on me, including death.'

3.2.3 Stem cell research in Australia[15]

The subject of stem cell research was also current in Australia at the same time with the Honourable John Lockhart, AO, QC, delivering findings to the Australian Government from the independent review of The Prohibition of Human Cloning Act 2002 and the Research Involving Human Embryos Act 2002. This occurred on 19 December 2005. The Lockhart Review not only recommended the continuing use of human embryos in stem cell research but also recommended, among other things, that somatic cell nuclear transfer, or therapeutic cloning, be legally permitted. This technique, also known as therapeutic cloning, creates tailored embryonic stem cells by removing DNA from a donor egg and replacing it with the DNA from a cell taken from the patient. We wanted to see how far the findings of the Lockhart Review were in line with community values, attitudes, and expectations.

> Q. 28: Our final topic to cover is the topic of stem cell research. Have you heard of stem cell research?

Table 35. Proportions aware of stem cell research.	
Response	**%**
Yes	89
No	10
Unsure	1
TOTAL	100

On the topic of stem cell research, it would seem that the vast majority of Australians (89 per cent) had heard of stem cell research.

> Q. 29: *There are two types of human stem cell research, namely taking stem cells from the patient's own body, and taking stem cells from human embryos which are left over from IVF treatment programs and which are destroyed in the stem cell removal process. Assuming that both types of research offered the same potential results and benefits, from an ethical point of view, do you have a preference for stem cell research using cells from the patient's own body or stem cell research using embryos, or no preference?*

Table 36. Preferences re method of stem cell research.	
Preference	**%**
Stem cell research using patient's own cells	40
Embryonic stem cell research	4
No preference	51
Can't say	5
TOTAL	100

A total of 40 per cent of the sample have a preference for stem cell research using the patient's own cells, with 4 per cent having a preference for embryonic stem cell research, and 56 per cent indicating no preference. This means that, given a preference, 96 per cent of the survey sample accept or prefer stem cell research using the patient's own cells, with 60 per cent accepting or preferring embryonic stem cell research.

Q. 30a: Do you support or oppose the cloning of human embryos as a source of stem cells?

Table 37. Opinions re cloning of human embryos.	
Opinion	**%**
Support	29
Neutral	12
Oppose	51
Can't say	8
TOTAL	100

A majority (51 per cent) oppose the cloning of human embryos as a source of stem cells, compared with 29 per cent support and 20 per cent neutral.

Q. 30b: Before it was mentioned today, were you aware that extracting stem cells from a human embryo causes the embryo to be destroyed in the process?

Table 38. Awareness re destruction of embryos.	
Response	**%**
Yes	57
No	43
TOTAL	100

While just over half (57 per cent) of survey respondents were aware that the embryo is destroyed in the process of extracting stem cells, a very substantial minority (43 per cent) were not aware of this fact.

Q. 30c: [IF NO] Now that you are aware of this, do you support or oppose the cloning of human embryos as a source of stem cells if it means that these embryos are destroyed in the process?

Table 39. Responses to cloning of human embryos.	
Response	**%**
Support	14
Neutral	13
Oppose	61
Can't say	12
TOTAL	100

Following this line of question and information sharing, it is clear that opposition to stem cell research increases when people are made aware that the embryo is destroyed in the process of extracting stem cells. That is, opposition to this process increases from 51 per cent to 55 per cent of the whole sample.

Part of the debate on 'therapeutic cloning' involves public reassurance that acceptance of this process will not lead to so-called 'reproductive cloning', the bringing to birth of a live, human, cloned baby. The distinction between 'therapeutic' and 'reproductive' cloning is directed towards giving just such an assurance. Are Australians convinced by these reassurances? Apparently not.

Q. 30d: Do you believe that research on cloning of human embryos will eventually lead to the cloning of human babies or not?

Table 40. Belief that cloning of embryos will lead to cloning of humans.	
Response	**%**
Yes	28
Probably yes	16
Possibly	24
Probably no	10
No	18
Don't know	5
TOTAL	100

This question shows that a total of 28 per cent of the survey sample believe that the cloning of human embryos will eventually lead to the cloning of human babies, with a further 16 per cent believing that this will probably occur, and a further 24 per cent believing that it is a possibility. This means, in total, 68 per cent of the sample believes that the cloning of human babies will definitely, probably, or possibly be an outcome of the cloning of human embryos. In short, Australians are not convinced that 'therapeutic' cloning can be finally quarantined from 'reproductive' cloning. And Australians simply do not approve of 'reproductive' cloning.

Q. 31: Do you support or oppose the idea of being able to clone or create genetically identical human beings from cloning?

Table 41. Responses re attitudes to cloning humans.	
Response	**%**
Support	6
Neutral	6
Oppose	86
Can't say	2
TOTAL	100

The results for this question clearly show strong opposition in the community to the idea of being able to clone or create genetically identical human beings from cloning (86 per cent oppose compared with only 6 per cent support). But would strong community feeling on this or any of the other issues we examined produce a shift in political commitments at the time of an election? Would people be prepared to consider shifting their vote on the basis of their attitudes to any of the four issues we examined?

Q. 37: Would any of the following issues have the potential to shift your vote at the next Federal election:

Table 42. Issues that may change voting.

Issues	Yes %	No %
The level of *funding* which different parties or candidates commit to *pregnancy-support services*	27	73
The stance that different parties or candidates take on the *abortion pill RU-486* and whether it should be legalised or not	35	65
The stance that different parties or candidates take on the issue of *embryonic stem cell research*	41	59
The stance that different parties or candidates take on the *legalisation of cloning of human embryos for research*	48	52

The results for this question show that there is significant potential to influence soft or swinging federal voters in terms of their vote intention, based on the issues that have been covered in this survey. For example:

- 48 per cent of voters potentially would change their vote on the issue of cloning human embryos for research;

- 41 per cent of voters potentially would change their vote on the broader issue of embryonic stem cell research;

- 35 per cent of voters potentially would change their vote on the RU-486 issue;

- 27 per cent of voters potentially would change their vote on the issue of party or candidate support for the introduction of new pregnancy-support services.

3.3 Summary observations

3.3.1 Abortion counselling services

The Federal Government can proceed with the introduction of the new services, confident that there is very strong public support behind the initiative, provided that it is made clear that women's right of access to abortion is protected in the process.

It is critical that some form of accreditation for counsellors is established, to give the public confidence in the objectivity and professionalism of the services. The most prominent evidence of this is the significant community concern identified in the survey about abortion clinics extending their services to include counselling about the alternatives to abortion. This may be because their core business is providing abortions.

3.3.2 RU-486

The strategy on RU-486, which a majority of Australians support, is to delay any decision on the drug until more is known about the risks. Support for this position is created by making the public aware of some of the risks associated with the drug, as well as the 'unanswered questions' that form the basis of numerous lawsuits in the US over RU-486.

Australians do not like the idea of blindly following the lead of other countries, or exposing Australian women to unnecessary risks (both the known risks such as those involved in medically unsupervised abortions occurring in the home and the unknown risks such as the unexplained deaths of ten RU-486 users in other countries).

The position on RU-486 which is supported by a majority of Australians is that:

- It is not fair on Australian women to expose them to both the known and unknown risks of RU-486.

- We should not blindly follow the lead of other countries on this.

- No one is worse off without RU-486. Australian women continue to have access to abortion via a procedure which pro-abortionists have argued consistently is safe, easy, and with a low risk of side-effects.

- There are unanswered questions about the risks of RU-486, as well as emerging evidence that it can lead to serious infection and even death.

- RU-486 will lead to medically unsupervised abortions taking place in the home which effectively will take Australian women back to the bad old days of 'backyard abortions'.

On this basis, Australians believed that it would be better to delay any decision about the introduction of the drug until more is known about the risks and until the lawsuits in other countries establish the facts behind the deaths of RU-486 users. This is at variance with the position adopted by the Federal Parliament, the representative of the Australian people.

3.3.3 Embryonic stem cell research

On the topic of stem cell research, Australians would prefer adult stem cell research when they know that embryonic stem cell research depends on embryo destruction and if there is a risk that embryonic stem cell research is going to evolve into the cloning of human babies (which they strongly oppose). Almost 7 out of 10 Australians believe that there is a risk that embryonic stem cell research involving cloned embryos will lead to the cloning of human babies, and more than 8 out of 10 Australians are opposed to the cloning of humans. The higher support for adult stem cell research is likely to be on the proviso that this research can deliver the same benefits as embryonic stem cell research.

So the typical view of Australians is that:

- all other things being equal, adult stem cell research is preferable to embryonic stem cell research (assuming that the benefits are the same);

- cloning of human embryos which are destroyed in the stem cell extraction process is opposed by a majority of Australians; and

- cloning of human embryos is seen as the 'thin end of the wedge' with a very real possibility that it will lead to the cloning of people which is strongly opposed by Australians.

Chapter 4

Understand, appreciate, protect: effective education in sexuality

Nicholas Tonti-Filippini

Helen McConnell

In this chapter we report the results of a literature survey on the effectiveness of sex education. We conclude that much education in sexuality focuses on avoiding unplanned pregnancy and preventing sexually transmissible disease. As a matter of pedagogy, there is little evidence that reciting the facts about harmful consequences and presenting a smorgasbord of sexual choices has a positive effect on the behaviour of teenagers in this matter. It may be that they attach much greater importance to identity issues, forming relationships and peer opinion than to sober messages about their health. There is also little to indicate that public health education messages are effective. Education in sexuality is much more complex because it deals with matters involving sexual identity, personal relationships, and personal morality.

We argue that in approaching education in sexuality, one ought to address the matter of what the *needs* of the target group are, what *objectives* may be drawn from those needs, what *methods* might be employed to meet those needs including who should be involved, and finally how to *evaluate* what is done in a way that respects privacy.

We then speculate on the basis of the little evidence available about the criteria that effective sex education would need to meet. We take the view that there is little point in preaching sexual taboos if you have not already established some more fundamental notions about the importance of being human, about making genuinely free choices that foster personal growth and development, and about respecting the human body and gender identity as a man or as a woman.

Our view is that if you want to do sex education effectively, then do not start with sex education (in the usual sense of what is meant). Rather, you start with matters to do with healthy living and behavioural notions related to identity as man or as woman, family relationships, friendship, self-worth and the worth of other persons. That then gives a context to matters that are causative in relation to behaviour, particularly in establishing behaviour that through being respectful of the person, including his or her body, is genuinely protective of the person and his or her physical and mental health. Our view is that the appropriate educational sequence is: understand, appreciate, protect.

For this chapter we undertook an extensive literature review to see what the evidence is for effective sex education. Of course, judging the effectiveness of sex education needs first a coherent understanding of what the needs are.

Though the needs are often portrayed simply in terms of preventing pregnancy and infectious disease, we thought that delaying sexual initiation is also a relevant factor. In addition, the sexual wellbeing of young people relates to a much wider range of matters including avoiding other harms such as risk of emotional harm, self-harm and suicide, risks to emerging gender identity, and risk of premature exposure to adult concepts and loss of childhood innocence. There is also a range of positive matters to do with the need for personal affirmation of young people and their self-confidence in matters such as gender identity, the acquired ability to make free and reasoned choices about sexual (and other) conduct, and to enjoy good relationships as a man or a woman and good dating. However, the available research seems to be more or less limited to factors related to protective behaviours in relation to sexually transmittible infection and pregnancy rates. There is also limited data on delaying sexual initiation.

4.1 Literature review

4.1.1 Context

During the past several decades, adolescent sexual and reproductive health has attracted special attention from international governments and researchers in the developed countries. To date, sexually transmitted infections (STIs), HIV and teenage pregnancy remain a considerable moral and economic problem for modern society.

Historically there has been an increase in sexual encounters at a younger age since the so-called 'sexual revolution' of the 1960s. Adolescent sexual activity has resulted in increased occurrence of sexually transmitted infections[1] and teenage pregnancy.[2] These consequences of the 'sexual revolution' gave an impulse to the creation of a number of national strategies and frameworks, which determine the key principles of sexual education in public and private schools.[3]

4.1.2 National strategies and programs in Australia and USA

In Australia there are federal programs such as the *National HIV/AIDS Strategy* 2005–2008: *Revitalising Australia's Response; the National Hepatitis C Strategy* 2005–2008, and the *National Aboriginal and Torres Strait Islander Sexual Health and Blood Borne Virus Strategy* 2005–2008. The first Australian National Sexually Transmissible Infections Strategy 2005–2008 was released by the Federal Department of Health and Ageing in 2005. Some states and territories employ their own guidelines, for example, in Victoria, *A Statement on Health and Physical Education for Australian Schools*[4] and *Health and Physical Education — A Curriculum Profile for Australian School National Framework*[5] has been adopted, and in Queensland

The Strategic Policy Framework for Children's and Young People's Health has been implemented.[6]

In the USA, an organisation called SIECUS (the Sexuality Information and Education Council of the United States) was established in 1964. In the last four decades, SIECUS has provided various sexual education programs and technical assistance to partner organisations around the world.[7]

4.1.3 The main directions of the research

The entirety of research in the area of teenage sexual education could be usefully divided into three directions: first, the rate of actual spread of STIs and HIV/AIDS among young people as an indicator of the effectiveness of sexual education; second, the incidence of pregnancy in teenagers who receive modern sexual education, and third, analysis of available curricula for sexual education in schools.

Aside from the published statistical reports and national surveys commissioned by the government, the above three indicators offer an important indirect measure of efficiency of sexual education.

4.1.4 Sexually transmitted diseases and sexual education

If left untreated, nearly all STIs eventually result in severe, long-term physical consequences. For instance, a chlamydial infection in females often ascends to the fallopian tubes, where it causes inflammation and potential infertility and ectopic pregnancy. In males, chlamydia may cause epididymitis and ensuing sterility.[8]

STIs have been increasing significantly in many developed countries in the last several decades. The following examples are derived from recently collected Australian data. The incidence of Chlamydia trachomatis in young people aged 12–24 years increased more than threefold from 98 to 338 cases per 100 000 of population between 1991 and 2001.

A similar tendency is found among young people of the same age diagnosed with gonococcal infection. Incidence of gonorrhoea increased by 150 per cent between 1991 to 2001, from 47 to 72 per 100 000 of population.[9]

The Third National Survey of Australian Secondary Students performed by La Trobe University has demonstrated poor or incomplete knowledge about HIV and STIs. More than 10 per cent of students did not know that HIV can be transmitted during sex between men: nearly 25 per cent did not know that pregnant, HIV-positive women could pass HIV to their children, and more than 15 per cent did not know that HIV-positive persons without clinical symptoms of disease could be a source of infection. An analogous situation exists in the area of STIs. The results emphasised similar lack of knowledge about chlamydia, gonorrhoea, herpes simplex and genital warts.[10]

In the United States, federal surveys for the Department of Health and Human Services have found a decline in sexual activity among adolescents 15 to 19 years of age during the last decade.[11] Nevertheless, overall rates of STIs in the United States are among the highest in the industrialised world. Every year approximately three million sexually active adolescents acquire STIs.[12] A recent population-based study found that 4.7 per cent of young women and 3.7 per cent of young men in the United States are infected by Chlamydia trachomatis.[13]

In recent research conducted in this area, the authors utilise the wide spread of STIs as an indirect evidence of effectiveness of different approaches in sexual education. It should be noted that at times researchers' conclusions may differ significantly.

An analysis of published studies utilising data from six surveys on sexual behaviour and surveillance of STIs in the date range from the 1970s to 2001 was conducted by A.E. Biddlecom in the United States. The results showed that incidence rates for gonorrhoea among adolescents declined in the last decade (1990s), notwithstanding the increased proportion of teenagers who have had sexual intercourse. In conclusion, the author emphasises that data sources were difficult to compare over most main indicators.[14]

Interestingly, according to the National Longitudinal Study of Adolescent Health in the US, younger individuals at first intercourse were associated with higher odds of STIs in comparison to older ages. However, both groups exhibited similar propensity for contracting STIs in later teenage years.[15]

It was proved that biological factors, health care, and social relationships contribute to the risk of contracting STIs.[16] There is no doubt that parents and the school play a significant role in adolescent life. Studies have revealed that adolescent girls who perceived that their parents disapproved of their sexual intercourse were less infected by STIs.

Furthermore, post-secondary school teenagers with better academic performance in school were less likely to have acquired STIs in six years time than those with lower academic grades. Consequently, the adolescents' academic success and parental disapproval of sexual intercourse could diminish the risk of acquiring STIs, particularly in girls.[17]

4.1.5 Teenage pregnancy and sexual education

Adolescent pregnancy, as mentioned earlier, could also serve as one indication of the effectiveness of sexual education. According to the Australian Institute of Health and Welfare, Australia's adolescent birth rate for females aged 15–19 years declined from 55 per 1000 of population in 1971 to 20 per 1000 of population in 1988 and has remained fairly stable since that time.[18] Australian indications are significantly lower than in the US at 87 per 1000 of population.[19]

Accurate statistics on the number of pregnancy terminations are difficult to obtain since both the Medicare data and National Hospital Morbidity Database are combined to provide statistical figures. In 2003, 13 855 women aged up to nineteen years had induced termination of pregnancy. This group represents 16.5 per cent of the total number of all performed abortions in Australia.[20] It also ought to be noted that abortions achieved early by chemical means using the morning-after pill and even later chemical abortions are usually not recorded as pregnancies or terminations of pregnancy.

An interesting investigation was performed in the United States by R. Barbieri.[21] The author examined the relationship between population density and the percentage of teenagers who electively terminated their pregnancy. Positive correlation between population density and percentage of adolescent termination of pregnancy was found. In particular, in areas of low population density teenagers preferred to give birth.

Consequences of teenage pregnancy are quite serious. Many studies demonstrate that teenage pregnancy and teenage maternity have a negative effect on the social and psychological adaptation of young women in modern society. This situation affects young mothers through often unstable family relationships and financial disadvantage,[22] low self-esteem, and postpartum depression.[23] Further, low interest in education and dislike of school are associated with subsequent risk of adolescent pregnancy.[24]

C. Seamark and D. Pereira-Gray performed a study which confirmed the hypothesis that pregnant teenagers are more likely to come from families with mothers who themselves had experienced adolescent pregnancy than their counterparts who did not become pregnant at that age.[25]

Children of adolescent mothers are at risk of pre-term birth, and developing future behavioural disorders.[26] It should be underlined that prematurity is the greatest single cause of the underdevelopment of an infant's internal organs and death after delivery.

The fathers in teenage pregnancy also undergo psychological stress. J. Quinlivan and J. Condon from Melbourne University examined anxiety and depression in fathers in the setting of teenage pregnancy.[27] The authors performed a cross-sectional cohort study comparing fathers in the setting of teenage (main) and non-teenage groups. It was shown that significantly more fathers from the main group have exhibited psychological symptomatology and required assistance services along with teenage mothers.

The widely accepted findings of the above studies serve to demonstrate the seriousness of the consequences of teenage pregnancy upon young people and have been generally relied on in the state and national educational programs in Australia and other countries.

4.1.6 School curricula and sex education

Effectiveness of sexual education is examined by analysis of curricula, involvement of participations in programs, timing of sex education, and impact of different external factors on adolescent sexual attitudes and behaviour. Interestingly, results and conclusions of studies in this specific area appear to differ significantly.

R. Lederman et al. studied effectiveness of participation in a sex education program by both school students and their parents.[28] It was found that this 'tandem' offers a promising approach to effective education about HIV and teenage pregnancy. In a different study, P. Borgia et al. assert that the sole apparent benefit of the peer-led intervention, compared to the education programs delivered by teachers, was a greater improvement in knowledge of HIV.[29]

The analysis on qualitative data from four primary Australian schools performed by J. Milton revealed that both mothers and teachers had difficulties discussing the sexuality issues with primary-school students owing to their insufficient prior training.[30] C. Somers and M. Eaves examined the hypothesis of probable harm of earlier sex education in a school in the USA.[31] The subjects in the study were 158 adolescents. The authors showed that sex education at a younger age could be beneficial, provided that topics and their interpretation are relevant to the specific age group.

The sources of sex education and their impact on adolescent sexual behaviour are very important in the technological era. In the present time alternative origins of information can be more authoritative than parents' opinions. In the past, sexual education has been provided as a formal school program. Nevertheless, children endeavoured to obtain sexual knowledge informally from peers, books, movies, TV programs etc.

Modern technologies provide opportunities for obtaining a wide variety of relevant information by users. In the last several years directed research has been performed in this area. G. Goldman identified and selected relevant websites, which were presented for sexual education in children and preschoolers.[32] In the following year the author introduced a comprehensive investigation considering the role of parents in sexual education today. It was underlined that learning should be actively shared by parents and children together. Computer-educated parents are seen to be more authoritative by children and thus are able to improve the quality of their sexual education.[33] Conversely, research performed by C. Somers and A. Surman has shown that earlier learning in school is more important for adolescents than other sources of sex education such as peers, media, and other adults.[34]

The impact of the media on adolescent sexual behaviours has been examined in the US by S. Escobar-Chaves et al.[35] The research was carried out by systematic review of the relevant biomedical and social-science literature and other sources on the sexual content of various mass media, published in English between 1983–2004. The effect of media issues on adolescent sexual behaviour was also imported into consideration.

The authors compared a group of American adolescents with a representative group of adolescents from other post-industrial English-speaking countries. They concluded that television was the only medium watched by teenagers with ongoing assessment of its sexual content. Other media were not considered in the basic investigations. Only 12 of 2522 research-related documents (less than 1 per cent) involved media and their youth-addressed effect.

The majority of studies were limited by express cross-sectional and sampling patterns and small sample size. Many crucial questions regarding the long-term effectiveness of various social-cultural technological and media approaches were not considered by the authors. In the concluding recommendations the authors showed concern over the development of adequate and comprehensive research methodologies and measures. Escobar-Chaves et al. finally conclude by noting that long-term studies should be the method of choice.

The influence of religiousness on the sexual attitudes and behaviour of adolescents has been under consideration by a wide range of researchers. The problems, which authors cover in their examinations, could be characterised by the following examples. S. Rostosky et al. completed a multifactorial analysis of studies published between 1980 and 2001 aimed at understanding the role and influence of religiousness of adolescents in relation to their sexual attitudes and behaviour.[36] The authors collected and examined approximately fifty studies, selected according to the authors' criteria. It was found that the vast majority of studies have used cross-sectional designs whereby crucial developmental changes in religious attitude, beliefs, and behaviour of participants could not be adequately described. Nevertheless, the results indicate that religious beliefs and practice delay the sexual debut of teenage girls. In conclusion the authors recommend improvement to examinations in this sub-field though utilisation of large-scale longitudinal study, which should ideally include the interaction of different systems.

A second group of researchers examined the connection between religious affiliation and frequency of attendance at religious services at age 14 years against a range of sexual behaviour among women aged 15–24. Indications included age at first intercourse; contraception used, timing of birth, and the number of sexual partners. The researchers exploited national representative data. Multivariate analysis verified that frequent attendance at religious services at age 14 years continues to have a strong delaying effect on the timing of first intercourse. Albeit in conclusion, the authors accentuated that the survey data and small sample size prevented them from gaining a complete understanding of associations between religious affiliation and reproductive behaviour.[37]

Among a number of approaches to sexual-education study, the abstinence-only program (abstinence until marriage) is central. Today this mode of education is wide spread in schools and is advocated by its proponents as unambiguously safe and effective. However, the last assertion is often questioned. According to the American Academy of Pediatrics, abstinence-only education programs have not demonstrated successful outcomes with regard to delayed initiation of sexual activity and decreased STIs among adolescents.[38]

The same opinion is expressed by Pinkerton, who asserts abstinence almost certainly has a failure rate.[39] His simulation studies suggest that abstinence appears to be about as good as condoms for the prevention of STIs. Prior to Pinkerton, a systematic review performed by A. DiCenso et al. allowed the authors to isolate a finding that primary prevention strategies, including abstinence-only did not delay the initiation of sexual intercourse or reduce the number of pregnancies in adolescents.[40]

On the other hand, the assertion of total ineffectiveness of abstinence-only programs appears to be at least inaccurate. The distinction between abstinence as an individual choice and abstinence induced by public intervention is not examined, albeit it is a crucial factor in its own right.

Logically, as a personal choice, abstinence is clearly 100 per cent effective in avoiding STIs and pregnancy. Conversely, abstinence by public intervention may and does provoke intrinsic protest in adolescents. J. Fortenberry supposes that, as a public health intervention used at a population level, abstinence almost certainly will have a failure rate, even if it is successful in a larger sense.[41] Sometimes failure of a program depends on absence of understanding of the essence of the subjects.

P. Goodson et al. studied how program directors and instructors define the term 'abstinence'.[42] Interviews were conducted with twenty-nine program staff (ten directors and nineteen instructors) from a sample of a federally funded abstinence-only-until-marriage programs. The results indicated substantial variability in the definition offered by the subjects. The authors concluded that this created difficulties in the development of the program as well as in the evaluation of its effectiveness.

4.1.7 Methodology of Research

The question of *methodology* utilised in studies of effectiveness of sexual education should be taken into consideration. As was mentioned above, the results of examinations can differ vastly. It is reasonable to assume that the cause could be hidden in the different approaches of each investigating author or group.

There are two types of epidemiological investigations: experimental studies and observational studies. The former includes randomised control studies in which similar individuals at the beginning are randomly allocated to two or more treatment groups, treated, and analysed; and the outcomes for each group are then compared after sufficient follow-up time. In an observational study, the allocation or assignment of factors is outside the control of the investigator, and the combinations are self-selected. For example, qualitative evaluation was used in studies seeking to determine the views of parents, teachers, and school counsellors about a) contraception, b) the usefulness of peer mentors in sexual education, and c) the association between sexual activity among urban adolescent girls and the four select measures of psychological adaptation.[43]

It should be noted, published observation studies are appreciably greater in volume then randomised control trials. G. Guyatt et al. performed a systematic review comparing the results of randomised trials with observation studies of interventions seeking to prevent adolescent pregnancy.[44] The authors found that the difference between the results of these types of studies were statistically significant in two out of eight outcomes. Observational studies exhibited greater reliance on estimates in assessing effectiveness of sex-education programs compared to randomised trials of adolescent pregnancy.

Besides objective difference in the results of observation there are methodological limitations of studies. For instance, some of the articles dealing with the effectiveness of education programs have been published in the format of a narrative review.[45] Further, the outcome data can be collected using improper questionnaires,[46] or an insufficient cohort of participators.[47] Jadad et al. established methodological procedure important for the development and validation of any health measurement.[48] In particular, Jadad's group argued that the quality of clinical trials should be assessed by blinded raters to limit the risk of bias in meta-analyses. They produced their own guidelines for assessment. The guidelines incorporate randomisation, double blinding (usually utilised in clinical treatment), and withdrawals and dropouts.

T. Furukawa et al., in analysing the sources of bias in diagnostic accuracy studies pays attention to the 'gold' or reference standard, used in medical trials.[49] A hypothetical ideal of a 'gold' standard test has sensitivity and specificity of 100 per cent. Unfortunately, the authors discuss utilisation of this test only for diagnostic purposes. Further significant limitations upon any given study are the time and funding constraints.[50]

4.1.8 What should be done for improvement of the research?

It should be noted that quality of research has improved simultaneously with the understanding of the importance of utilisation of adequate methodologies for investigations. Nevertheless, sometimes the conclusions as to the effectiveness of education are contradictory and difficult to interpret. Accordingly, the quality of research may be ameliorated by adopting varying approaches.

The utilisation of reliable primary data is the basic requirement for achieving trustworthy results. It has been suggested that use of thoroughly designed questionnaires is preferred to the use of reports prepared ad hoc by individual participants.[51] Randomised control trials are deemed to be a method of choice for the testing of interventions in sex-education programs. Observational studies, both longitudinal and cross-sectional are recommended for use only in the situations where randomised control studies are not available as a first alternative.[52]

A major disadvantage for authors of meta-analyses and systematic reviews is that the assessment of the quality of their investigations depends on the information available in the collected reports.[53] Sometimes, the inappropriate description of the methodology of the trial could create an impression of deficiency of data, where this may not be the case.[54]

4.1.9 Types of programs for young people: what works

We have been able to categorise programs roughly as:

- safe sex/condom promotion to prevent STIs (often including promotion of contraception also);

- abstinence only;

- abstinence plus — abstain, but use condoms if not;

- delay first intercourse programs — full information, including prophylaxis and contraception but also including effects of early sexual initiation, plus behavioural program, including group Cognitive Behavioural Therapy (CBT), some use of pledge to delay (e.g., six months renewable).

Another factor to be assessed is the involvement of parents in school curricula. As we discussed earlier, the limited research available on parent participation in school-based programs is very positive.

A concern we have about promoting so-called 'safe sex' is that it gives young people the impression that using condoms makes sexual intimacy safe. It may make sexual intimacy safer in relation to infection and pregnancy, but it certainly does not make sexual intimacy completely safe in that respect, nor does such promotion address the wider issues such as risk of emotional harm, self-harm, and suicide, risks to emerging gender identity, and risk of premature exposure to adult concepts and loss of childhood innocence. Such programs also do not address positively the need for personal affirmation of young people and their self-confidence in matters such as gender identity, the acquired ability to make free and reasoned choices about sexual (and other) conduct, and the enjoyment of good relating as a man or a woman and good dating.

Condoms are not even safe in relation to pregnancy and infection. They have a Pearl index of 3–15 pregnancies per hundred women years. The rates are higher in youth, and the rate of STI transmission from infected persons is higher again than the pregnancy rate. Condoms reduce chances of sexually transmissible disease with the heterosexual HIV transmission rate reduced by 80 per cent,[55] but only 50 per cent reduction in rates for genital herpes and genital warts viruses because they are spread from the genital area.

Since 1984, condom promotion to young people has been universal in Australia in schools, public advertisements, community education and higher education. But the uptake and continuance rates are mixed. A basic question to ask is whether STIs in young people fell. In fact, rates for the common STIs, such as chlamydia, genital herpes, and the human papilloma virus, are increasing in young people.

Overall, the assessment of prevention programs for youth is not very encouraging. A review commissioned by the World Health Organisation indicated dismal results for current sex-education programs.[56] A. Grunseit et al. reviewed forty-seven studies (published between 1974 and 1995) that evaluated sexuality-education interventions implemented in various countries. All studies addressed the behavioural impact of programs. Twenty-five reported that education neither increased nor decreased sexual activity and attendant rates of pregnancy and STIs; seventeen reported that education delayed the onset of sexual activity, reduced the number of sexual partners, or reduced unplanned pregnancy and STI rates; and three found increases in sexual behaviour associated with education (one of these was an abstinence-only program, one had potentially significant selection bias, and one reported correlational results, which did not imply causality).

Our view, based on reviewing the research, is that programs like the 'safe sex' programs that focus on avoiding or minimising harm have not been shown to be effective. Similarly there is little evidence that abstinence-only programs are effective. However, programs that present the facts *and* have values and behavioural components, like the pledge or delay-first-intercourse programs, have been shown to have some success.

The pledge or delay-sexual-intercourse programs are an interesting and very positive phenomena. These programs have:

- full information about risks and prevention, and a behavioural component (e.g., group CBT) addressing factors that lead to early sexual initiation, and

- short term focus (e.g., six-month pledge) that gives renewable protection, delays risk, and encourages more considered sexual decisions.

They are thought to be more realistic than abstinence-only programs but may have more social and behavioural content than most sex-education programs.

There is much evidence that the pledge or delay-first-intercourse programs have had some success. Michael Resnick et al., using a longitudinal study, showed that the effects of a virginity pledge in reducing sexual activity were statistically significant at the 99.9 per cent confidence level.[57] Andrew Doniger showed that 'Not Me, Not Now',an abstinence-oriented, adolescent pregnancy prevention communications program produced both shifts in attitudes and a decline in sexual activity rate over the intervention period that were statistically significant at the 95 per cent confidence level.[58] The difference in the rate of decline in adolescent pregnancy in Monroe County, when compared to other geographic areas, was statistically significant at the 95 to 99 per cent confidence levels. Elaine Borawski et al. showed similar results for delay-first-intercourse programs.[59] Peter Bearman and Hanna Bruckner showed that the effects of a virginity pledge were shown to be statistically significant at the 95 per cent confidence level.[60] In a six-month follow up for Intercourse Delay Program, Stephen Jorgensen et al. showed that the effects of the program in reducing the rate of onset of sexual activity were statistically significant at the 94.9 per cent confidence level.[61] The effects of the program on specific areas of knowledge were significant at the 95 per cent confidence level and above.

The quantity of sexual education programs and analyses of their effectiveness has increased significantly in the last several decades. Western society has increasingly turned to resolving the problems of adolescent sexuality and the associated increase in STIs. Teenage pregnancy and its social consequences have also drawn public attention. The investigation of improvements in teenage sexual health may potentially play a crucial role in defining the problem of the effectiveness of programs and approaches. Quality research is the way to improve sexual education of adolescents, whereupon a healthier society can be maintained.

However, the focus seems to have been on evidence in relation to factors that lead to avoiding teenage pregnancy and sexually transmissible infection, and has included, to a limited extent, a focus on factors that delay sexual initiation or 'debut'. It is not at all clear that that focus reflects the actual needs that young people have in relation to education in sexuality. What is needed first, is research on what those needs are. From that research it would be possible to draft educational objectives based on those needs, and then to develop and evaluate the effectiveness of various methods aimed at meeting those objectives.

4.2 Education in sexuality: needs, objectives, and methods

4.2.1 The goals of education in sexuality

The review of the literature would seem to indicate that effective sex education is holistic, containing information, values and behavioural components. We suggest that, in fact, education about sexual intimacy is a small component of sexuality education. A basic question to ask is: what are the goals of sexuality education? But before that question can be answered, there is the prior question: what are the needs of the target groups?

The reality is that, though we may to a large extent understand the biology, human sexuality is a mystery emotionally, cognitively and spiritually. It is a mystery that unfolds throughout life. The differences between men and women are a part of that mystery and constitute the phenomenon of complementarity. Being man or woman is part of our identity, and our sexuality affects all aspects of being an individual who is at one and the same time both a bodily and a spiritual being. Sexuality especially concerns affectivity, the capacity to love and to procreate, and in a more general way, the capacity to form bonds of communion with others.

Education in sexuality thus begins with the first relationships that a child forms with his or her parents and siblings. There a child normally feels secure, is recognised and loved, and learns to become a lover, one who gives of himself or herself to others. In the first instance, guidance in human sexuality thus happens by the example of the parents and their love for each other and the creation of an environment of respect for the human person and individual dignity.

Sex-education programs therefore are an adjunct to a process that is already well established by the time a child begins formal education. There are of course numerous other influences that are formative of a child's capacity to relate and to enter into communion with others. They include:

- peers
- television
- movies
- internet (chat and download)
- computer games

- magazines
- newspapers
- books
- busybodies

An obvious need in education in sexuality is to respect the dignity of the individual who is the focus of the education. Crucial to that education is the surety that content is age appropriate, appropriate to the level of maturity of the child. Looked at from that perspective, much of the education that comes from 'other' sources is not respectful of the dignity of the child, for it is designed to serve other goals. It is also not controllable. Much of the need for education in sexuality is thus remedial or preventative, a response to content that is of an exploitative nature.

While sex-education programs are invariably directed to adolescents, the foundations for a well-adjusted individual are laid much earlier than that. Along the way one hopes that a child's education in sexuality would have:

- fostered positive self-image and self-esteem,
- formed confidence in his or her gender identity (male or female),
- protected innocence,
- responded encouragingly to curiosity,
- provided a home environment in which he or she can appreciate parents' love for each other and thus has good behavioural models for the way in which men and women relate to each other,
- established the capacity in knowledge, values, skills, and behaviour to understand, appreciate, and protect his or her health, including fertility, to develop friendships and to respect the dignity of others,
- assisted the child to regard sexual intimacy as purposeful, significant, and powerful in its capacity

to express and receive love, but also vulnerable and needing to be protected and reserved for those committed circumstances in which it is an expression of love rather than of use.

These then are some general goals for sex education. However they do to an extent represent an idealistic view. We know that the reality for many children is not so positive. A reason for the focus on sex education is the fact that, as a community and as parents and teachers, we often fail our children. One of the greatest fears every parent has is that a child will be so maladjusted and unhappy as to commit self-harm. The evidence about the causes of self-harm and suicide is compelling. We know that there are strong associations between social factors, self-harm and suicide.

The National Health and Medical Research Council's review of youth suicide identified major social factors in relation to youth suicide including: low socioeconomic status, poor educational achievement, parental separation or divorce, parental psychopathology, family history of suicidal behaviour, parental discord, childhood abuse, and poor parental care.[62] Other factors include mental illness, sexual orientation, interpersonal losses or conflicts, legal or disciplinary crises, other life events, and unemployment.

The goals of education in sexuality are inseparable from the general goals that parents have for their children: for them to be secure, happy, well-adjusted, and developing as persons in truth and love toward greater freedom. Education in sexuality is a part of seeking happiness and fulfilment, and it is obviously subject to whatever conclusions have been drawn about what constitutes happiness and fulfilment.

Our view of happiness and fulfilment is a religious view. We hold that religious values are important to education in sexuality because religion portrays sexual intimacy positively as an opportunity to develop in the image and likeness of God. Religious values recognise that human beings find fulfilment in outreach to others. Marriage is a gift of self to one's spouse and that gift of love may become the gift of a child as an embodiment of that loving union. Marriage is thus a God-like role being a *self-sacrifice*, giving oneself as Christ gave himself to all humankind, *covenantal* as God's relationship to us is covenantal, and *creative* in giving and nurturing life so that those children develop in love and truth as free individuals in the way in which the creator made us free. The religious values exclude notions of use and exploitation and replace them with notions of loving and giving. Central to that divine imagery is the notion of a community of persons, the community of persons of the Trinity, the community of persons of a marriage, the community of persons of one's family, and the local and wider communities.

But whether or not one takes a religious view, one can recognise the importance to human fulfilment of developing human virtues. The human virtues are the acquired personal attributes necessary to develop as a human being. Their premise is the notion that individual human development is important. The core virtues are about being able to discern what is good for human development and to choose how to achieve it (wisdom), about recognising the needs of others and acting justly towards them (justice), about having the courage in the face of difficulties to pursue goodness, and about achieving self-mastery of the will over one's instincts (temperance). These virtues are said to be core, firstly, because they are common to all reasoned approaches to morality; secondly, because they are essential to good community life; and thirdly, because, if one pauses to reflect on them, one can see that the complete absence of any one of them would in fact constitute a mental illness!

These virtues are also essential to being a good lover. To be able to give oneself to another, one needs to be able to discern goodness so that one can serve the other by pursuing what is good for his/her development and for one's own development. To love someone, one also must be just towards the other. Giving oneself in love also requires a great deal of courage, because love makes us vulnerable and more easily hurt. Finally, and very importantly, giving oneself in love is a reasoned choice in which one masters one's own instincts and redirects one's drives for the sake of the other. Classically this aspect of loving is known as chastity.

Chastity is the successful integration of sexuality within the person. To be a good lover, one must first have mastered one's sexual instincts and directed them towards the unified goodness of one's entire person as a physical, emotional, intelligent, and spiritual being. Only then is one able to make a complete gift of oneself to another. Chastity is important for it allows the bodily aspects of sexuality to become personal and truly human by being integrated into the relationship of one person to another, in the complete and lifelong mutual gift of a man and a woman. In this way, the sexual joining of a man and a woman is expressive of their personhood at all levels and not just at the biological level, because it is giving rather than using. The virtues make it possible for a person to be at ease with himself or herself, to achieve self-mastery, and to experience joy in leading a morally good life. Goodness becomes that person's normal practice, and he or she is fully free because not impeded by vice. A vice is a disposition toward practices that impede, obstruct, or destroy human development.

Our view is that a central objective of education in sexuality is to guide young people to be good lovers. To be good lovers they need to acquire the core virtues, and chastity is an element of those core virtues. This is not, of course, an isolated goal. The evidence would suggest that abstinence-only programs are ineffective. More than that, we would suggest that they do the child or the young person a disservice because the virtues are aspects of human development that are interrelated.

The problem of imbalance in sex education arises, we think, in sex education being something of a remedy for failures in education or a response to the age inappropriate and exploitative education that is the effect of the media. The task, we suggest, is a much broader task and begins the moment, as an infant, a child starts to relate to others. The task is to guide a person toward an appreciation of the goodness of human existence and human development, toward a desire to know the truth (including self-knowledge), a lively interest in and awareness of the needs of others, and a desire for self-mastery. This is basically what sex education is about, and we do them a disservice if we focus only on one aspect. Education forms a person in knowledge, skills, attitudes and behaviours. Education in sexuality ought to address each of those components.

4.2.2 Partners in sex education

Obviously parents have the primary role in the broad notion of education in sexuality presented here. They form the child's first relationships, and they usually provide the first example to the child of manhood and womanhood and of a giving relationship between a man and a woman. Their love for the child and for each other is thus formative.

The role of parents is, in a strong sense, God-like: initiating life, providing the environment for the new life, and nurturing directed towards the child ultimately gaining the freedom that comes from knowledge, acquiring skills and behaviours, learning to value, and deciding to act in ways that foster human development. Their love for the child gives them the natural authority to lead in the development of their child. The parents' role is so primary that any other person intervening should be seen as partners with the parents rather than as independent of them. In that respect our view is that those conducting education in sexuality should first seek that partnership with the parents and work through the content of proposed programs with them, seeking their approval, collaboration and support. It follows, then, that schools and public education programs should see themselves as primarily supportive of the parents' role. As professional educators, teachers have access to resources and new developments in teaching methodology that help to inform behaviour and values. By working closely with the parents, teachers can assist them in their task.

Crucial to good programs is the assessment of need so as to determine what is age appropriate for children at the level they are and given the exposure they have to events inside and outside the home. Parents are intrinsic to that assessment as they are likely to know their individual child and his or her circumstances better than anyone else. Respecting the age of innocence, and allowing children to be children, is important and a child's right.

That said, parents may find educating their children in sexuality a difficult and embarrassing task. In our experience, parents often turn to the school to provide resources and support in this respect. Teachers and schools can assist by imparting knowledge and up-to-date resources suitable for parents to use.

Public educators, including those considering a state-wide or national program, would be well advised to address their material to parents for them to use with their children. In our experience, one of the most effective forms of education is the worksheet designed for children and parents to work with together. If material is provided to parents, they, then, can decide when particular material is suitable for their child and introduce it in the safety and security of the parent-child relationship.

4.2.3 Foundations of education in sexuality

In our view, the foundation of an education in sexuality is the notion that our sexuality reflects our capacity to be given love and to give life, and the primary value is the worth and dignity of each member of the human family. Also foundational is the reality that sexuality involves the whole person and that respecting human dignity means both respecting a person as a body and as a chooser.

For that reason, we hold that sexuality should occur across the key learning areas and not be seen as the prerogative of any particular area. It is a grave mistake to see sexuality education as a matter of health-science alone or of physical education or of social science and history or of religious studies. Each has a part to play in the development of the child. Adequate education in sexuality is not fragmented. The biology of reproduction, for example, and matters of reproductive health, ought not be taught without reflecting on human love and supportive relationships.

That points to the need for education in sexuality within a school to be formally coordinated. Information should be appropriate to the different phases of a child's development and delivered in a context in which the child feels comfortable and not embarrassed. Sensitivity should be shown towards those aspects of sexuality that are best treated individually. Dependence on the role of parents, in that respect, is important for they normally provide a relationship of friendship and trust. The intimate details of sexual union are never matters for classroom discussion.

Presentation of material of an erotic or arousing nature to children or young people is exploitative. No one should ever be invited, let alone obliged, to act in a way that could offend against modesty or against his or her own sense of delicacy or privacy.

Educators in this area need to be particularly sensitive to the cultural and family environment in which a child lives. At the same time, it would be a mistake for educators to endorse an exploitative cultural or family situation.

4.2.4 Methods of education in sexuality

Education in sexuality warrants the attention of our best minds in teaching and learning methodology. Creativity and innovation should be encouraged but supported by sound research and comprehensively evaluated to ensure that it is meeting the broad goals of education is sexuality. However, it is important that that creativity not breach fundamental principles in relation to what is age appropriate and respectful of the age of innocence and what is respectful of human dignity and the love-giving and life-giving meaning of sexuality. Interventions that promote an irresponsible or recreational attitude to sex or treat it at the level only of a bodily function are not only not helpful, but are dangerous to the emotional, physical, and spiritual well-being of young people.

As has been shown by the research review, there is no evidence to show that so-called 'safe sex' programs are effective when they do not also teach the dignity of the human person and the meaning of sexuality. While hygiene concerning bodily fluids should be taught at an appropriately earlier age, the sexual transmission of disease needs to be handled sensitively, using accurate medical information. It should be introduced with care only at an appropriate age and discussed in the context of the meaning of sexuality and a holistic understanding of the human person and human relationships. Sexuality programs need to be integrated so that they encompass the development of the whole person.

4.3 Ethics and the evaluation of effectiveness of education in sexuality

Systematically gathering information about children or young people is research and raises a number of important issues including:

- freedom of participation - discerning whether they are in a dependent relationship (teacher-student, for instance),

- confidentiality,

- suggestive effects of raising sensitive topics with children.

In Australia, there are national guidelines on the ethics of human research. The guidelines have been published by the National Health and Medical Research Council and endorsed by the Australian Vice Chancellors Committee and the Australian Research Council. The guidelines should govern the conduct of research on the effectiveness of education in sexuality.

Of particular note is the fact that if teenagers are asked about their sexual (or other behaviour) they may disclose information about crimes such as sexual or violent abuse or illegal drug taking. Under state law that information may not be held confidential by those in mandated professions, but is required, under the mandatory reporting provisions, to be reported. If one is asking questions in those areas then, under our law, one may not guarantee anonymity. The individuals remain re-identifiable usually, in any case, if the information is of an intimate or descriptive nature.

Basically anyone conducting such research would be well advised to seek approval for a formal protocol from:

- an NHMRC-registered human research ethics committee,
- the school principal and the education authority (or the leadership of the youth group to whom the program is being delivered), and
- the parents of each child.

The protocol would need to include the plain-language statement to parents. It would need not only to specify anonymity and confidentiality, but also the conditions under which disclosure would be made, such as, if a young person was discovered to be at risk of abuse, or other matters of a criminal nature. The plain-language statement would also need to specify how the information was to be handled, the purposes for which it would be used, how long and how it would be stored, what efforts would be made to de-identity it and how re-identification would be prevented, who would have access to it, and how statistical data gathered from the information would be used, especially information that related to a particular group.

Chapter 5

Reframing the anti-abortion message: pro-life and/or pro-woman?

Brigid McKenna (Vout)

The secret is out — one in four pregnancies in Australia ends in induced abortion and seven out of ten Australians think that this rate is too high. Australians are publicly talking about abortion again. Additionally, women who are hurting as a result of their abortion experiences are courageously breaking the silence and causing us to question whether abortion is the panacea that it was promised to be. For the pro-life movement in Australia, this renewed dialogue brings opportunities, as well as challenges. 'Whereto from here?' we ask (or we should be asking!). How can public discussion of abortion move from statistics to morality, from tolerance to change, from acquiescence with the culture of death to building the culture of life? One suggestion for strengthening anti-abortion attitudes and behaviour is for the pro-life movement to adopt some of the 'women-centred' strategic proposals to emerge from the USA over the past fifteen years: to become more pro-woman in order to become more pro-life! This chapter attempts to look closely at the overall rationale and underlying reasoning of women-centred strategies, by listening to their critics as well as their advocates, in order to assess their role in the abortion debate in Australia.

What are women-centred, pro-life strategies? Why are they being used? Women-centred, pro-life strategies aim to reduce the acceptance and incidence of abortion by drawing attention to the harm that abortion does, not to the foetus, but to the woman who aborts. They begin with the claim that most women neither want nor benefit from abortion — that most women do not really 'choose' abortion but are pressured into it by others, only to experience a range of negative physical and psychological effects after abortion. These claims are used to:

- redefine the abortion debate in terms of the legitimate needs and welfare of pregnant women rather than in terms of an exclusive focus upon the unborn;
- limit the harm that abortion causes women by working to:
  - improve *free* and *informed* consent by minimising coercion and increasing awareness of the physical and psychological risks involved with abortion.
  - promote programs of practical assistance to pregnant women and social policy, which ensure that women are provided with real alternatives to abortion.
  - promote compassion and assistance to women after abortion.

Emphasis upon these concerns and activities, it is claimed, represents an important shift in focus for the pro-life movement, which for the past thirty years or so has concentrated most of its effort on dispelling the notion that abortion destroys only a 'bunch of cells', not a human being. The movement has primarily employed a 'foetal-centred strategy', which hinges on the message that 'abortion kills a very young human being'.

A vast amount of money, time and effort has been employed to educate the public about the humanity of the unborn child, with good results. Major research into Australians' attitudes to abortion found that 58 per cent of Australians do not accept the 'foetus is not a person' argument.[1] In the United States nearly 80 per cent of the public now admit that abortion involves the destruction of a human life.[2]

Yet while this 'foetal-centred' approach to abortion has successfully raised awareness of what happens during an abortion, this has not translated into a significant reduction in the number of abortions. Fifty-eight per cent of Australians accept that the foetus is a person, but 70 per cent agree with arguments for legal access to abortion based upon women's rights and the idea that abortion is a 'necessary evil', while 75 per cent agree with the argument that it gives women control over their own lives.[3] Foetal-centred approaches might have helped to educate the public about the humanity of the unborn, but the public is still not convinced that the 'rights' of the foetus are more important than those of women, especially women 'in crisis'. Instead, there is an 'ambivalent majority' who agree in a soft and general way that abortion is wrong, but believe it must be tolerated as an 'evil necessity'.

Recognition of this phenomenon in the USA during the 1990s led to a major rethink of the pro-life message. Some leaders in the pro-life movement began to ask how it was that people could be against abortion personally, yet in favour of keeping it legal. Why hadn't acceptance of the humanity of the foetus converted into public opposition to abortion? These questions prompted new research into attitudes to abortion that challenged assumptions about how the pro-life movement should approach the abortion debate.

Some pro-life researchers sought to understand more about the reasons why women choose abortion and how to identify and assist those who were most at risk of having abortions. One study found that even though 70 per cent of women who abort acknowledge that abortion is morally wrong, 52 per cent felt coerced by an outside source such as a boyfriend, family member, or doctor, while 83 per cent said they would have carried their baby to term had they received support from boyfriend, families, etc.[4]

Other research found that many women are unable to see any good coming from an unplanned pregnancy. Instead they perceive motherhood as a threat — and as one so serious as to represent a 'death of self' with the result that abortion is the least of three perceived evils: motherhood, adoption, and abortion.[5] These women do not think in the same way a pro-lifer would think, often weighing up the choice as 'either my life is over or the life of this new child is over' or believing that given the difficult circumstances into which he or she would enter the world, often the child is better off aborted.[6] Commenting on this research, Paul Swope observed that 'it is not so clear that our culture is guided by the moral absolute, "It is always wrong to take the life of an innocent child", precisely because there is the perceived "death" to the woman as well, which greatly alters the moral equation in the public mind'.[7] This research also found that pro-life slogans and educational presentations that focus almost exclusively on the unborn child, not the mother, have tended to build resentment towards their message, not sympathy, particularly among women of childbearing age.[8] Much of this seems to correlate with the finding that in Australia the strongest pro-abortion arguments are about a woman's right to choose and her empowerment to make a decision that may be bad, but is, in all circumstances, justifiable.[9]

Armed with these insights, strategists began to search for a way ahead between the extremes of the polarised pro-choice versus pro-life debate, which focused on reaching and persuading those who are on ambivalent middle ground.[10] Swope observed that:

> The current dynamics of the public debate work against this: in politics the middle ground is rejected; in the media pro-lifers are portrayed as violent extremists and thus utterly alienated from the middle ground; in the pro-life movement itself moral principles allow no room for a middle ground; and the 'pro-life' and 'pro-choice' labels portray the debate as a tug-of-war between extremes. In all four arenas pro-lifers are not persuasively communicating with the very group that has the potential to move in our direction.[11]

Frederica Mathewes-Green noted that the pro-abortion people had largely abandoned speaking of abortion as 'liberating'. Instead they had 'hung a lantern on their biggest problem'—that abortion was a painful rather than exhilarating experience—convincing America that women were already suffering enough and that the least they deserved was to be left alone to decide for themselves.[12] The so-called 'pro-choice' movement in the USA had already reframed their message. Was it time for the pro-life movement to do likewise?

Swope, Mathewes-Green, Reardon and others decided that it was time. Observing that people are generally open to the concerns of women above the life of the foetus, they began to use arguments on behalf of the pregnant woman in crisis or the suffering post-abortive woman to challenge their moral ambivalence. They began to present the public with hard evidence and moving stories about post-abortion harm to challenge the majority opinion that abortion should be tolerated as a 'necessary evil'. Swope described it this way:

> Pro-lifers disdain the term 'pro-choice', but we need to understand that when a woman vulnerable to abortion uses the term, she uses it not in the sense of 'freedom to kill a baby', but rather 'freedom to preserve my own life'. We may be quick—and rightfully so—to prioritise the real death of the unborn child over the imagined death of the woman, but to do so is to miss the key ingredient that affects society's attitude to abortion, namely, the welfare of the woman involved.[13]

It was time to 'reframe the message' and 'redefine the abortion debate' by focusing (as the pro-abortion movement does) on the issue of defending the interests of women. Using stories of women's negative experience of abortion[14] and good epidemiological studies about the physical and psychological harm caused by abortion,[15] women-centred strategists set about dispelling the central claims of the pro-abortion movement—that abortion ensures women's autonomy and well-being.

Responding to the belief that abortion should be tolerated so that women can at least retain some control over their lives and their bodies, women-centred approaches began to challenge the pro-abortion movement's rhetoric of choice by drawing attention to the incidence of unwanted abortions. They argued that most women do not want abortions; that most women who have abortions do not freely choose abortion.

In response to the belief that abortion should be tolerated for the sake of helping women who find themselves in difficult circumstances (e.g., mental health problems or rape), women-centred approaches argued that women do not benefit from abortion. They began to emphasise negative effects of abortion on women—physical, psychological, relational, cultural and spiritual.

5.1 Some pro-life criticisms

Women-centred approaches are, however, not without controversy. Within the pro-life movement, questions have been raised, often with great passion, about whether it is strategically misguided and possibly even morally wrong to concentrate the public's attention on anyone other than abortion's primary victim, the unborn child.[16] Can a pro-woman strategy really shift public opinion away from support for abortion? Can a pro-woman strategy be pursued without compromising moral opposition to abortion?

Francis Beckwith argues that this attempt to reframe the abortion debate, or adopt what he terms the 'new rhetorical strategy' (NRS),[17] overstates the extent that practical problems drive women to act against their conscience and choose to have an abortion. Beckwith questions whether the practical problems of motherhood would also cause women to commit infanticide or child homicide at an equally high rate as they weighed up the equation 'either my life is over or the life of my child is over'? Swope, Reardon, and others, he says, are mistaken in thinking that the majority of the public is convinced of the humanity of the foetus and that pregnant women seeking abortions see their foetuses on the same moral plane as they see either themselves or their already born children.

Beckwith also questions the quality and interpretation of the research upon which the NRS is based. He argues that Mathewes-Green's oft quoted Real Choices Project,[18] which sets out to discover the practical reasons why women have abortions, is not representative of the general population of women who have abortions because it draws largely upon information from pro-life pregnancy centres and women involved in post-abortion support groups. He criticises Swope's claims about the ineffectiveness of the traditional pro-life strategy as unsubstantiated and points out that Swope 'does not have counterfactual knowledge of how the world would have been if the pro-life movement had not emphasised foetal humanity from its genesis'.[19] He also questions whether attitudinal studies test for real or apparent pro-life sentiments, noting that even if the NRS can reduce the number of abortions, it does not follow that the culture is actually becoming more accepting of the pro-life message: 'Although an appeal to self-interest may persuade some women not to have abortions, the choice not to abort for this reason is not the same as a moral conversion and intellectual assent to the pro-life perspective.'[20]

Even more seriously, Beckwith suggests that an emphasis on appealing to the pregnant woman's self-interest to persuade her against abortion could actually nurture and sustain the very moral presuppositions that allow for abortion. He points out that Swope and others have no principled argument against abortion in circumstances where, morality aside, abortion is in the pregnant woman's relational, financial, physical, educational, or professional best interests. Even if the new rhetorical strategy were to result in fewer abortions, it 'may have the unfortunate consequence of sustaining and perhaps increasing the number of people who think that unless their needs are pacified, they are perfectly justified in performing homicide on other members of the human community'.[21]

5.2 How do women-centred pro-life strategists respond to such criticisms?

David Reardon counters these arguments by insisting that the pro-woman approach is not only consistent with the pro-life moral imperative, but a fuller expression of it. Reardon points out that it is only the mother who can directly nurture her unborn child; all the rest of us can do is nurture the mother. He talks, therefore, of a unified 'pro-woman/pro-life agenda', which is guided by the principle that the best interests of the child and the mother are always joined (even if the mother does not initially realise it). Thus, the only way to help either the mother or her child is to help both. Conversely, if either is hurt, both are hurt. Reardon believes that women-centred strategies do not undermine moral opposition to abortion so long as a focus on post-abortion issues subsumes, but not replaces, the issue of the unborn child's human rights. He thinks that it is time for the pro-life and pro-choice movements to overcome the individualistic assumptions of the 'old abortion debate' that has tended to pit the rights and interests of women and unborn children against one another. He challenges both sides by insisting that women and unborn children have *shared* rather than *rival* interests. As such, we should be helping each other to understand that abortion is morally wrong because it is an attack against the life of an unborn child and an attack against the integral well being of the woman, because it kills the unborn and harms women physically, psychologically, and spiritually.

At another level, Reardon argues that rather than sidestepping the immorality of abortion, women-centred arguments actually have a greater chance of achieving moral conversion. He proposes that because the interests of a mother and child are permanently intertwined, when we begin to talk about post-abortion issues, we are implicitly beginning to talk about the physical and behavioural symptoms of a moral problem. He believes this is our greatest chance of drawing the ambivalent majority back to recognise the root cause of the problem: the injustice of killing the unborn. Why? Because, whenever others cannot be convinced to acknowledge a moral truth for its own sake, the second best option is to appeal to their self-interest and help them to see that unethical acts are injurious to their happiness.

Mary Cunningham Agee justifies women-centred arguments on similar grounds when she writes:

> In a society in which moral standards are dismissed as a matter of personal opinion, defending human life based on the fifth commandment's proscription 'Thou shall not kill' is not likely to change many minds. In a civilisation in which objective truth is considered to be unattainable or merely subjective, how much credence would an exclusively rational argument be given? In a culture in which only 'feelings' are widely accepted as real or valid, an argument (against abortion) based exclusively on what is 'right and reasonable' is unlikely to be persuasive.[22]

The key to prying open (in her case, American) closed minds is through an emotional appeal to personal — and therefore, irrefutable — experience, such as the suffering woman's experience after abortion. According to this approach, we need to replace objective, deductive and principled moral argumentation with subjective, inductive and experiential ways of coming to understand moral truth.[23]

It remains to be seen whether or not Australian 'pro-lifers' will choose one approach over the other, or seek to strike an effective balance between them. Failing to try new strategies may result in losing unborn lives and not preventing further women, families, and communities from bearing the long-term scars of abortion. On the other hand, placing too much faith and energy into these new strategies may increase public awareness of what abortion does to women but fall short of advancing the understanding that the reason why abortion harms women is because it is a violation of the natural moral order. There is clearly a need for further attitudinal studies and sound philosophical reflection about some of the risks involved in placing too much confidence in the subjective, inductive and experiential nature of modern hearts and minds.

It could be dangerous if the dominant public argument against abortion was that 'abortion causes harm to women'. Isn't the reason that we have a culture that supports abortion partly due to the systematic rejection of objective, inductive and principled ethical thinking? Could the overly enthusiastic uptake of a message that essentially says 'abortion is wrong because of all the bad effects that it has upon women' further compromise our stance against a 'results are all that counts' ethic? Is it enough to appeal to self-interest over recognition and observance of objective, moral principles? As we ponder these questions we should remember that some, perhaps many, abortions do not result in an experience of suffering or harm to the women who have them, yet their abortions are still morally wrong. Furthermore, sometimes decisions to continue with a pregnancy are accompanied by genuine suffering or harm to women, yet their choice remains morally right. Doing good may require that one suffer more than if one did either evil or no good at all.[24]

How too, will an appeal to self-interest help us to address other moral decisions about human life, such as destructive embryo research, genetic enhancement, euthanasia, or assisted suicide?[25] The new rhetoric might work to save an unborn human being's life, but it could leave the parents, at least morally and intellectually, where they were. Clever marketing and reframed messages might change some immediate attitudes and behaviour, but the general impoverishment of ethical reasoning might corrupt future choices.

5.3 Some pro-abortion responses

Ironically, the pro-abortion movement also alerts us to some of the strengths and weaknesses of women-centred pro-life strategies. If some people within the pro-life movement have doubts about the motive and effectiveness of women-centred strategies, the pro-abortion movement seems to be quite clear about their motive, as well as being concerned about their effectiveness. One Australian commentator recently wrote:

> A certain amount of kudos must be given to the religious right for listening to the voices of women. They have finally heard our concerns, listened to our fears, and acknowledged the inequalities in our lives. Now, after taking detailed notes, they have stolen our slogans for their own conservative gains.[26]

Leslie Cannold has warned the pro-abortion movement that it is 'imperative that pro-choice feminists develop an integrated analysis of this strategy and an effective response to it' that includes 'not only literal rebuttals based on evidence, but also information and arguments that are able to counter its ideological power'.[27] She draws attention to the fact that many women-centred strategists are reluctant to identify themselves with the broader pro-life movement and 'have pragmatically dropped religious justifications and adopted feminist principles and concepts like informed consent in order to broaden their support base'. This is, she thinks, 'surprisingly effective,' but something that can be easily undermined by the production of documentary evidence linking women-centred activists with the 'anti-choice movement and anti-choice beliefs'.

> Presenting such hard evidence in the media enables questions to be asked about the motives women-centred activists have for denying their anti-choice connections and about their trustworthiness on other issues. More importantly, connecting women-centred strategy with anti-choice activists and the anti-choice agenda makes it clear that the strategy is designed to exploit women's negative experiences with abortion as a means to anti-choice ends.[28]

It is likely, therefore, that abortion supporters will try to undermine a women-centred pro-life strategy with charges of deception and exploitation, strengthened by their assessment that: 'Feeling that their own and other women's experiences are being used to pursue an anti-choice agenda—and that anti-choice activists are seeking to disguise this fact—increases women's resentment of the anti-choice movement'.[29] Nothing less than transparency and active genuine compassion for women, combined with clever rhetoric, will be required to meet these charges.

Cannold also believes the women-centred strategy implies that if a woman who fully understands all the necessary information makes a voluntary decision to have an abortion, then that decision and the resulting abortion would be (morally) legitimate. She knows that this does not sit well with most 'pro-lifers' and that it could give rise to serious division within the movement. Additionally, she is not convinced that attempts by pro-life strategists, such as David Reardon, to avert this by combining women-centred claims and tactics with foetal-centred ones will be as effective because 'the power of a women-centred strategy comes from its reversal of unpopular elements of the foetal-centred approach, and linking the two seems to facilitate women's recognition that 'anti-choice concern' about women's abortion grief is grounded in the aim of prohibiting abortion'.[30]

Yet there are signs that abortion supporters and providers are threatened by an increased focus on women's negative experience of abortion, and have begun to re-examine their practices and rhetoric. *Newsweek* recently carried an article titled 'Politics of Choice' which described pro-choice activists and abortion providers striving for greater transparency by seeking to make the parents of pregnant teenagers more involved in abortion decisions, branching into post-abortion counselling, and adopting words like 'baby' and 'killing' when referring to abortion because they acknowledge that this is how many women seeking abortions speak and feel.[31] One abortion clinic director in Pittsburgh, Pennsylvania, USA, has begun employing chaplains to arrange baptisms for aborted foetuses, setting up mediation or prayer spaces in clinics and developing a website where women can write messages to their aborted baby. The article quotes Frances Kissling, head of Catholics for A Free Choice, as saying: 'It's hard to trust us when we present ourselves as callous… If we were more honest about the ambiguities and the conflicts, people would feel they could trust us and wouldn't need to pass all those laws against us.'[32]

5.4 A way forward

It appears that there is an important role for further reflection and discussion if pro-life women-centred strategies are to have positive and lasting impact upon the abortion debate in Australia. These final six points are suggestions as to how the integrity and efficacy of these strategies might be strengthened.

1. Strategies should be integrated with traditional pro-life strategies and arguments. A range of different pro-life voices and messages need to be promoted. There will always be a need for principled arguments against abortion: arguments about the humanity of the foetus and the inviolability of human life. There seems also, to be a good case for women-centred arguments: arguments about the harm that abortion does to women, about the legitimate rights of women and the need to support mothers—young or old, married or single, and especially when they are alone, abused, overwhelmed, or undervalued. As Pope John Paul II insisted, it is necessary for those who oppose abortion to become courageously 'pro-woman.'[33]

There will be a time, a place and an audience for women-centred arguments over foetal-centred arguments, and vice versa. But wherever possible, our preference ought to be to link statements about care and concern for women with our commitment to protect the unborn. It is not enough to say 'abortion is wrong because it hurts women'. We have to mean what we say and say what we mean: 'abortion is wrong because it hurts women and kills unborn children'.

One reason for this is that authentic love, made manifest in care and concern for the other, should be radically inclusive of women and their children. If human life is sacred and inviolable at every stage and in every circumstance where life is involved, charity cannot tolerate bias and discrimination.[34] Additionally, if we always stop short of arguments on behalf of the foetus as well as women, we risk leaving too many people behind by abdicating our individual or collective responsibility as moral educators or, as abortion supporters remind us, by further alienating people by arousing their suspicion and distrust. In our desperation to reach the middle majority who has been closed to the traditional pro-life message, we must not completely abandon consistent and principled ethical arguments.

2. They require us to continue to grow in, and demonstrate, genuine compassion for women. Women-centred pro-life strategies provide us with an opportunity to correct the public image of 'pro-lifers' as judgmental and uncompassionate. But we must be honest about ourselves and our communities and ensure that walls of judgmentalism and condemnation, particularly towards post-abortive women, have in fact been broken down. Most importantly, we must never be deserving of the pro-abortion movement's criticisms that we are 'exploiting' the suffering of post-abortive women for our own ends.

3. They should be linked to existing or new programs of practical assistance. We need to put our money, our time, and our efforts where our mouth is.[35] The pro-life movement has in fact recognised this for a long time — pregnancy counselling and support services have provided women with much needed assistance and love for many years, often at great sacrifice. But perhaps one area that has been

too long overlooked is public policy. One of the challenges which lies at the heart of a women-centred approach is working to ensure that society rethinks big questions regarding maternity and paternity leave, educational and workplace practices, childcare, tax structures, and other social policies that need to be much more woman/child/family friendly.

4. They should include and engage men. Too many men already feel unable to contribute to social debate or individual decisions about abortion. Yet when surveyed, 76 per cent of Australians thought that men and women had the right to participate equally in the abortion debate.[36] The modern feminist movement has deliberately alienated all men in order to punish a few. Ironically, women-centred pro-life strategies represent an opportunity to bring men back into the picture, by focusing upon the needs of pregnant women and the particular responsibility of fathers to meet these needs. Genuine progress is impossible without men.

5. They should be a part of a broader cultural approach to reducing abortion. The Australian Catholic Bishops' most recent general statement on abortion draws upon some of this wisdom when it speaks of the 'need to build a culture that respects the link between life and love, welcomes and esteems children and families, and supports women in every way'.[37] It is also reflected in statements like this one from Serrin Foster of Feminists for Life America which says that we must work to 'reverse the negative attitudes toward children and parenting that have become so prevalent in our culture. Our society once again needs to cherish motherhood, champion fatherhood, and celebrate the benefits and rewards of parenthood.'[38] A pro-woman culture must be integrated within a vision for a pro-children, pro-family culture.

6. They should be part of a broader approach to life issues and efforts to promote respect for the dignity of the human person which recognises the interconnectedness of attitudes

and practices that animate our current 'culture of death': the practical materialism which breeds individualism, utilitarianism, and hedonism and spawns acts of terrorism, euthanasia, abortion, abuses of biotechnology, etc. These are all attacks on human life and dignity; they are all linked; they must all be addressed.[39]

These, then, are a few reflections about how to advance a pro-woman pro-life agenda. There is of course much more to study, reflect, discuss, and decide upon in this area. Hopefully, people with great wisdom and experience, as well as people with fresh ideas and new energy will undertake this task together. Too much is at stake for us not to unite and clarify our own ideas about how best to protect and promote the life and dignity of women and their unborn children.

Chapter 6

Moving beyond the polarised debate on abortion: the way of the future

Marcia Riordan

The debate on abortion in Australia is changing and changing for good. For too many years the debate was polarised into a battle over the rights of the child verus the rights of the woman. Too often, slogans and rhetoric were all that was heard and the public became largely disengaged, uninterested, disillusioned. And the debate went nowhere. Sometimes attempts to bring about a renewed public debate were met with claims that it is a battle that has already been won and that there is no need to revisit it.

In the past, little attempt was made to engage the general public in the debate by assessing public attitudes and responding to those attitudes. Recent research by John Fleming and others (see chapter two) provides important insight into the Australian public's attitudes to abortion. For instance, while 62 per cent of the public may say that they support abortion on demand, this figure drops when different circumstances are considered and when they are asked how strongly they support such a position. A poll has also demonstrated that 63 per cent of Australians either oppose or are not strongly supportive of abortion on demand, and that 64 to 73 per cent of Australians think that the abortion rate is too high.

If the debate is to be advanced, the findings that 87 per cent of Australians believe that it would be a good thing if the numbers of abortions were reduced while at the same time protecting existing legal rights to freely choose abortion, is of some significance. This shows that Australians are conflicted with respect to the issue of abortion. It demonstrates that while they do not like abortion and wish abortions did not occur, they are not going to stop anyone from having an abortion. It also demonstrates that they will not vote to support legislative bans at this point in time.

Importantly, Fleming found that 94 per cent of Australians think that all the alternatives should be seriously considered before choosing abortion, and 99 per cent thought that women should have access to counselling before an abortion. Yet surprisingly, he found that although the public thought that a woman considering abortion should seek advice from more than one source, for example, a health professional with no ties to the abortion clinic, friends or relatives, or professional counselling service, most (58 per cent) did not know where to refer a woman for support.[1] This shows that there is clear public support for pregnancy counselling and support programs and that much more needs to be done to ensure that abortion becomes a last resort not the first.

If a move is to be made away from the old slogans and rhetoric and toward nurture of the new debate, the survey's findings, that only 22 per cent of Australians think that they are not well informed on the topic of abortion and 71 per cent support greater public discussion, become important. It means that new ways of educating and informing the public about abortion need to be found without resorting to slogans, rhetoric or heated debates.

This survey provides renewed reasons to hope that it is possible to move the debate forward. If many of the findings in the SCBI survey are taken up, the general public may become engaged and reignite the debate in ways not possible only a few years ago. But there are also other reasons to hope. The USA is witnessing a fairly dramatic change in public opinion, and this change has occurred in a relatively short space of time.

> It was just a typical week in Middle America where the decades old debate of abortion rights has become a full-blown battle. But even as they continue to raise money and march around state capitals, the view from the pro-choice side is this is a fight they are losing.[2]

The last ten years have seen abortion once again become a significant issue in the United States, and an issue that is far from settled. And 'when a rap singer is urging young women "to make the right decision and don't go through with this knife incision", America's abortion wars are in a different psychological place'.[3]

The first quote is from *Reuters News Service* from Sunday 29 January 2006 and the second is from the *Boston Globe*, 2005. Neither of these organisations could be accused of having a pro-life bias. Yet the climate is changing in the US to the extent that the pro-choice side along with some of the secular media are admitting that they are starting to lose the battle for hearts and minds on abortion. Is this the beginning of a cultural change, where abortion will once again become unthinkable? Is it the beginning of a generational change in attitude to abortion?

6.1 Evidence of change in the US

The SCBI survey shows that support for abortion on demand is not as strong as may have been thought. Attitudes also seem to be changing in the US. Already a shift in the opinion polls is evident as the debate moves away from the old polarised abortion debate.

The polls seem to be showing a consistent trend, and this change in public opinion is no accident. Polls taken of Americans' attitudes to abortion in 1995 found that 33 per cent of those surveyed described themselves as pro-life. By the year 2000, 45 per cent were describing themselves as pro-life.[4] By 2003, 61 per cent of those surveyed could be described as pro-life, with 19 per cent of those wanting a ban on all abortions and 42 per cent saying that they thought abortion should only be allowed in a few circumstances.[5] This represents a significant shift in public opinion in only a few years.

Two more recent polls taken by Wirthlin World Wide and Zogby also found that around 55–56 per cent of those surveyed in the US would ban or restrict abortion to circumstances of the life of the woman, rape, or incest.[6] Again this represents a significant change from the Gallop poll taken in 1995. As Susan Wills of the United States Conference of Catholic Bishops (USCCB) says 'We're winning the battle for the hearts and minds, but don't count on the mainstream media to get the story straight. That's your job and mine'.[7]

This change in opinion is also translating to a change in student support for abortion. A poll taken of UCLA students in the year 1999 found that 50 per cent of 'freshers' or first year students were opposed to abortion.[8] Another poll taken in January 2006 found that 67 per cent of high school seniors thought that abortion was always or usually wrong.[9] They also supported proposals that would give women alternatives to abortion: 72 per cent of this same group of female seniors would not consider an abortion if they became pregnant.

Other polls have shown interesting results. A poll taken by Opinion Dynamics for *Fox News* found that there was strong support for laws that either required abortion clinics to obtain parental consent for a minor (78 per cent) or to at least notify parents about the abortion (72 per cent).[10]

Polls taken of American Catholics are also of some interest. A poll taken by Quinnipiac in 2004 found that most Catholics agreed with Pope John Paul II's strong pro-life position.[11] They also found that two-thirds opposed abortion in all or most cases and that 80 per cent thought that Catholic Church teaching on the 'life' issues should stay the same.

How much notice should be taken of opinion polls? They can be manipulated or biased depending on what questions are asked and who asks the questions. The polls briefly looked at above are thought to be reasonably reputable. But there are also other indicators of change.

6.1.1 The abortion rate is dropping in the US

Another measure of change is the number of abortions that are performed each year. In 1990, 1.61 million abortions took place. By the year 2000, these numbers had dropped to 1.31 million abortions.[12] While, 1.31 millions is still an alarming number, not something anyone could be pleased about, it does show a significant turn around in the number of abortions that are occurring. Another measurable change is the number of doctors willing to do abortions. By the year 2000, the number willing to do abortions had dropped by 11 per cent. This is the lowest number of doctors willing to do abortions since 1974, possibly because of the hostile political environment.[13]

6.1.2 What is behind these changes?

What could be behind these changes in attitude in the USA? There are possibly many ways of looking at this, and many people will come to different conclusions. Yet it is clear that the 1990s saw a major *rethink* of the pro-life message. Key leaders in the pro-life movement started to ask some hard questions. For instance, they were puzzled: how could women (and the public) be against abortion personally, yet in favour of keeping it legal? Many people also saw abortion as a 'necessary evil'. There is evidence of a similar attitude in Australia from the SCBI survey.

Key pro-life leaders realised that the pro-life message had convinced many that the foetus was a person, not just a blob of tissues, yet this was still not *converting* into opposition to abortion or into women choosing life for their children. They also realised that the public debate over abortion tended to pit women against children, with children often viewed as the enemy. They realised too that, in the past, pro-lifers thought that they just had to convince the public of the humanity of the unborn. Yet it was proving to be much more complicated.[14]

Research done around this time in the US found that many women do not see any good coming from an 'unplanned pregnancy'. They do not think the way a pro-life person thinks, especially if they are feeling alone, abandoned, fearful, and panicky. Instead the researchers found that such women perceive the unplanned pregnancy as a 'death of self' and abortion as the least of three evils: the three 'evils' being motherhood, adoption, and abortion. They may often weigh up the choice as 'either my life is over or the life of this new child is over'. They may view motherhood as a loss of control over their lives and may not be able to think rationally. In such instances abortion may be viewed as the way to self-preservation, as the way to 'getting on with her life'. The researchers also found that the emphasis on babies, whether dismembered foetuses or happy newborns tends to deepen the women's sense of denial, isolation and despair—the very emotions that will drive her to choose abortion. They found that the pro-life movement's tendency in the past to focus almost exclusively on the unborn child, not the mother, tended to build resentment, not sympathy, particularly among younger women. This led these women to view the pro-life movement as judgmental and uncaring about them and their situation.[15] (An image, which the media is only too happy to exploit!)

US pro-life strategists also realised that in the past they had tended to think that they should be working to change legislation and court rulings. They had tended to have an 'all or nothing' approach. Some of them realised that there were many other initiatives that they could be trying even though it was not yet possible to overturn *Roe v. Wade*. The SCBI survey has similarly reported that public opinion becomes polarised as soon as any mention of legal restrictions is made.

The 1990s saw the development of new strategies in the US based on some of the new research. Pro-life researchers had learnt more about the reasons women were choosing abortion and had valuable insights from women who had already had an abortion. Important in the development of these new strategies was the growing realisation that it is the mother that will make the life and death decision, so that it is the *mother* more than anyone who needs to hear compassionate words. They realised that it was important to target those who were most at risk, or those most likely to have an abortion. These new strategies have been called 'women-centred strategies'.

6.2 The influence of John Paul II

The personal witness of Pope John Paul II should never be underestimated in the development of the new pro-life strategies. Around the same time, in the mid-1990s John Paul II published his encyclical *Evangelium Vitae*, or The Gospel of Life.[16] Apart from clearing up any misunderstanding about the Catholic Church's consistent and unchanging teaching on abortion and being a shot in the arm for the pro-life movement, his encyclical was more. It also gave the pro-life movement a much deeper and clearer understanding of the problems when dealing with abortion. Significantly, he encouraged all to work for cultural change and described that great drama that was the cultural battle between the 'culture of life' and the 'culture of death'.

John Paul II described the current culture as one of death. Briefly, he said that it is one that tends to reject life and that this was evident in the increasing acts of violence, terrorism, euthanasia, abortion, human cloning, and IVF. These, he argued, are all attacks on human life; they are all linked and they ultimately lead to alienation and despair. The opposite is the culture of life, John Paul II said. In this culture, every human life is welcomed, honoured, and respected; every human life has a purpose and is intended for eternity. In an interview with an Italian journalist, Vittorio Messori, John Paul II left us with some clear insights into solving the problem of abortion. This series of interviews was later published in 1994 under the title *Crossing the Threshold of Hope*. He writes:

> It is necessary to become courageously 'pro-woman,' promoting a choice that is truly in favour of women. *It is precisely the woman, in fact who pays the highest price, not only for her motherhood, but even more for its destruction, for the suppression of the life of the child who has been conceived* [emphasis added]. The only honest stance, in these cases *is that of radical solidarity with the woman*. It is not right to leave her alone.[17]

The key message he has for all people of good will, if they truly want to create a new culture of life, is that they must become radically pro-woman and radically pro-life. He argues that this new culture can only be built through love and genuine compassion.

6.3 Key strategists in the US in the 1990s

A number of key people in the pro-life movement in the United States clearly responded to Pope John Paul II's call. It appears that they were already heading in a similar direction before *Evangelium Vitae* was published, and it certainly encouraged them that they were on the right path. These included Frederica Mathewes-Green who published *Real Choices: Listening to Women, Looking for Alternatives to Abortion*[18] in 1994. Mathewes-Green set about researching what was driving women to seek abortion in the first place and what it might take to break the cycle of violence. She surveyed pregnancy counsellors and the women who sort help from pregnancy centres but she also listened to women who had abortions. A new conversion had begun.

David Reardon's *Making Abortion Rare: A Healing Strategy for a Divided Nation* was another landmark work, published in 1996. He made what was a radical claim at the time, that post-abortion issues were the key to converting hearts — the key to winning the battle for life,[19] that every aspect of the pro-life battle could be transformed and energised by better understanding of post-abortion issues.

Paul Swope's article in *First Things*, 'Abortion: A failure to communicate', was another key work.[20] In it he analysed the effectiveness of pro-life strategies to date (as already mentioned) and made a number of suggestions, based on research and experience, about how we could reach those who had so far not heard our message — how we might persuade women to choose life and how we could better take our message to the world.

6.4 What are women-centred pro-life strategies?

These new strategies have been called 'women-centred strategies'. They are a type of pro-life strategy. They aim to reduce the acceptance and incidence of abortion by drawing attention to the harm that abortion does, not to the *foetus*, but to the woman who aborts. They begin with the claim that most women neither want nor benefit from abortion but are pressured into it by others and then experience a range of negative physical and psychological effects after abortion.[21] They are not a 'compromise' or a 'sell out' to the pro-abortionists but they are, more than anything, a change in emphasis.

They are being used to try to redefine the abortion debate in terms of the legitimate needs of women rather than an exclusive focus upon the unborn. Proponents aim to directly limit the harm that abortion causes women by addressing issues of consent and by minimising coercion, through the promotion of practical assistance to women, through the development of better social policy. They are also being used to promote compassion and assistance to post-abortive women.

This all adds up to a new strategy of working to make abortion unthinkable or at least very rare. It is a long-term plan. It is not an all-or-nothing plan, but a plan to make changes where possible, based on what is realistically achievable. Working to change the culture means taking the message to every walk of life, to every profession, everywhere. Every conversation must be about building a new culture of life. Working to create such a big cultural change in thinking means more than just marching or lobbying politicians although there can be a time and a place for that too, but it really means changing to become people of life. Transformation is needed.

There are a number of primary reasons why a change is becoming evident in the US:

- There is a growing realisation that abortion harms women as well as children.

- A number of programs have been developed to help women heal the profound wounds of abortion.

- There is an increasing awareness that it is only the mother who can directly nurture her unborn child, and all anyone else can do is to nurture the mother.

- They are working to provide alternatives to abortion and better support for women.

- 3D ultrasound is increasingly showing the humanity of the child.

In addition other factors are important in helping create such changes. The development of the new strategies was based on research. They aimed to convert the 'middle ground' or the many, many people who are not pro-abortion advocates. They challenged the pro-abortion rhetoric and language. They provided alternatives to abortion and they raised awareness of women's experience of abortion. They started to develop a new feminism and continued to educate the public about the humanity of the unborn child. They continued to build pro-life networks and associations, and worked on coordinated campaigns. They developed new public policies, and they began to use the media, the

Internet, and the World Wide Web to get the message out. Lastly, they worked to keep the debate alive. In other words, there are many ways that both sides of the debate can work to achieve the same ends.

6.4.1 How effective are the new strategies?

There is a growing realisation that abortion is not the answer. And the issue of abortion is once again gaining political importance in the United States as can be seen in the drawn out debate in the United States Congress over the Partial-Birth Abortion Ban Act. Partial birth abortion was eventually banned by Congress and voted into law by President Bush in 2003 but was ruled unconstitutional in 2006 by the US Appeals Courts. Although they still have not completely succeeded in banning partial-birth abortion, the nation was involved in a big debate and many unsavoury facts about abortion were brought into the light and drawn to public attention.

In addition they have managed to have John Roberts and Samuel Alito appointed to the Supreme Court in 2003 and 2006 respectively. The Bush government has also cut funding to UN population control policies arguing against the vague term 'reproductive health' which can be interpreted to include access to abortion. Hilary Clinton, for years a strong supporter of a woman's right to abortion, recently made this most interesting statement:

> There is an opportunity for people of good faith to find common ground in this debate. We should agree that we want every child in this country to be wanted, cherished, and loved…. We can all recognise that abortion in many ways represents a sad, even tragic, choice to many, many women.[22]

While Hilary Clinton has not become pro-life, there is evidence that she is focusing more on women and considering other options than abortion for unplanned pregnancies.

With this subtle shift of focus giving more attention to the plight of the woman, the two sides of the abortion debate may be able to find some common ground and make some progress.

6.5 What can be learned from the new strategies?

There have been significant new insights into why so many people have viewed abortion as a 'necessary evil' in the past. There is now a better understanding of why many Australians hold such conflicting views on abortion — not prepared to block a woman's access to abortion yet wishing that there were not so many abortions and prepared to support measures designed to reduce the rate of abortions. The evidence from the US that strategies aimed at supporting vulnerable women can and do work. Well thought out, constructive strategies designed to make a long-term impact and reduce abortions are already starting to make inroads in the United States. Many women will not have an abortion if given genuine support and alternatives. But what about Australia?

There are many reasons to hope. Leslie Cannold, an Australian pro-abortion activist and spokesperson for Reproductive Choice Australia thinks that women-centred strategies possess 'ideological power' and can be 'surprisingly effective'.[23]

Too often the temptation has been to blame religious leaders or the government and declare that *they* need to do something. But the past cannot be changed, and the future can be changed. To move on from the old polarised debates, constructive alternatives must be found. It is too important to leave this just to religious leaders or the government, although of course their role is significant and sends a message. Pope John Paul II called on everyone to play a part in this great new struggle to build a culture of life and love.

Australia has one of the highest rates of abortion in the Western World. It is estimated that at least 1 in 4 pregnancies end in abortion. It is a significant issue for Australia. This is finally being recognised, and organisations are emerging that are taking up these new women-centred initiatives. Examples of these initiatives are outlined in the following sections.

6.5.1 Pastoral responses to abortion

In November 2004 the Australian Catholic Bishops Conference announced the appointment of a taskforce on pastoral responses to abortion to investigate ways in which the Church could improve its support for women, their partners and families so as to enable and encourage them to continue with an unexpected or difficult pregnancy.[24] Members included bishops and representatives of various organisations and sectors within the Church, such as the Commission for Australian Catholic Women, Catholic Women's League, Respect Life Offices, and health, welfare, and education offices. The taskforce welcomed the renewed public debate over abortion, sparked in part by the Federal Minister for Health, Tony Abbott. They welcomed the continued discussion about ways of reversing the spiral of abortion. 'The Church', they said, 'stands ready to help shape a positive new approach to problem pregnancy. Catholics join others in opposing all violence to women and children, before or after birth.'[5] They called on 'churches, government, and charities to join with them, in ensuring that all pregnant women have real options'.[26]

> We support the establishment of a national forum to consider practical ways of assisting them and of promoting constructive discussion within the community. No woman should have to choose between her own well-being and the life of her child. The well-being of a pregnant mother and her child cannot be separated. To harm one is always to harm the other; to care for one always requires caring for both. Yet too often women report being pressured by their circumstances into having an abortion: they feel they have no other option.

> Women with unplanned pregnancies need to be offered genuine alternatives to abortion. They need access to good counselling and support, health care, welfare, and housing. Educational facilities and work places must be more accommodating of the special needs of pregnant women and families. [27]

The taskforce investigated practical and pastoral ways of responding to women in need. It reviewed academic research and current practices and services within the Church and set up a consultation process inviting women to share their experiences. It sought to better understand gaps in services and identify ways the Church might better respond to future challenges. The taskforce made a series of recommendations to the Australian Catholic Bishops Conference and eagerly awaits the final outcome. It is hoped that any initiatives that result from the work of the taskforce will build on the efforts that many generous people have already made in support of vulnerable women and their families.

6.5.2 Pregnancy support services

In December 2004, following the renewed debate over abortion and the establishment of the Australian Catholic Bishops Taskforce on Pastoral Responses to Abortion, George Cardinal Pell of Sydney asked Centacare, the Church's welfare arm, to develop a pregnancy support program. 'Women need real alternatives to abortion, and while the Catholic Church provides many family services, this new pregnancy support program is targeted to meet the specific needs of women contemplating abortion', he said.[28] The late Cardinal Thomas Winning of Scotland and the late Cardinal John O'Connor of New York set up programs for women in need and have now helped many hundreds of women. In another exciting development, Archbishop Denis Hart has invited Centacare Melbourne to develop a similar program for the Archdiocese of Melbourne and this was due to commence in late 2006.

6.5.3 Stories from experience

Here in Australia women who have experienced an abortion are starting to tell their stories. Canberra journalist, Melinda Tankard-Reist published a landmark book in 2000, *Giving Sorrow Words,* about women who have been traumatised by abortion.[29] Reist lifted the lid on what until then had been a taboo — women whose lives had not been enhanced by their abortion. These women suffered lasting emotional shock and were not prepared for the intense suffering they were to experience. Their stories are confronting, heart breaking and disturbing. Their suffering was compounded by the fact that they had no one to turn to afterwards, nowhere to go to try to start rebuilding their lives.

Since writing her book, Melinda Reist has heard from many hundreds of other women who contacted her to share their experiences. Her book has sold out twice and is being reprinted and a documentary is also on the way. Meeting many of these women and hearing their stories first hand is helping to shift the abortion debate towards the women involved. The women themselves have displayed great courage in speaking out about their experience and have given us unique insights into the Australian situation. There is much to be learned from them to help provide women with better alternatives in the future. Reist has since published another important book called *Defiant Birth*: *Women who Resist Medical Eugenics.* In this book she documents the experience of women who kept their babies despite medical advice and often pressure from others to abort their children because they were viewed as 'not perfect'.

6.5.4 Women's Forum Australia

Determined that the renewed debate sparked by Federal Minister for Health, Tony Abbott would continue so that pro-life women's voices might be heard, over a thousand women gathered in Sydney in December 2004 under the banner 'Pro-Woman and Pro-Life'. They represented:

> a new generation of women, who have watched many friends and sisters, endure the torment of abortion. They are aware of the pressure of motherhood and the demands of the corporate world. They know too that abortion is a quick, cheap response to a desperate woman—but that its effects can be devastating. They called for a new debate and for change. They don't want abortion—they want a world that accepts them and their bodies. They are part of a grassroots movement that has coalesced into Women's Forum Australia.[30]

And they are growing.

6.5.5 Federal government initiatives

In March 2006 the federal government announced it would fund measures designed to reduce the number of abortions occurring each year in Australia. The government recognised that many women were unaware of alternatives to abortion and services that were available to them. Federal money was to be made available to fund a twenty-four-hour, seven-day-a-week National Pregnancy Support Telephone Helpline to assist women access services and explore pregnancy options.

In addition non-directive professional counsellors, allied health professionals, and general practitioners would be able to apply for a *Medicare Benefit Schedule* for pregnancy support counselling. One of the government requirements is that counsellors be professional with no financial ties to abortion clinics. These new initiatives are expected to cost fifty-one million dollars over four years. Health Minister Tony Abbott said:

> The government does not support changing the abortion law nor does it support restricting Medicare funding for abortion. Nevertheless, the government wants to give more support to women who are or who have been uncertain about continuing a pregnancy.[31]

6.5.6 Alternatives and support

Religious organisations and the federal government are becoming increasingly aware of the need to offer alternatives to abortion. The public too is slowly realising that abortion has all too often been the only choice women are offered. If the rate of abortion is to be reduced in Australia then vulnerable pregnant women need a genuine *choice*. They have a need for more information on where to find help and more places offering help so that they can truly echo the words of Patricia Heaton who says, 'Women who are experiencing unplanned pregnancy also deserve unexpected joy!'[32]

Thanks to the work of SCBI, there is a much better understanding of the conflicting views Australians hold over abortion. We have new evidence that one of the keys to solving Australia's abortion rate is to offer women a choice other than abortion and at the same time offer help to those who have had an abortion. Constructive strategies designed at making a long-term impact are the best chance of transforming the culture into a culture of life. In summary, it seems that new woman-centred approaches to trying to stem the tide of abortion would be supported by the Australian public.

Chapter 7

An evidence base for counselling, social policy and alternatives to abortion

Selena Ewing

We set out to forge new ground in the Australian abortion debate by seeking areas of common ground, from which constructive public policy could be developed. In this chapter, some of our key findings will be discussed and built upon with peer-reviewed research.

When the politics of abortion have become a bitter impasse, debate being artificially cast as 'pro-life' versus 'pro-choice', there are no winners. This is particularly true for women who become pregnant under difficult circumstances and proceed to seek information to assist them in the decision that they must make about motherhood.

More than ten years ago, two Australian researchers, supportive of abortion, observed that:

> fear of sabotaging the case for women's right to choose abortion has meant that the distress and ambivalence experienced by women facing a problem pregnancy and abortion has been understated or disregarded by some writers in the area despite clinicians' and researchers' ready observation of its prevalence.[1]

Perhaps because of the severely polarised debate in Australia over past decades, the fact that abortion is often a traumatic decision has become something of a pawn in the battle. But it does not necessarily follow from this fact that abortion ought to be made illegal. Rather, the logical policy response is to provide assistance to women faced with the decision. When abortion is widely available, as in Australia, all pregnant women must make the decision to continue or to terminate. Women having difficulty making this important decision must be given resources, information, and support. They need professional counselling and accurate information about all their options, not just the option of abortion.

In our representative survey of twelve hundred Australians, 99 per cent were in favour of counselling being provided about the risks and alternatives prior to abortion. Seventy-eight per cent said there should be counselling before this decision, and 21 per cent said it should be available on a voluntary basis only. To achieve this, counselling providers need to be aware of the complexities of motives for abortion and the decision-making process.

7.1 Decision making in pregnancy

Over past decades there has been a view that to concede that abortion has a dark side would be to side with the pro-life lobby. Thus, abortion service providers and lobbyists have tended towards painting abortion as a positive experience with few negative effects. Counselling, it is sometimes suggested, ought to simply affirm the woman's decision and provide a referral for the procedure. Proposals for breathing space, or 'cooling-off periods', were in the past flatly rejected by abortion supporters as being patronising toward women.

But a review of research on how women experience the abortion decision reveals that ambivalence and conflicting feelings are common. Many researchers have found that the decision to abort is marked by a high degree of ambivalence (being unsure, or 'in two minds').[2] This is normal in almost all major life decisions, of which abortion is one.[3] However, ambivalence within the abortion decision-making process should still be of concern to policy makers and service providers. This is because of the solid evidence of potentially severe effects of abortion for women who were unsure about their decision. It also highlights the need for women to be fully informed about abortion and all alternatives before making a decision.

Ambivalence is common in early pregnancy, even for many women whose pregnancies are specifically planned or wanted. Women's attitudes towards the pregnancy and the baby appear to change over time, even during pregnancy.[4] Some researchers report:

> Of particular concern is the finding that women who reported their pregnancies as mistimed or unwanted were so much more likely to change their reports over time (to report the pregnancy as wanted) than were women who initially said that their pregnancies had been well-timed.[5]

Nearly one third of all women in a Swedish study who were seeking abortion reported contradictory feelings, both positive and negative, towards their pregnancy. Nearly half (46 per cent) of all the women seeking abortion expressed a conflict of conscience in seeking abortion.[6] Among 1446 women applying for abortion in Sweden, almost one in ten changed their minds.[7] Another Swedish study, involving 854 women one year after abortion, found that 19.8 per cent were still undecided as to whether they had made the right decision.[8]

It is of concern that one large study by B. Major and colleagues found a decreasing level of decision satisfaction over a two-year period after abortion. At one month post-abortion, 10.8 per cent of women were dissatisfied and felt they had made the wrong decision, and 10.5 per cent were neutral about their decision. At two years, 16.3 per cent of women were dissatisfied and felt they had made the wrong decision. Nineteen per cent of women said they would 'definitely not' or 'probably not' have the abortion again if they had to make the decision over, and 12 per cent were undecided.[9]

In a Swedish study, women who were ambivalent about their decision more often stated that their decision might have been different under alternative personal circumstances, for example, if the partner had wanted the baby or if finances had been better. Among these women, ambivalence about the abortion decision was associated with pressure from other people, particularly the male partner, and a negative attitude towards abortion.[10]

Personal finances, housing conditions, and pressure from a partner were significant reasons for abortion among ambivalent women in another study.[11] However, finances and housing may be more difficult to overcome than pressure from a partner. H. Söderberg et al. showed that Swedish women who changed their minds about abortion (i.e., applied for abortion but did not go through with it) were most often initially motivated to have an abortion because their partner did not want the baby.[12]

Among 196 women who had a termination for foetal abnormality in the Netherlands, 8 per cent reported feelings of regret, and 10 per cent reported feelings of doubt about their decision.[13] Among eighty-three women having abortion for foetal malformation in Germany, eight expressed retrospective doubts about the decision, and one felt she had made the wrong decision.[14]

Ambivalence among pregnant women, including those seeking abortion, is common and should inform considerations about abortion service delivery. The prevalence of ambivalence is a concrete indicator of the complexity of decisions made during pregnancy and underscores the need for information, accessible counselling, and professional support to aid a woman's decision making by presenting alternative strategies to address external coercive factors such as finances, housing options or lack of support.

Moreover, a substantial evidence base shows that ambivalence and difficulty arriving at the decision to abort are risk factors for long-term psychological distress following abortion.[15] For example, among US college students (including women who had had an abortion and men whose partners had had an abortion), the only predictor of increased anxiety after abortion for women was a lack of feeling comfortable with the decision.[16] A Dutch study showed that women who reported feelings of doubt about their decision were over-represented in the group with post-traumatic stress symptoms. The authors of this study emphasise the importance of adequate psychological support and guidance from the caregiver during the decision-making process 'in order to avoid impulsive and not fully internalised decisions'.[17]

There is no doubt that some of the respondents in our opinion poll were women who had experienced abortion. Half were women, and it is estimated that one in three Australian women will have an abortion in her lifetime. The research showed that Australians are ambivalent about abortion; while they want abortion available as a legal option, they generally prefer that women choose one of the alternatives to abortion, including adoption. This same ambivalence is found among many women who seek abortion, making the decision difficult and traumatic.

7.2 'Unwanted,' 'unplanned,' and 'unintended' pregnancies

Pregnancy 'intendedness' is a notion that cannot be used accurately in discussions of abortion.[18] Much research literature uses the terms 'planned,' 'unplanned,' 'intended,' 'unintended,' 'wanted,' 'unwanted,' and the concept of 'planning' as self-evident and unproblematic.[19] But for a growing number of researchers, the concept of *pregnancy intendedness* is in transition: it is no longer thought correct or useful to assume that becoming pregnant is a rational activity based on planning and forethought.[20] For this reason, a simplistic focus on contraception and sex education to reduce the unintended pregnancy rate, and therefore to reduce the abortion rate, is unlikely to be successful on its own. For example, in one empirical study, the 'intendedness' of a woman's pregnancy and her adjustment to, and happiness with, her pregnancy did not appear to be closely linked.[21]

In a 2002 study of UK women who had either given birth or had an abortion, most did not use the terms 'planned,' 'unplanned,' 'intended,' 'unintended,' 'wanted,' or 'unwanted' to classify their pregnancies. Only thirteen of the forty-seven women interviewed used these terms at all. Three women used the term 'intended'; all were married, over thirty, and held university degrees. Eight women used the terms 'unplanned' or 'unintended.' These women varied in age from 17 to 37, varied in education, and had pregnancies that were either carried to term or terminated. The researchers conclude that women do not spontaneously use these terms. Many women found it difficult to define a 'wanted' pregnancy, and the term 'unwanted' provoked a strong emotional reaction and disagreement among women.[22]

Only eight of the forty-seven women applied the term 'unwanted' to their pregnancies, and some with reservation. All were terminating. Eleven of the nineteen women having abortions chose *not* to apply the term 'unwanted'. One woman expressed it thus:

> It's not that I don't want the baby, it's that I can't have it…. Well not 'can't', that's another word I should put in, but it's not within my means to have it, and I think it's for the baby's best. But I think 'unwanted'…, it's not that I don't want it at all. I love it just as much because, you know, if I could have it, and I would love to be able to have it, so I think 'unwanted' is a bit of a kind of harsh word in my head.[23]

G. Barrett and K. Wellings noted that 'women's reluctance to apply the term 'unwanted' is interesting in light of the way in which the term 'unwanted' is often used in the medical literature as a euphemism for pregnancies ending in abortion.'[24] Barrett and Wellings concluded also that the women in their study expected four criteria to be met for a pregnancy to be 'planned'. These criteria ensured that the women had:

- a clear intention to become pregnant;
- not used contraception, in order to become pregnant;
- discussed and agreed with their partners that they would try to conceive;
- made wide lifestyle preparations or reached the right time in their life.

They also found that some women did not want to plan pregnancy — they wanted it to be a surprise. There was evidence of resistance to family planning among some women.

L. Williams et al. conducted a unique study in the US in 2001 that considered women's retrospective attitudes towards their children's births.[25] Over time the women's attitudes changed, more often toward more favourable reports (15 per cent more positive versus 10 per cent more negative). The authors found that:

> there was a disturbingly high frequency (from the point of view of consistency) — 19 per cent for last pregnancies and 27 per cent for next-to-last pregnancies — of women whose pregnancy was reported as 'unwanted' who said they reacted to the event by being happy, thrilled or glad or by thinking how nice it was.[26]

The results suggest that women were likely to reclassify their unintended or unwanted pregnancies later as 'wanted' or 'intended'. Women rarely reclassified their originally 'intended' pregnancies. The authors conclude that 'it suggests considerable inconsistency between prospective and retrospective measures of the same event, either in the form of rationalisation of the result, or in widespread changes of intention'.[27]

Some studies have also found that many women do not use any method of birth control despite their lack of conscious or stated intention for pregnancy.[28]

It seems at present that many health professionals believe that the only valid approach to abortion is to work towards ensuring that all pregnancies are the result of planning and conscious decisions by women. When evaluated against published research, this emerges as a narrow and naive strategy. While 'unintended', 'unplanned', and 'unwanted' pregnancies are discussed by family-planning and sexual-health experts, women's real lives demonstrate that pregnancy decision making is far more subtle and complicated, and that a range of factors impact on the decision to initiate and proceed with having a baby.

7.3 Alternatives to abortion

The 'backyard abortion' concept suggests that if women are not provided with legal and affordable termination facilities, they will seek out illegal and potentially more dangerous procedures, rather than continue their pregnancies. This spectre has been highly influential in garnering support for legal termination services funded by Medicare.

But this is also one of the most compelling arguments for a debate on how social and economic policies impact on women's reproductive decision making. If women are indeed willing to break the law and endure unhygienic, painful, and secret procedures to end their pregnancies, they must surely be desperate. It speaks not of free choice, but of coercion by external factors. It suggests a lack of alternatives.

Despite a lack of evidence that women would behave this way, it is a scenario worth considering. The 'backyard abortion' argument is sometimes used as emotional blackmail to ensure support for access to abortion, when it should really be an argument that begins a discussion about the reasons why women seek abortion. It should signal that women do not feel free to give birth to their own children, and it should be clear that simply providing abortion services will do nothing to enhance these women's freedom.

Interestingly, there is evidence that a substantial number of women have abortions despite being personally opposed to abortion.[29] In an Australian study, five of the twenty women interviewed (all of them attending a clinic for an abortion) stated: 'abortion is against my beliefs'.[30] In a Norwegian study, 13 per cent of women undergoing abortion were opposed to the law allowing abortion on demand.[31]

It is, therefore, reasonable to assume that there were other powerful influences in these women's lives that motivated them to seek abortion, rather than abortion being a free, uncoerced choice or a straightforward and preferred option. Attention should be given to the pressures causing women to seek abortion.

7.4 Motives underlying abortion decisions

Reasons women give for why they seek abortion are often far more complex than simply not intending to become pregnant.[32]

Abortion decisions are not random occurrences. There are differences in demographic and social patterns among women who have abortions and women who do not.[33] These patterns provide clues as to how to address and relieve some of the pressures that can bias a decision in favour of abortion.

Evidence demonstrates that 'unintended' pregnancy is not the simple cause of abortion. Women's decisions are not independent of their circumstances and the influences of people around them. Research suggests that abortion is considered by women because of a lack of freedom to pursue motherhood, lack of emotional and financial support and other barriers to giving birth. (See the following sections on finances, study and work, and relationships.)

Specified medical conditions, foetal abnormality, and rape are 'hard cases' that motivate relatively few abortions.[34] Notwithstanding the difficulties and challenges involved in all of these situations, the vast majority of abortions are performed on healthy mothers and babies.

An Australian research project suggests that women primarily have abortions because they perceive that having a baby would jeopardise their future, they believe they could not cope with a baby, they do not want others to know they are pregnant or they cannot afford to have a baby.[35] For women of all ages, relationship problems are an important factor in abortion decision-making.

The following table summarises some of the findings from a 1995 Australian research project, involving women presenting at an abortion clinic:[36]

Table 1. Endorsement of 'pro-terminate' items of balance sheet (n=20).			
Statement	True for situation %	Considered %	Considered very much %
Continuing would jeopardise future	100	100	80
Believe my right to choose	100	90	60
Know termination of pregnancy safe, simple	95	75	60
Could not cope	90	90	70
Not want others to know pregnant	85	60	35
Can't afford financially	75	70	60
Know women who aborted, did well	75	70	40
Pregnancy has no real form yet	75	70	45
Important others would suffer	65	55	35

Partner could not cope	65	55	25
Would be a single mother	55	40	35
Too young	45	45	24
Relationship unstable or new	45	45	30
Do not have support to continue	45	40	20
Worried not be a good mother	40	40	35
Relationship at risk if continue	35	25	10
Others say should terminate	35	20	15
Really scared of childbirth	35	25	20
Coped well with previous TOP	30	25	10
Health would suffer	20	15	10
Do not ever want (more) children	20	15	10
Too old	15	15	10
Not want involvement with partner in conception	5	0	0
Result of forced sex	5	5	5
Worried about health of pregnancy	5	5	5
Not want others to know had sex	5	5	5

A lack of support features prominently in this list: 'could not cope', 'can't afford financially', 'do not have support to continue', and 'relationship at risk if continue'. Other reasons are related to lack of self-confidence: 'could not cope' and 'would not be a good mother'. From a cognitive behavioural perspective, it is interesting to note that some of these statements may not be true facts, though this does not, of course, invalidate the woman's perception of them as true (e.g., 'know termination of pregnancy safe, simple', and 'pregnancy has no real form yet').

Other statements may also represent beliefs or fears (e.g., 'too old', 'too young') relating to the individual's circumstances and feelings, rather than being objectively true across the population (e.g., others of the same age may not seek abortion). Coercion, explicit and implicit, is also evident (e.g., 'others say should terminate', 'result of forced sex', 'relationship at risk if continue', 'do not want others to know pregnant', and 'partner could not cope').

It is noteworthy that all twenty women seeking abortion believed that giving birth would jeopardise their futures. This belief, however, is not an inevitable outcome but, rather, a subjective assessment of how pregnancy and motherhood, to the best of her knowledge, might fit with a woman's hopes, dreams, and aspirations. On the other hand, few women were aware of the potential harm. This demonstrates the critical importance of fully informing a woman, before she proceeds with abortion, about all the possible effects of abortion on her health and well-being, and on all the options and alternatives available to her.

7.5 Key factors

7.5.1 Finances

Research suggests that one of the most common motivations for abortion is financial concern, that is, the reality or perception by the mother that she cannot afford to raise a baby.[37] This might be related to the costs of raising a child, or to lost earnings, or both. In New South Wales, in a study of 2249 women having abortions in 1995, 60 per cent gave the reason 'can't afford a baby now'.[38] This was by far the most common motivation.

In Australia and overseas, older women are more likely to cite as reasons for abortion: completed family, work (pressures of work, or necessity to earn an income), and problems in their relationships with the partner as reasons for abortion.[39] This may indicate that women feel they cannot have as many children as they want, frequently on affordability grounds. Anecdotal evidence from abortion providers suggests that increasing numbers of partnered women over thirty in Australia are choosing to limit their family size by terminating pregnancies for economic reasons.[40]

Australia could be similar to other developed countries where the high cost of housing can affect women's options for caring for children. One Swedish study showed that women living in crowded housing situations chose abortion more than twice as often as women living in spacious conditions.[41] The high cost of housing may force women to work when they would rather have children or care for their families at home. It may also force women to live in smaller homes than they would need.

In Scotland, a retrospective study sought to identify women who were at risk of repeat abortion. The authors found that deprivation was the most important independent predictor of repeat abortion.[42]

7.5.2 Study and work

The desire to study and work is often a reason given for abortion,[43] suggesting that many women feel that pregnancy and motherhood are not compatible with study and work. This could be because structural barriers prevent them from achieving both, or that women want to devote most or all of their time to their family when they have one. All twenty of the women (who were attending for abortion) interviewed in an Australian study agreed with the statement 'continuing the pregnancy would jeopardise my career, study or future plans'.[44]

Younger women are more likely to cite youth, career, single parenthood, and changes to lifestyle as a reason for abortion.[45] This might simply reflect their preference for abortion over childbearing. However, there are alternative interpretations, for example, schools, universities, workplaces, and careers may not be welcoming of mothers. Relationship instability, including the threat of abandonment by men, is certainly a real problem for young women. Perhaps young women fear an unknown future, dramatic changes to lifestyle, and the perceived 'loss of self' when becoming a mother.

7.5.3 Wanting the best for their children

International research shows that some termination decisions are motivated by the desire to provide children with a safe and positive environment. If a woman is poor, or in a dysfunctional or violent domestic situation, she may seek abortion because she does not feel able to provide her child with a suitable upbringing.[46] There is evidence that women do not want to raise children as a single mother, whether because of potential practical, financial, or emotional difficulties, or stigmatisation.[47] There is also evidence that women believe their children have a right to be wanted and loved by both parents and raised in a caring environment.[48]

Again, these findings may relate to a lack of emotional, financial, and community support for women to have children. They suggest frequent abandonment of women by men, communities that are economically and professionally structured such that single motherhood seems too difficult to pursue and a perception that women are inadequate if they provide anything less than the perceived ideal.

7.6 Relationships

7.6.1 Relationships and abortion

Problems with the quality of intimate relationships, including lack of commitment from a male partner, or physical, psychological, and sexual violence, appear to be a major contributor to abortion in Australia and overseas.[49]

A major factor in a woman's decision about her pregnancy is the influence of the people closest to her, especially her partner. Research shows that in making the decision, women assess the likely level of emotional and financial support from their partner. If the partner does not want the pregnancy, or will give no financial support, the woman is more likely to view her pregnancy as 'unwanted'.[50] Research suggests that the male partner has a direct influence on a woman's desire for pregnancy and childbearing and on a woman's attitude towards an unplanned pregnancy.[51]

An Australian study of teenagers' pregnancy-resolution decisions found that most young women, whether choosing abortion or childbirth, reported that they arrived at the decision entirely on their own. However the authors stated that it was clear that these decisions were occurring within the context of a family and partner relationship, and in reality these external factors influenced the teenagers' decisions. Most significant was direct influence from the partner.[52]

Women who changed their minds about abortion (i.e., applied for abortion but did not go through with it) were most often initially motivated to have an abortion because their partner did not want the baby, according to Söderberg et al.[53] This suggests that these women were at first prepared to have an abortion because of lack of support, or perhaps even a request or demand, from their partners. However, given some time, the women decided not to accede to this pressure.

Another study found that, among 103 women undergoing termination, 'partner relationship' was the most common reason given. This included a relationship with no future or viewed as too recent, the ambivalence of the partner towards a pregnancy, his non-commitment to paternity, or a pre-existing situation of crisis such as separation or divorce.[54]

Relationships can also influence a woman's perspective on whether her pregnancy was planned or unplanned. For example, a US study of pregnancy 'intendedness' found that:

> those who had been unmarried at both interviews were more likely to shift their reports from intended to unintended than were women who were married at both interviews. This may be the result of disappointed expectations regarding the stability of the relationships out of which the babies were born.[55]

The strength and quality of women's relationships are important factors in the abortion decision. An Australian study found that 30 per cent of women having an abortion had considered, as an argument *against* having an abortion, that the partner relationship was stable and caring. Feeling that her partner could cope with a baby was also an important argument against abortion for these women. This Australian study is extremely useful in identifying the correlation between women's feelings about motherhood and the realities of their lives. In relation to the women's own, present decisions to have an abortion, the statement 'I could not cope' was strongly related to 'I do not have emotional and practical support'. Eighteen of the twenty women said that they could not cope with a baby, and this was an important reason for having an abortion.[56]

7.6.2 Domestic violence and abuse

Abortion, particularly repeat abortion, has a strong, established relationship with domestic violence in many countries, including Australia.[57] A woman who is a victim of domestic violence may have an abortion for various reasons related to the abuse:[58]

- the current or past pregnancies precipitated increased violence,

- fear that the foetus will be harmed by violence,
- coercion from an abuser,
- the pregnancy was the result of rape,
- her lack of desire to have a child with an abuser, and/or her fears regarding this prospect.

Research has found that it may be that pregnant, abused women do not want their children to suffer in the same abusive domestic situation and therefore seek abortion, or that these women are more likely to experience coerced sex, or that they are coerced into abortion, or all of these at once.[59] Also, an English study found that almost 2 per cent of requests for termination may have been due to forced sex.[60]

In an Australian study, 1014 women were interviewed during pregnancy and followed up after delivery. Women reporting past abuse or abuse during pregnancy were compared with non-abused women. The study found that abused women had a higher incidence of two or more pregnancy terminations.[61]

Another recent study of 14 784 Australian women aged eighteen to twenty-three years found that pregnancy loss, whether miscarriage or termination, was associated with the experience of violence. The authors recommend that when young women present with pregnancy, health providers should inquire about violence and be prepared to offer support.[62]

A sample of 486 women seeking abortion in the US found that the prevalence of self-reported abuse was 39.5 per cent. Women with an abuse history were more likely than non-abused women to cite relationship issues as a reason for seeking termination. This study also found that women were much more likely to identify themselves as 'abused' when given a paper survey compared with being asked directly, a relevant finding for screening and intervention programs. The authors suggest that past or present abusive relationships influence women's decisions to seek abortion.[63] Several researchers recommend systematic identification of a history of abuse among women seeking abortion, with the concurrent provision of information about interventions, safety, and referral for counselling.[64]

A Canadian study investigated the possibility of universal screening for domestic violence in an abortion clinic, and found it to be feasible but challenging.[65] The authors note that simply asking questions about abuse is an intervention, because this communicates that domestic abuse is an important issue. This study found some difficulties in universal screening at the abortion clinic. Staff compliance with the policy was low, with staff asking the questions of only 254 of the 499 women attending for abortion. About half the reasons given for not asking were 'patient-centred' reasons, such as poor English skills, the partner being present or the woman being too emotionally distraught. About half the reasons were counsellor-related, such as the counsellor feeling rushed during the session, or feeling that rapport was not established. In some cases the counsellors 'ran out of energy' to ask the questions. Nevertheless, the counsellors found that overall, women were receptive to the screening.[66]

Other studies recommend routine prenatal visits as opportunities for trust-building between women and health-care professionals, and therefore counselling and intervention for those who disclose abuse.[67] However, the presence of an abusive male partner or other perpetrator at pre-abortion interviews may well present an insurmountable problem for women in disclosing abuse or coercion, as may the lack of a trusted relationship with the abortion provider.[68]

A recent Australian report on the social, economic, and safety needs of women during pregnancy provides a detailed picture of the extent, level and nature of violence against women during pregnancy. The author cautions against careless implementation of screening programs in the context of pregnancy health-care services. Her research and experience suggests that women will only discuss violence in the context of a trusted relationship (unless the violence is severe and the woman has already sought help). Hence, routine screening may or may not create the appropriate safe environment for women to speak freely about abuse.[69]

Angela Taft wrote an important paper on violence against Australian women in pregnancy and after childbirth in 2002. She states that 4–9 per cent of pregnant women experience domestic violence, and that a higher proportion of abused women than non-abused women seek abortion. She argues, however, that 'we do not have the evidence to recommend partner-abuse screening as policy at present' (referring to health services in general, not specifically to abortion services). This recommendation is based partly on evidence suggesting that most women do not disclose abuse; and if the response from a health professional is unsupportive or judgmental, it may discourage the woman from seeking help for a long time.[70]

The relationship between abortion and domestic violence is disturbing, and there is a great need for a new approach. Simply improving access to abortion is inappropriate; the woman will return home having lost her baby but still having been exposed to violence. It is clear also that counselling arrangements in the past have failed to identify and help many women subject to abuse and seeking abortion as a result. Improved counselling may greatly assist in these cases; women need confidential, high-quality counsellors who have plenty of time to listen and who are aware of the pressures and difficulties in situations of abuse. Additional funding would be necessary for the appropriate training and time requirements.

7.6.3 Rape, incest and coerced sex

While abortion for rape or incest is relatively uncommon, sexual coercion is alarmingly common in Australia. In a recent representative sample of Australian women, 21.1 per cent of women had experienced sexual coercion (i.e., forced or frightened into unwanted sexual activity) and 10.3 per cent had been coerced when aged sixteen or younger.[71] A Swedish study found that 12 per cent of women seeking abortion had become pregnant in a situation where they had felt pressured or threatened by the man.[72] Overall, there is very little research on this topic, perhaps due to an assumption that abortion is always the best option for a woman pregnant through rape. However it is premature to assume that a woman pregnant through rape and incest will benefit from abortion. There is currently no evidence that it heals the woman's pain or provides any other benefits.

There is also very little documentation of the experiences of women who have become pregnant as a result of rape and have chosen either abortion or birth. However, one book documents the experiences of almost two hundred women who were raped and became pregnant, including women who continued the pregnancy as well as some who underwent abortion. Nearly all the women interviewed said they regretted aborting their babies conceived through rape or incest. On the other hand, among the women who carried their pregnancies to term, not one expressed regret about that choice.

D. Reardon writes that:

> many women report that their abortions felt like a degrading form of 'medical rape'. …Abortion involves a painful intrusion into a woman's sexual organs by a masked stranger…. For many women this experiential association between abortion and sexual assault is very strong…. Women with a history of sexual assault are likely to experience greater distress during and after an abortion than are other women.[73]

There is some evidence from India that abortion as an option facilitates and perpetuates the continuation of rape and violence in intimate relationships.[74] While this sample is socially and demographically different from Australian women, it highlights the potential for such situations here.

7.7 Mental and emotional factors

7.7.1. Depressed mood during pregnancy

Depressed mood during pregnancy is common, although often temporary, and is related to hormonal changes during pregnancy as well as the stresses of pregnancy, impending birth and other coincident life events. L. Bonari et al. cite estimates of prevalences ranging from 10 to 25 per cent of pregnant women (who did not seek abortion).[75] S.M. Marcus et al. found that 20 per cent of pregnant women (not seeking abortion) experience depressed mood, yet few are diagnosed with clinical depression or seek treatment.[76] J. Evans et al. studied a population of 14 541 pregnant women in England, and found depressive symptoms in 11.8 per cent at eighteen weeks and 13.5 per cent at thirty-two weeks gestation. The rate of depressive symptoms after childbirth was lower than during pregnancy.[77]

In a study of women undergoing second-trimester abortion for foetal abnormality, there was a high rate of depression at enrolment in the study (61.9 per cent of women electing surgical termination, and 53.8 per cent of women electing medical termination). At four months the prevalence was 23.5 per cent for surgical versus 14.3 per cent for medical, and 27.3 per cent for surgical versus 20 per cent for medical at twelve months.[78]

L.E. Ross et al. propose a biopsychosocial model of depression during pregnancy and the postpartum period, suggesting that:

> variance in depressive symptoms can be best accounted for by the indirect effects of biological risk factors on psychosocial variables

and anxiety. These biological variables could alter sensitivity to environmental stressors, such as lack of social support, and in this way, determine the threshold for developing symptoms of depression or anxiety during pregnancy.[79]

Depression and other types of mental illness can be related to cognitive distortions that may affect decision-making capacity.[80] It is therefore highly relevant to consider the possibility of undetected and untreated depression amongst women seeking abortion. There are effective non-pharmacological interventions for depression, including counselling, physical activity and support services. Antidepressants may benefit pregnant women with severe depression.[81]

Academics and health professionals are considering and proposing routine screening for depression in prenatal clinics.[82] In Australia, this includes the *Beyond Blue* Postnatal Depression Program, which is trialling the use of a simple screening tool to identify pregnant women at risk of antenatal and postnatal depression.[83] Similar research might also be beneficial if directed towards women considering abortion.

7.7.2 Risk factors for psychological harm and emotional distress

Research has identified particular risk factors among women seeking abortion that are predictive of negative psychological and emotional outcomes of abortion, giving further impetus to the provision of counselling and social policy support for pregnant women.

Swedish researchers found that women are more likely to suffer psychologically and emotionally from abortion if they are living alone, have poor emotional support from family and friends, experience adverse post-abortion change in relationship with partner, have underlying ambivalence or adverse attitudes to abortion, or are actively religious.[84]

In another Swedish study, an absence of emotional distress immediately after the abortion was reported by women who had made the decision without a conflict of conscience and without pressure.[85] Other researchers have found that ambivalence about the abortion and difficulty with the decision are predictors of post-abortion psychological harm.[86] Clinicians should note that delaying the decision is a marker for ambivalence.[87]

Abortion for foetal abnormality is known to be associated with psychological morbidity.[88] Relationship violence also predicts particularly negative responses to abortion.[89] In a study of abortion and post-traumatic stress disorder in Russian and American women, more negative responses to abortion in American women were related to being younger, having a history of divorce, not having been employed full time, having more years of education, having bonded to the foetus, not believing in a woman's right to have an abortion, not being counselled before the abortion, having felt pressured into the decision, and having experienced more abortions. Among Russian women, negative responses were associated with having bonded to the foetus, not believing in a woman's right to abortion, having a partner who desired the pregnancy, experiencing health complications, feeling pressured into the decision, having experienced ambiguity surrounding the decision, not having received counselling before the procedure, and being further along in the pregnancy.[90] Pre-pregnancy history of depression consistently predicted poorer post-abortion mental health, and more negative abortion-related emotions and evaluations. Furthermore, younger women evaluated their abortion more negatively, as did women who had more children at the time of abortion.[91]

A study of 13 261 women with an unplanned pregnancy in the UK found that women with a history of psychiatric illness were found to have higher rates of such illness after both abortion and childbirth (although in this study, psychiatric disorders after childbirth were found to be artificially inflated by poor coding). The rate of deliberate self-harm, however, was found to be significantly higher after abortion than childbirth, among women with no history of self-harm.[92]

A recent comprehensive review of the psychology of abortion summarises research on 'mediators in psychological processes'. This means 'how characteristics of the individual or experiences are able to partially or fully explain relations between specific predictor variables and outcomes'.[93] The reviewers found evidence of several mediators in current post-abortion psychology literature:

- *Self-efficacy* – the woman's judgment, taking into account her knowledge and her confidence, that she has the ability to execute the actions necessary to successfully complete various life tasks.

- *Attribution of blame* – the degree to which the woman feels the situation may have been modifiable.

- *Subsequent reproductive events* – including another abortion or other forms of perinatal loss such as miscarriage or stillbirth, difficulty conceiving, problems with a desired pregnancy, and giving birth.

Counsellors, doctors and abortion practitioners need to be particularly alert to women who are seeking abortion yet express some enjoyment in being pregnant or a desire to have the child.

7.8 Abnormalities in the foetus

7.8.1 Abortion for disability or disease in the foetus

Abortion for congenital abnormality or other health indications in the foetus comprise relatively few of state and national totals. Nonetheless, these occurrences are worthy of research attention and consideration of more supportive and beneficial policies and practices. Currently, research and women's experiences highlight the routinisation and expectations of participation in prenatal screening and abortion,[94] a lack of information for women undergoing screening or who have received positive results,[95] subtle and not-so-subtle pressure on women to choose abortion if their baby has suspected disability or disease,[96] and a commonly noted lack of support for families and individuals living with disability in our community. This growing body of evidence suggests that the reasons for women's choice of abortion in these situations are more complex than simply not wanting to have a child with that particular disability.

Some research has questioned whether women feel that abortion for suspected abnormality is even a free choice. A Netherlands study involved interviews with thirty women who underwent abortion at twenty-four weeks or later (compared with thirty women who underwent induced delivery resulting in perinatal death). Of the abortion group, eighteen reported that this was the outcome of a decision process, while twelve (40 per cent) reported that they 'had no choice'.[97]

There are significant pressures on women, apart from personal preference, to avoid being mothers of children with disease or disability. New prenatal testing technologies mean that women now have the responsibility to make the decision to give birth or not. It is therefore reasonable to predict that women will be increasingly seen as *responsible* for the births of children with disability or disease. Furthermore, if children are considered to have an illness that is perceived to be 'preventable', they may be considered less worthy of help both by health professionals and others.

A multi-national study has already provided evidence that this is happening. T. Marteau et al. explored the idea of *attribution* in relation to the birth of disabled children. Attribution is the tendency for people to seek an explanation for an unexpected and negative event. Specifically,

> attribution theory predicts that more help will be given when dependency is attributed to factors such as lack of ability on the

victim's part (internal but uncontrollable cause), than when it is attributed to a lack of effort on the victim's part (internal and controllable cause).[98]

Marteau's study involved the completion of hypothetical case studies by three groups: pregnant women, men and women from the general community,and geneticists, from Germany, Portugal and the UK (also included were obstetricians from the UK). In all three countries, and for all study groups, the mother's history of prenatal screening was the single most important factor influencing attributions of control and blame following the birth of a child with Down syndrome. These results suggest that both health professionals and lay people make judgments about women's roles in the birth of children with disabilities. The authors conclude:

> The results of the current study would suggest that less help will be given to parents who decline testing because the outcome, giving birth to a child with a condition for which prenatal screening and selective termination are available, is seen as preventable.[99]

Lippman has similarly argued that 'the provision of prenatal testing for foetal abnormality and selective termination of affected foetuses will result in mothers being blamed for giving birth to children with disabilities'.[100]

As genetic research and prenatal screening technology develops, the range of available prenatal tests will expand, including probably the range of tests that become routine in Australian antenatal care. Women will therefore be faced with more decisions about what, if any, testing should be undertaken on their children and whether or not to proceed with an abortion in the case of detected or suspected abnormality.

7.8.2 Abortion for suspected or confirmed disability or disease in the foetus

Our research found overwhelming support for abortion in the case of foetal disability both as a legal option and as a morally acceptable option. Eighty-five per cent of Australians support women obtaining abortion when the foetus has a severe disability, and 60 per cent when the foetus has a mild disability. We did not find out whether this support relates to considerations of the mother's wellbeing, for example, an assumption that she would benefit from an abortion, or considerations of the child's well-being — paradoxically that the child would benefit from never being born. One can hypothesise, however, that strong community support for abortion in such circumstances may translate into a *lack* of community support for women who choose to continue the pregnancies when the child born will experience disease or disability. It is not widely known that for women who abort because of suspected or confirmed disability or disease in the foetus, the procedure and the years afterward can be extremely traumatic and characterised by grief and guilt.[101] Thus, the provision of counselling, alternatives and social policy support are imperative for these women.

A Scottish study of women's reactions to second-trimester abortion for foetal abnormality found that, despite its acceptance in the community, the procedure 'remains an emotionally traumatic major life event for both the father and mother', involving turmoil, ambiguity and reticence. Particularly vulnerable groups were found to be: a) young and immature couples; b) women with secondary post-abortion infertility and those with a reproductive conflict; and c) vulnerable personalities and those who are unsupported. The authors recommended that all of these require early identification and support.[102]

S. Elder and K. Laurence tested the effects of a support program for women undergoing second trimester termination for foetal abnormality in the UK. Describing women's reactions to the procedure, they found that 78 per cent in one group (detection at ultrasound or early blood test) and 90 per cent in a second group (detection at amniocentesis) experienced an acute grief reaction. Five women from group two had prolonged periods of grief lasting up to two years. The authors conclude that abortion for foetal abnormality in the second trimester 'should be regarded as no less serious than a stillbirth and that acute grief reactions by the parents must be expected,' bearing in mind that this will be compounded by feelings of guilt for having chosen the procedure.[103]

Dutch researchers found that, among 196 women aborting for foetal abnormality, grief and post-traumatic symptoms did not decrease between two and seven years after the event. In their cross-sectional sample, with a relatively high response rate of 79 per cent, pathological post-traumatic scores were found in 17.3 per cent of participants. Advanced gestational age was associated with more psychological distress. Grief and regret were reported by 8 per cent and 10 per cent of participants respectively. The authors emphasise the importance of 'adequate psychological support from the caregiver during the decision-making process in order to avoid impulsive and not fully internalised decisions'.[104]

Similar results were found by other researchers who investigated eighty-three women terminating due to foetal malformation and compared them with women terminating for non-medical reasons and women giving birth. They found that termination of pregnancy due to foetal malformation is an emotionally traumatic major life event, which leads to severe post-traumatic stress response and intense grief reactions which are still evident two to seven years after the procedure. Contrary to expectations, women's experiences of traumatic stress four years after the procedure were not significantly different from women's experiences fourteen days afterwards.[105]

A metasynthesis of qualitative research involving women who had experienced abnormal prenatal tests found that couples chose to terminate their pregnancies for reasons including 'the availability and acceptability of termination and the perceived certainty of foetal death'. Factors contributing to the choice to terminate included ambivalence about the ability to parent an impaired child and altruistic concerns about the foetus, other children and marriage and family life. The authors note that:

> no matter what they ultimately chose to do, couples felt pulled to make the opposite decision and justify it to themselves, to close and distant members of their social network, and to health-care providers. Couples continuing their pregnancies felt pressure from providers to terminate their pregnancies, and all couples felt the need to explain or explain away their choices.[106]

They found that the intimate links between choice and loss involved in prenatal testing and abortion created a paradoxical situation that did not support a simplistic notion of 'choice'.[107]

A. Kersting et al. conducted a detailed analysis of three women's experiences of termination for foetal abnormality. The authors conclude that such an event is to be seen as a severe trauma that may entail a pathological grieving process. Health professionals should be aware of the varying responses and coping methods.[108]

M. Sandelowski and J. Barroso note that:

> positive prenatal diagnosis was devastating for women as it—and its aftermath—were embodied experiences for women, that is, prenatal testing, quickening, the continuation or termination of a pregnancy with an impaired foetus, and postpartum leaking of breast milk happen in women's bodies.[109]

The authors also state that:

> couples experienced selective termination as a technologically induced, historically unique, and paradoxical form of suffering entailing the intentional loss of a desired pregnancy and killing to care.… Couples, health-care providers, family, and friends underestimated the intensity and duration of feelings of loss following selective termination.[110]

They concluded that 'couples experienced selective termination as traumatic, regardless of the prenatal test revealing the foetal impairment or stage in pregnancy in which the termination occurred'.

In a 1993 study, C. Zeanah et al. concluded that:

> women who terminate pregnancies for foetal anomalies experience grief as intense as those who experience spontaneous perinatal loss, and they may require similar clinical management. Diagnosis of a foetal anomaly and subsequent termination may be associated with psychological morbidity.[111]

Similarly, a 1997 study on the long-term effects of abortion for foetal disability concluded that 'the long-term psychological stress response in women to pregnancy termination following ultrasonographic detection of foetal anomalies does not differ from the stress responses seen in women experiencing perinatal loss'.[112]

Prenatal diagnosis and abortion of foetuses with disease or disability has been assumed beneficial for women, but the psychological consequences of these procedures has been a neglected area of research.[113] In particular, recent research (V. Davies et al.) questions the assumption that early detection and termination of foetal anomaly has better outcomes for women in psychological terms.[114]

7.9 Social policy supporting the choice of motherhood

Historically and rhetorically, the phrase 'a woman's right to choose' has referred to making abortion available, in terms of its legality as well as access to services. The right to choose to give birth has received little attention. It may be assumed that giving birth is the default choice, the easiest choice, or not even a choice at all. But where abortion is readily available, all pregnant women are forced to choose. Women's stories and research suggest that in some cases choosing motherhood seems too difficult, and for them abortion becomes the path of least resistance.

Anecdotally, some women report their abortion decisions as being uninformed or coerced, and often distressing.

Empirical evidence also suggests that women frequently find the decision difficult, and have conflicting desires and emotions in relation to motherhood, their unborn children, and other aspects of their lives. In such cases, women concerned about the circumstances in which they are pregnant may need a listening ear, and non-judgmental advice and information about their options. They may need someone to help them draw out and sort through the myriad complex issues involved in their decision making about motherhood. It is clear that the idea that pregnancy counselling ought to simply validate a woman's decision is inappropriate for women who have not yet decided what to do.

We found that Australians overwhelmingly support the provision of counselling to women considering abortion. This is not to suggest that women who are seeking abortion need counselling to change their minds. Rather, a woman considering abortion clearly has major life issues which are inhibiting her perception that she could continue with her pregnancy. Research shows that women always have particular reasons for undergoing abortion; it is not the sole fact that she is pregnant, but the circumstances in which she is pregnant that present her with a dilemma.

The breadth of published research also demonstrates that a decision about pregnancy encompasses far more than simply the medical risks and benefits of the abortion procedure or pregnancy and delivery. Finances, housing, welfare, relationships, study, employment, violence, mental health, morals, and beliefs are all entwined; the pregnancy decision does indeed fit the biopsychosocial model. Health information from a general practitioner is important but only part of what a woman may need to make her decision. She may also need someone who has the time to listen and the resources to advise about many other aspects of her life. In particular, this listening ear and source of advice must not have a vested interest in providing her with an abortion.

In our survey, 99 per cent were in favour of counselling being provided about the risks and alternatives prior to abortion. Seventy-eight per cent said there should be counselling before this decision, and 21 per cent said it should be available on a voluntary basis only. Given that compulsory counselling would be in some cases coercive and therefore counterproductive, and in acknowledgment of the fact that many women may have had support, dialogue, and information from her own personal networks, voluntary counselling appears to be a more appropriate response.

In this chapter I have used peer-reviewed research to demonstrate the need for continued debate as well as the provision of counselling and a range of policy responses for pregnant women. Evidence shows that the abortion decision is not always straightforward or simple; that many women are unsure about their decision both before and after, and that there are many influences in women's lives which severely restrict their reproductive decision-making. Strong community support for counselling and alternatives is therefore well founded and worthy of consideration in public policy.

Chapter 8

Post-coital intervention:
from fear of pregnancy to rape crisis[1]

Nicholas Tonti-Filippini

Mary Walsh

In the practice of family medicine, women requesting what they usually call 'the morning-after pill' often confront Catholic and pro-life physicians. This usually follows a broken or slipped condom or natural (unprotected) intercourse. The requests for post-coital intervention have arisen from concerted efforts to promote to young women the need to have post-coital hormonal intervention or 'emergency contraception', as it is often called in such circumstances, to prevent pregnancy. Post-coital intervention is even made available without medical prescription in some jurisdictions, despite there being significant, relatively common medical contraindications and drug interactions.

A longer-standing problem has been the problem of rape crisis. Catholic rape crisis centres meeting the needs of women with dignity and compassion would seem to be an appropriate calling for Catholic health-care services. Yet in developed countries, there are few, if any, Catholic rape crisis centres. The obvious reason for Catholics to have withdrawn from that field is the lack of development of a morally acceptable alternative way of dealing with the risk of pregnancy following rape, in societies in which abortifacience is the recommended solution. Seemingly, Catholics and Catholic institutions wanting to abide by Church teaching have been frightened from the field.

8.1 Case study

A patient, three months postpartum and breastfeeding, requested the 'morning-after pill' (post-coital hormonal intervention to prevent ongoing pregnancy) after experiencing condom breakage on the previous evening. The birth of her child had occurred after she had had a similar event and been prescribed post-coital intervention which had failed.

It was unlikely that the previous night's event would result in pregnancy, given that she was breastfeeding, but she expressed a strong need for reassurance, her anxiety partly driven by the previous experience with combined condom and post-coital intervention failure.

Her circumstances led her general practitioner (GP) down an unexpected course. She decided to explore whether the patient's likely infertility could in fact be identified with certainty, thus avoiding the need for her concern and for any further action. The GP arranged for serum progesterone and oestrogen tests and contacted an endocrinologist, Professor Emeritus James Brown, Ph.D., M.D. (University of Melbourne), whom she knew had a research interest in this area. He was able to inform her that the test results indicated that the patient was not in the ovulatory phase of her cycle, the oestrogen levels being far lower than would be the case if she were in a fertile phase, and the progesterone so low as to indicate that she was not immediately postovulatory. The GP was able to offer her the reassurance that there was little if any likelihood that she could become pregnant from the event of the broken condom.

This episode raises the question as to whether, on many of the occasions that the 'morning-after pill' is requested, its use would needlessly expose women to its side effects, discomfort, and disruption. There is the option of serum or urine ovarian hormone testing to determine whether the patient was in a fertile phase at the time of the incident. Luteinising hormone tests might also be used but are much less informative and less reliable than testing progesterone levels. (See discussion below.)

In the discussions with endocrinologists that followed, it emerged that there are nonabortifacient alternatives to the Yuzpe regimen or the newer progesterone-only formulations for post-coital intervention. The use of oestrogen-only formulations to delay ovulation, well tried in the development of the oral contraceptive pill, would seem to be a morally acceptable defence against the pregnancy effect of rape. Unlike the combined progesterone-oestrogen formulation in the Yuzpe regimen, or the newer progesterone-only formulations (such as Postinor-2), a moderate dose of oestrogen would not disrupt the endometrium and potentially cause embryo loss. (See discussion below.)

8.2 A common problem

The requests for post-coital intervention often arise from condom mishaps. Catholic doctors find themselves embroiled in a mess largely made by government and other public health education efforts directed at young people and aimed at so-called 'harm minimisation' which largely avoid the central issue of avoiding the medical and moral personal disasters created by early sexual initiation and sex outside marriage.

Condoms are presented as the universal safety precaution. But even with perfect use to avoid pregnancy the medical evidence indicates a Pearl index for pregnancy for condoms between three and fifteen per hundred woman-years.[2]

Studies on perfect condom use are usually done on adults, there being ethical difficulties with undertaking such a study on teenagers. Consequently, it is much more difficult to obtain condom effectiveness figures for teenagers. Teenagers lack experience, may be more likely to be experimenting, and, often enough, change partners relatively frequently. One would expect condom efficacy in relation to pregnancy and disease to be different in teenagers.

In a major study on condom use by two hundred sexually active girls between the ages of 14–21, median 17 years, M. Christ et al. found that a very high proportion reported problems with condoms in the past year, 31 per cent had experienced a condom breaking; 39.5 per cent had experienced a condom falling off; and 6 per cent had become pregnant with a condom. Eighty-five per cent reported negative experiences, including broken condoms or condoms falling off, pregnancy, condom painful or too tight, unpleasant smell, interrupted sex, and reduced sensation.[3]

Avoiding pregnancy and disease are justifiably major sources of worry for sexually active adolescents, but condoms do not alleviate those worries. Their experience with condoms often does not tally with the assurances that educators often give that condomised sex is safe. In general practice, girls often present distressed, requesting assistance after natural (unprotected) intercourse or after a condom problem has occurred.

8.3 Post-coital intervention

Post-coital intervention may be given as a double dose of one of the higher dose combined pills taken twelve hours apart, the so-called 'Yuzpe regimen'. It normally causes a shedding of the endometrium resulting in loss of the embryo if fertilisation occurs in that cycle. The Yuzpe regimen may also suppress or delay ovulation. This latter contraceptive effect would, of course, be ineffective in preventing fertilisation, if ovulation was occurring or had already occurred at the time of the intervention. In that case, the regimen's effect would be on nidation (implantation).[4]

It is unlikely that the Yuzpe regimen would cause changes to the cervical mucus sufficient to completely prevent sperm from reaching the fallopian tube. Even the normal natural rise in progesterone, which begins eight hours before ovulation, does not prevent residual channelling in the cervix which is capable of allowing the passage of sperm on the third day after the rise in progesterone and the peak day of mucus.[5]

More commonly, a progesterone-only formulation (marketed as Postinor-2 in Australia) is being advocated for post-coital intervention. The manufacturer is vague about the method of action of the main ingredient, levonorgestrel. There are three main possibilities:[6]

- altering the lining of the uterus so that the embryo, when it reaches the uterus at about six days old, cannot implant;

- preventing ovulation (likely to be less than a 33 per cent chance of preventing ovulation and may be as low as 19 per cent[7]); or

- preventing the sperm from reaching the ovum by altering the production of mucus-carrying sperm in the cervix (the neck of the womb).

The first is not a contraceptive effect but an abortifacient effect. High doses of levonorgestrel have been shown by electron-microscope scanning of the endometrial surface to cause detectable changes affecting the receptivity of the endometrial surface.[8] The impact of those changes would be to prevent the implantation of the embryo, which takes place when the embryo has reached the stage at which differentiation of the cells into organs has just begun (at least 4–6 days old).

Preventing ovulation will not happen in most women following Postinor-2 use. The main ingredient in the combined contraceptive pill that prevents ovulation is oestrogen. Postinor-2 is progesterone only (levonorgestrel) and has a reduced effect on preventing ovulation.[9]

If preventing or delaying ovulation was all that was wanted, then a moderate dose of oestrogen is all that would be required. The ovulation-delaying effect of estradiol benzoate in oil was known as early as 1928 and well-known in the 1930s and '40s when it was used as a treatment for a variety of hormonal disorders. Its ovulation-delaying effect was a major focus in the early development of the contraceptive pill before the synthetic progesterones became available and Gregory Goodwin Pincus, Frank Colton, and others developed the combined pill. Estradiol benzoate reliably delayed ovulation, but an oestrogen-only pill was never marketed because many women would ovulate soon after the oestrogen was stopped at day twenty-one. It was only when the progesterone was added that ceasing the active pills at day twenty-one reliably produced bleeding rather than ovulation.[10] There is no evidence that oestrogen has abortifacient effects. The effect of oestrogen on the endometrium is to promote its development.

Taking oestrogen only would be likely to prevent pregnancy from occurring from an act the night before, provided that ovulation and fertilisation had not already occurred.[11] To meet the needs of rape victims, there is a need for greater research on treatments that affect ovulation and sperm transport without affecting the endometrium. An oestrogen-only post-coital intervention would be less effective than the Yuzpe regime or the high dose of levonorgestrel, but only because it would not also be abortifacient. If the moral requirement were to limit intervention to contraception and not abortifacience then there would be no justification for taking either the combined or the progesterone-only formulations.

One of the acknowledged possible affects of levonorgestrel is a higher incidence of ectopic pregnancy possibly due to its effect on the cilia in the fallopian tube, which are involved in the transit of the embryo.[12] This adds to the moral and medical concern about using it. Its use would be irresponsible, potentially endangering the women as well as the embryo. If it were not for the ideological commitment to abortion, there is no way that levonorgestrel would be medically permitted to be used post-coitally. It should be noted that there is no evidence available that oestrogen has an effect on the cilia and seemingly no reports of ectopic pregnancy associated with oestrogen use.

Preventing the sperm from reaching the ovum by altering the production of mucus-carrying sperm in the cervix is a known effect of progesterone if it is administered on a daily basis ahead of sexual intercourse. However, if intercourse happened the night before, it is a little late to try to prevent the passage of sperm if the woman is at a fertile time. The mucus channels that transport the sperm will already have been formed.[13] Sperm can be found within the fallopian tube within twenty minutes of sexual intercourse.

If the woman is in the period just prior to ovulation, some sperm may be stored in the crypts in the cervix.[14] One contraceptive possibility would be that the high levonorgestrel dose might trap those sperm by changing the character of the cervical mucus. However, a search of the literature yielded no publications to support that claim.

There has been some suggestion that levonorgestrel might affect the sperm itself. Some changes to straight-line velocity of sperm and to sperm-oocyte fusion have been observed in sperm treated with levonorgestrel but only at high concentration. W. Yeung et al. conclude that these effects are not likely to contribute significantly to emergency contraception.[15]

There have also been suggestions that the effect on the cilia and contractions of the fallopian tube might so delay the transit of the embryo that, when it arrives at the endometrium, nidation cannot occur due to the later arrival of the blastocyst. I can find no publications or research finding that would support this suggestion.

From this it would appear that the abortifacient effect, destroying a six-day-old embryo, is the most likely effect of Postinor-2. The postfertilisation effects thus have implications in such areas as informed consent, emergency department protocols, and conscience clauses.[16] This is especially significant for Catholic hospitals.

A Catholic, or at least pro-life, rape crisis centre ought not to include post-coital preparations containing only levonorgestrel as an option, given its abortifacient effects and the availability of other options that are not abortifacient or are at least less abortifacient. The Yuzpe regime is more likely to be contraceptive than the progesterone-only formulation, but only if administered prior to ovulation. At the time of ovulation or after ovulation the effectiveness of the combined oestrogen and progesterone formulation relies on anti-nidation.

Since a woman is infertile most of the cycle, there is an issue whether post-coital intervention is in fact unnecessary. The Yuzpe regimen and the levonorgestrel alternative are not without significant medical side effects. They are certainly not recommended as a routine way of controlling fertility.

If it were possible to identify that:

(a) an act of intercourse in the previous twenty-four hours could not have resulted in fertilisation;

(b) ovulation and hence possible fertilisation might yet occur in the near future unless there is intervention; or

(c) ovulation had already occurred and the ovum was already likely to have been exposed to sperm, and that fertilisation, if it was to occur, had already occurred;

then this would seem to be useful information to determine whether any intervention were necessary and to allow the woman to make an informed moral choice based on identifying the morally significant aspects of the options made available to her in a society that accepts the practice of abortifacience.

8.4 Identifying fertile and infertile phases

The search for reliable methods of natural family planning has resulted in the capacity to identify the infertile and the possibly fertile phases of the cycle, and ovulation. A woman's own observation of the presence of mucus at the vulva and the sensation it produces, allows her to recognise when she is infertile, when possibly fertile, and the occurrence of ovulation.

The phases of the cycle are also identifiable by testing for urine estrone glucuronide and urine pregnanediol glucuronide using the Brown monitor.[17] The Brown monitor is readily available in Australia as a home kit. It is my understanding that it may not be so readily available in the United States.

Serum testing of estradiol and progesterone also can be used to confirm the phases of a woman's cycle. In our experience, if the request is specified as urgent, a result can be obtained from a pathology laboratory within two to four hours.

Much of the literature on this topic tends to focus on testing for luteinising hormone (LH). It should be noted that the progesterone test is far more reliable and much more informative. LH indicates only that the pituitary is sending it out to attempt to cause the follicle to rupture, and that may or may not be successful, and the ovary's response may or may not be delayed. There is ample evidence of luteinised unruptured follicles. When that happens, the woman does not ovulate then but may progress to ovulate at a later time when there is subsequent LH surge within that cycle. The progesterone level indicates the ovary's response to the LH surge and the precise timing of ovulation. Higher levels also conclusively indicate that she is in the postovulatory infertile phase. Relying on LH testing is a little like asking parents what they told the child to do, rather than simply observing what the child is doing. The progesterone rise is a precise indicator of ovulation, the LH surge is an indication of the pituitary's attempt to cause ovulation.[18]

The oestrogen test is vital for precisely determining whether the woman has entered a potentially fertile phase. The progesterone test is vital for determining when ovulation occurs and the end of the potentially fertile phase.

It is our view that a Catholic rape crisis centre providing post-coital intervention would have an obligation to ensure that it had the capacity to undertake serum oestrogen and progesterone tests or urine estrone glucuronide and pregnanediol glucuronide tests, or at least to have rapid access to the tests by another agency.

Macroscopic analysis on internal examination can identify whether cervical mucus is present and whether it is of a consistency that indicates possible fertility. Low power microscopic analysis of the cervical mucus would confirm the mucus type,[19] but obtaining the sample (in a procedure similar to obtaining a sample for a Pap-smear test) does require experience.

Finally, ultrasound can be used to identify ovulation. Working independently,

- Professor James Brown, charting the ovarian hormonal levels and correlating them with the women's charting of when intercourse occurred in relation to pregnancy occurring, established the relation between the ovarian and pituitary hormones and the different phases of the cycle;[20]

- Professor Erik Odeblad undertook biophysical assays of cervical mucus and identified the roles of the different types of cervical mucus in fertility and infertility;[21]

- Drs Evelyn and John Billings studied women's observations of their symptoms and correlated those charted observations of the mucus symptom with whether pregnancy resulted from sexual intercourse during the different phases of mucus symptom.[22] They devised a set of rules to avoid or achieve pregnancy on that empirical basis. According to the standards of evidence-based medicine, the Billings rules to avoid pregnancy have a method related Pearl Index of 0–2.2 pregnancies per hundred woman-years in initiates.[23]

When these three areas of research were combined, they were mutually reaffirming, and each complemented the other in developing a full understanding of the relationship between the cervix, follicular development, and ovulation. Together, the Billings, Brown, and Odeblad have reviewed hundreds of thousands of women's cycles. More than 750 cycles have been monitored for ovarian hormone levels and contrasted with the women's charting of the mucus sensation at the vulva.

It is possible to offer to women who are in distress over an event that happened during the previous twenty-four hours, and which they fear may result in pregnancy, the possibility of identifying whether they are in fact infertile, or alternatively, whether they may conceive or may already have conceived.

Table 1 (see page 265), which was developed with assistance from Professor Brown, Dr John Billings and Dr Evelyn Billings, describes the woman's cervical mucus symptoms and what might be found if an internal examination were to be done. An examination is often done for forensic purposes after rape. If a woman had been charting her symptoms, it would be unnecessary to undertake further examination or testing, but she might want further confirmation or, as is the norm unfortunately, she may be ignorant of her symptoms and how to interpret them.

Table 1 also shows serum estradiol and progesterone levels for each phase. Pathologists usually offer a service, including an after-hours service, for serum estradiol and progesterone testing. If marked 'urgent', the result can be available in the same time that it takes to receive the results of early pregnancy tests (testing hCG), a matter of three or four hours.

Also shown in table 1 are the urine estrone glucuronide and pregnanediol glucuronide ranges for the different phases of the cycle. If the woman, according to these indicators, falls into the areas of the preovulatory infertile phase or the luteal infertile phase, then she can be reassured that pregnancy is most unlikely from an event occurring during the previous twenty-four hours. It would be possible, if thought necessary, to add an ultrasound examination of the ovaries to gain further confirmation of the stage or absence of follicular development and whether or not ovulation was about to or had occurred recently, but either serum or urinary results would be sufficient.

From table 1, it is evident that a woman who has a serum estradiol less than 440 pmol/L and serum progesterone less than 4.9 nmol/L, or a serum progesterone greater than 12 nmol/L, is in an infertile phase of her cycle. These figures are conservative, erring on the side of caution. There is a grey area when the progesterone is between 7 and 12 nmol/L which further research may narrow.

The symptoms of a woman who was charting would indicate whether she had ovulated. This information would more precisely identify the possibly fertile period. A woman who was charting adequately would not need confirmatory serum or urine testing. Though not trained to chart, a woman may nevertheless be able to provide some details of her cycle during the history-taking. The doctor may rely on the latter in conjunction with his or her examination and the blood or urine tests. A second blood or urine test taken a day later would also define more precisely the direction in which the trend in the serum or urine values was, and thus provide a basis for a more precise assessment. This is not necessary for the purpose of identifying whether a single act of sexual intercourse in the previous twenty-four hours may result in pregnancy. However, it would provide more information for the woman and possibly greater reassurance.

Further it should also be confirmed with the woman that there were not earlier incidents by which she may have conceived.

A WHO study on identifying fertility by the mucus symptom showed that the probability of pregnancy in relation to the peak day (determined by the mucus symptom alone) was 0.67 if intercourse occurred on peak day, 0.5 one day before peak day, 0.5 one to three days before peak day if there is slippery mucus, and 0.5 if there is only sticky mucus, 0.4 one day after peak day, 0.2 two days after peak day, and 0.1 three days after peak day. Outside the fertile period (commencement of mucus change to three days after peak day) the probability of pregnancy was 0.004.[24] The latter figure is especially significant for these purposes.

Most recently, D. Dunson et al. studied the daily probability of intercourse resulting in pregnancy for each day of what they called the fertile window. Their study involved 782 healthy couples and 5869 menstrual cycles. They used a rise in basal body temperature (BBT) (retrospectively) to recognise that ovulation had occurred. Nearly all pregnancies occurred within a six-day window with peak fertility occurring two days before the day of temperature rise.[25]

The corresponding WHO data for the Billings Ovulation Method (above) indicates the peak day identified by the mucus symptom may be a slightly stronger indicator of the day of peak fertility than the BBT rise minus two days, with a greater probability (0.67) of pregnancy resulting from intercourse on the peak day in the WHO study compared to probability (0.5) of pregnancy from intercourse two days before the BBT rise in the Dunson study for the most fertile age group, and lower probabilities for the older groups. However, there may be sampling differences.

The use of ovarian hormone testing gives a very accurate picture of what is happening in the woman's cycle. This is useful either to confirm the woman's own knowledge of her cycle, or in the absence of such knowledge, to determine whether or not she is at a potentially fertile phase of her cycle.

In the circumstance of rape, one would expect that it would be particularly reassuring for a woman, who is in either of the infertile phases, to be told that her cervix is closed with a G-mucus plug and that her vagina is naturally hostile to sperm. The information would also be reassuring for women who had simply had an unplanned exposure to the risk of pregnancy.

With this knowledge it becomes clear that one would have no need to use post-coital intervention during either of the infertile phases. Further, one can identify with some precision whether ovulation has occurred or is imminent, and thus, the time at which the contraceptive effect of the post-coital intervention would no longer be operable and the effect of preventing a birth would result rather from the abortifacient action of the post-coital intervention.

8.5 An alternative to abortifacience

The period of possible fertility prior to ovulation remains to be examined. A double dose of a high-dose combined progesterone and oestrogen pill might not be the treatment of choice if the aim were only to achieve contraceptive cover for the previous evening's happening. It is relatively easy to delay or suppress ovulation beyond the stage at which intercourse in the previous twenty-four hours might result in pregnancy.

In my discussion with him, Professor Brown suggested that an obvious agent to use to delay ovulation (given the early research on the pill) would be a single, moderate dose of oestrogen only. This would be unlikely to cause harm to the pregnancy if ovulation had already occurred and would be unlikely to cause significant problems for the woman, especially if a natural oestrogen were used—though there needs to be some further exploration of this possibility and even a trial to see what dosage would be required. It should, however, be born in mind that there is a dearth of well-researched information about the effects of the existing post-coital interventions and their actions. More is known about the ovulation-delaying effects of a moderate dose of oestrogen, which were widely researched over an extensive period prior to the development of the combined pill, than about the dosage and pharmacological effects of a double dose of the combined pill repeated over two days, or of the large dose of a progesterone-only formulation.

8.6 Managing pregnancy scares

The information about identifying the phases of the woman's cycle is very useful for those who ask for the morning-after pill after a condom mishap or natural sexual intercourse. A first step in such cases is to attempt to exclude the possibility that she is already pregnant. Second, by taking a history and undertaking a clinical examination and, if necessary, testing the ovarian hormones (by blood test or by urine analysis), the doctor could tell her whether pregnancy from the recent event would be improbable (see table 1). Most of the time it is. The doctor could also tell them if pregnancy is possible on this occasion and, if so, discuss with them at that early stage, the implications.

In most instances, knowing that pregnancy is improbable, the woman can choose to avoid the unpleasantness—the nausea, vomiting, severe abdominal pain and cramping, and heavy bleeding of the post-coital intervention, and the moral and psychological issue in relation to having done something possibly abortifacient. By using knowledge of the ovulatory cycle, the woman can be freed of anxiety in many instances and perhaps learn something about her physiology and reproductive health—information which few women appear to have.[26]

In practice, it makes sense to offer women who request the 'morning-after pill' the option of a serum test for oestrogen and progesterone levels and the possibility of being able to determine whether in fact pregnancy would be an improbable outcome without intervention. This option not only avoids the difficulties of the morning-after pill, it also assists them to better understand their own fertility and infertility.

A Catholic doctor may not formally cooperate in evil by prescribing contraception to prevent pregnancy, and especially not abortifacients. In the circumstances of a request for post-coital intervention, by taking steps to identify the likelihood of fertility or infertility, the doctor can narrow down the dilemma to a much smaller number of cases. In doing so, the doctor can develop a much better understanding of the woman and her needs and take the opportunity of the interaction to give her sound medical advice about the difficulties created by sexual intercourse outside of the circumstances in which she has a relationship within which a child would be welcomed. This can be an exercise in much needed primary health care, especially in relation to the increasing incidence of sexually transmissible infection.

8.7 Rape crisis

Providing care and support to those who have been raped is properly a function of Catholic health facilities. The medical component of that care needs to address the physical and mental trauma, and it needs to deal with the risks of pregnancy and of sexually transmissible disease.

In our societies where there are many immoral technological options that are lawfully offered, Catholic practitioners or facilities, for their own protection, need to make plain, publicly and on the occasion in which assistance is sought, that the service is conducted according to Catholic moral principles especially with respect to abortifacients, and that such services, though available elsewhere, will not be available from the facility.

A particular need for a woman who has been raped is that of information. Offering the woman pregnancy testing (testing for human chorionic gonadotrophin), in case she was already pregnant, and testing for the ovarian hormone levels can provide her with valuable information. In particular, it would be reassuring for her to know, as would usually be the case, that she was at an infertile time, and the cervix was blocked with mucus that prevents sperm and diminishes the chances of sexually transmissible infection. Given that any technology can malfunction, it is important that the level of reliability of the tests offered is also communicated to her.

It has long been accepted by orthodox Catholic moral theologians that it is legitimate in the circumstances of rape to attempt contraception as a defence against the effects of the aggressor including the presence in her body of his sperm. The goods of the marriage relationship that are destroyed by contraception do not exist in the circumstances of rape.

However, once fertilisation has occurred, then there is the matter of a new life having formed. By determining whether ovulation has yet occurred, it is possible to differentiate between contraception and abortifacience. A Catholic rape crisis facility could confidently reassure most that post-coital hormonal intervention is unnecessary, after determining that that was so by testing the ovarian hormone levels and taking a history. In the event that the woman's cycle was in a fertile phase approaching ovulation, Brown suggests that a moderate dose of an oestrogen-only formulation could be offered to delay ovulation beyond the capacity of the sperm to survive. Further research would determine with greater certainty the effectiveness of oestrogen in that application using contemporary standards of analysis. At no stage of the cycle would it be morally appropriate to use a treatment that also contained progesterone given the probability of its antinidation effect on the endometrium. The use of levonorgestrel as a post-coital intervention is never morally appropriate.

In rape crisis, the option of combining ovarian hormone testing, medical counselling and nonabortifacient contraceptive interventions would need to be integrated within complete professional support for a woman so violently used. It would also be important that the woman be informed that a Catholic or pro-life agency would manage her care differently from the way in which it may be managed elsewhere. A Catholic agency would do nothing that would endanger embryonic human life.

	Basic Infertile Pattern	Possibly Fertile Phase	Luteal Phase
Woman's Vulval Sensation and Observation	Woman reporting dry sensation at vulva or unchanging discharge and no change yet this cycle.	• Change at vulva to moist or slippery sensation; • Following three days after peak, dry sensation at vulva.	Dry or sticky sensation (not wet or slippery).
Clinical Examination	• Clinical examination not necessary but if being done (e.g., for forensic purposes), no strings of mucus should be seen macroscopically. • Microscopic analysis of a sample taken from the cervix (by experienced doctor) would show G-type mucus	• L and/or S-type mucus in cervix, possibly with motile sperm; • Following three days after peak, G and some S mucus in cervix on clinical examination.	G-mucus in cervix.
Serum Confirmation	• Serum estradiol <440 pmol/L • Serum progesterone level < 4.9 nmol/L	• Serum estradiol >440 pmol/L • Serum progesterone 0.5–4.9 nmol/L • After ovulation, a serum progesterone <7 nmol/L – may still be fertile	• Serum progesterone >12 nmol/L
Urine Confirmation	• Urine estrone glucuronide <100 nmol/24 hrs • Urine pregnanediol glucuronide <4 micromol/24 hrs	• Urine estrone glucuronide >150 nmol/24 hrs • Urine pregnanediol glucuronide <7 micromol/24 hrs	• Urine pregnanediol glucuronide >12 micromol/24 hrs
Advise Patient	Pregnancy most unlikely if intercourse <24 hours before (p<0.004).	Pregnancy possible (p<0.5).	Pregnancy most unlikely if intercourse <24 hours before (p<0.004).

Table 1. Determining whether pregnancy is unlikely when sexual intercourse has occurred in previous 24 hours.
(Table prepared with assistance of Professor James B. Brown [University of Melbourne] and Drs John and Evelyn Billings.)

Chapter 9

What rights, if any, do the unborn have under international law?[1]

John Fleming

Barristers and solicitors have traditionally looked to case law as an important source of interpreting domestic law. With the increasing globalisation of world trade, tourism, the breaking down of language barriers, and improvements in international relations, international law has emerged as a further important influence. International law has traditionally focused on governing relations between independent nation states. However, in the aftermath of the Second World War, the United Nations was formed on the basis of a Charter which committed the members of the UN to 'take joint and separate action in cooperation with the Organisation' to achieve 'the purposes set forth in Article 55 [of the Charter]'.[2] Article 55 committed the UN to promote 'universal respect for, and observance of, human rights and fundamental freedoms for all without distinction as to race, sex, language, or religion'.[3]

One important consequence of this major development in international relations has been:

> the demise of Oppenheim's doctrine that 'States solely and exclusively are the subject of International Law' ... [I]t is [now] ... the case that inter-state treaties are increasingly concerned with the 'trans-national' affairs ... of private individuals and companies.[4]

D.J. Harris, in a later discussion of the activities of the UN Commission on Human Rights, also points out that 'the idea that the treatment of a state's own nationals is a matter within its own jurisdiction has been abandoned'.

The practice of the Commission shows clearly the acceptance by the states, as they respond without question to allegations against them, that *the protection of human rights is now within the domain of international law.*[5]

A further important consequence of these developments in international law has been the increasing number of Declarations and Conventions which can potentially affect Australian municipal laws. The areas of domestic law which are potentially influenced are immense; they include administrative law, family law (especially custody matters), discrimination laws, medical negligence, succession, immigration and refugee law, criminal law, and human rights.

Practitioners need to be aware of how this may be relevant. The High Court in the *Minister for Immigration and Ethnic Affairs v Teoh*[6] held that entry into a treaty by Australia creates a 'legitimate expectation' — in administrative law — that the Executive Government and its agencies will act according to the treaty, even where those terms were *not* incorporated in Australian law.[7] Moreover, there is a presumption that the legislature intends to give effect to Australia's obligations under international law. Where a statute or subordinate legislation is ambiguous, it should be construed in accordance with those obligations, particularly where they are undertaken in a treaty to which Australia is a party.[8] These rulings of the High Court can profoundly influence many aspects of Australian municipal law. I will look at these issues in the context of the rights of the unborn, if any, under international law and their implications for Australian domestic law.

In 1996, considerable public controversy about the legality of abortion arose when the High Court of Australia was called upon to consider an appeal from the judgment of the New South Wales Court of Appeal in *CES v Superclinics (Australia) Pty Ltd.*[9] The Court of Appeal, by majority, approved, but did not apply, the principle in *R v Wald.*[10] Devine J. in that case had held that: first, an abortion may be lawful if the person performing the abortion, or the woman upon whom it is performed, has an honest belief on reasonable grounds that what was done was necessary to preserve the woman involved from serious danger to her life, or physical or mental health, which the continuance of the pregnancy would entail, not merely the normal danger of the pregnancy and childbirth; and second, a woman upon whom an abortion is performed is not guilty of aiding or abetting that act if she honestly and reasonably holds the appropriate belief, irrespective of the beliefs of the person performing the act. The High Court granted Special Leave to Appeal on 15 April 1996[11] and the Court subsequently granted representative interest groups leave to intervene. The proceedings were, however, settled during the course of argument, and the Court was not called upon to give judgment. But the case highlights an instance where international law may be relevant to domestic laws. The issue of the unborn has again arisen in the context of the United Nations Convention on the Rights of the Child 1989.

On 28 August 1995 the Attorney-General of Australia referred to the Australian Human Rights and Equal Opportunity Commission and the Australian Law Reform Commission (the Commissions) 'for inquiry and report, matters relating to children and young people and the legal process'.

In May 1997 a Draft Recommendations Paper entitled 'A Matter of Priority: Children and the Legal Process' (the 'Paper') was jointly published by the Commissions. This chapter, based largely on submissions to those Commissions by Dr Michael G. Hains and me, considers the rights of the unborn under international law. These considerations are even more appropriate in the twenty-first century as particular elites continue their campaign for a universally recognised 'right to abortion', usually pursued under the rubric of 'the right of access to reproductive health-care service' or, to use the apt words of Richard Wilkins, 'illusive legal constructs' such as 'forced pregnancy'.[12]

In 1997 the Commissions adopted the definition of 'child' used in the United Nations Convention on the Rights of the Child 1989,[13] (i.e. a person under the age of eighteen). Despite that definition, the paper did not consider the rights of all children under the age of eighteen, failing to discuss the rights of unborn children and the issue of abortion. The implication here is that this is a group of human beings who are not to receive moral consideration as human beings with fundamental rights and nor are they to be afforded the protection of the law.

So, while the Paper emphasised the importance of the Convention on the Rights of the Child (CRC), it failed to acknowledge that it must be interpreted in the light of the Charter of the United Nations,[14] the Universal Declaration of Human Rights 1948,[15] the International Covenant on Civil and Political Rights 1966 (ICCPR), the Declaration of the Rights of the Child 1959, and other fundamental human rights documents. This is a common mistake and a serious one indeed since, as we shall see, those foundational documents have much to say on the rights of the unborn bearing directly on ambit claims being made for the recognition of a 'right to abortion'.

The fact is that the rights of the unborn were discussed in the drafting stages of the Universal Declaration of Human Rights 1948 (UDHR)as well as in the drafting stages of the CRC. The matter is also referred to in the International Covenant on Civil and Political Rights 1966. That this subject did not merit discussion by the Commissions is, therefore, a cause for great concern. It is also a matter for concern that academic lawyers seem unwilling to deal with these issues, preferring instead to simply assert that the UDHR and the ICCPR contain nothing that would suggest that the unborn have rights.

The importance of the abortion issue in the Australian legal context is further underscored by the fact that the Declaration of the Rights of the Child 1959 was attached as a Schedule to the Human Rights and Equal Opportunity Commission Act 1986 (Cth.) following discussions with the Right to Life Association,[16] such was the importance of this matter. As a consequence, the Declaration of the Rights of the Child 1959,[17] is part of Australian municipal law, although what legal rights to which this may give rise is debatable.[18] Accordingly it is not good enough within the Australian context to simply describe the Declaration on the Rights of the Child as 'a non-binding international instrument'.[19]

9.1 Human rights and the unborn child

9.1.1 The convention on the rights of the child and abortion

The CRC, adopted by the General Assembly of the United Nations on the 20th November, 1989, and ratified[20] by Australia,[21] reiterates the positions taken by the Universal Declaration of Human Rights 1948, which have been adopted and proclaimed by Australia, about the 'equal and inalienable rights of all members of the human family' as the 'foundation of freedom, justice and peace in the world', and that the 'United Nations has proclaimed that childhood is entitled to special care and assistance'.[22] In particular the CRC asserts: 'States Parties recognise that every child has the inherent right to life'[23] and that 'States Parties shall ensure to the maximum extent possible the survival and development of the child'.[24]

Regarding abortion, the CRC bears in mind that, 'as indicated in the Declaration of the Rights of the Child, "the child, by reason of his physical and mental immaturity, needs special safeguards and care, including appropriate legal protection, before as well as after birth" '.[25] Does it necessarily follow from this that the right to life of the pre-born child is protected? Senator Gareth Evans, the then Minister for Foreign Affairs and Trade, told the Australian Senate on 26 October 1989 that the Australian Government understands the reference to the rights of the child 'before as well as after birth' in a way that does not preclude abortion. However, Australia made no such reservation or interpretation[26] at the time of ratification.[27] Acknowledging that the reference to the rights of the child 'before as well as after birth' does appear in the Preamble in the then draft Convention, 'at the same time a statement in the *travaux préparatoires* - the preparatory materials - makes it clear that the contentious issue of the child's rights before birth is a question to be determined by individual states parties'.[28]

Senator Evans' statement on this matter is seriously misleading. When they were debating this aspect of the Preamble, some delegations supported it precisely because it offered protection to the unborn child.[29] Other delegations, of which Australia was one, opposed:

> what in their view amounted to re-opening the debate on this controversial matter [abortion] which, as they indicated, had been extensively discussed at earlier sessions of the Working Group with no consensus achieved. It was also pointed out by some delegations that *an unborn child is not literally a person* whose rights could already be protected, and that the main thrust of the Convention was deemed to promulgate the rights and freedoms of every human being after his birth and to the age of 18 years.[30]

As a consequence of the debate they amended the Preamble such that the text would no longer say, 'Recognising that …' but 'Bearing in mind that …' (as indicated in the Declaration of the Rights of the Child 1959) 'the child, by reason of his physical and mental immaturity, needs special safeguards and care, including appropriate legal protection, before as well as after birth'. Further, the following statement was, by agreement, placed in the *travaux préparatoires*: 'In adopting this preambular paragraph, the Working Group does not intend to prejudice the interpretation of article 1[31] or any other provision of the Convention by States Parties.'[32] No doubt this is the statement to which Senator Evans referred. However, this was not the end of the matter.

The representative of the United Kingdom sought 'confirmation from the Legal Counsel that the statement would be taken into account if, in the future, doubts were raised as to the method of interpreting article 1'.[33] That advice was annexed to the report of the Working Group. It gives no such assurance and by no means allows the matter of abortion to be automatically reserved to the judgment of states parties.

The Response of the Legal Counsel certainly allows such an interpretative statement to be included in the *travaux préparatoires*. However, the Legal Counsel cautioned that:

> seeking to establish the meaning of a particular provision of a treaty, through an inclusion in the *travaux préparatoires* may not optimally fulfil the intended purpose, because, as you know, under article 32 of the Vienna Convention on the Law of Treaties, *travaux préparatoires* constitute a 'supplementary means of interpretation' and hence recourse to *travaux préparatoires* may only be had if the relevant treaty provisions are in fact found by those interpreting the treaty to be unclear.[34]

It is by no means certain that those international courts that have to interpret international law will find the treaty unclear, especially as it is to be understood, not by itself, but with reference to and guided by the Universal Declaration of Human Rights 1948, the International Covenant on Civil and Political Rights 1966 and other international covenants.

In his account of the abortion debate, in the context of the CRC, Philip Alston claims that:

> the acceptance of a preambular paragraph recognising that 'the child needs special safeguards and care, including appropriate legal protection, before as well as after birth' cannot be interpreted as an indirect reversal of that explicit rejection [of proposals to recognise the right to life of the unborn]. To do so would be to attribute to the preamble an importance considerably in excess of that which may reasonably be accorded to such broad policy pronouncements.[35]

Alston believes that the CRC leaves the matter of abortion as an open question such that those States that wish to prohibit abortion and those that wish to approve it are on an equal footing. He believes that existing international human rights law does not provide for the status of the unborn child, and that the CRC is in conformity with that position. But Alston overlooks the fact that a reference in the Preamble is part of the treaty itself,[36] whereas the *travaux préparatoires* is a supplementary means of interpretation to be used in limited circumstances.[37]

Alston is simply not entitled to this conclusion on the basis of the facts that he, himself, has outlined. As we have already noted, some delegations favoured the inclusion of the words 'the child … needs special safeguards and care, including appropriate legal protection, before as well as after birth' precisely because they believed that it offered protection to the unborn child while others opposed it because they saw it 're-opening the debate on this controversial matter (abortion)'.[38] The fact is that with a minor change in words ('Recognising that' was changed to 'Bearing in mind that') these contentious words were included in the Preamble of the CRC. That clearly means the abortion issue was left on the table as both those who opposed its inclusion and those who favoured its inclusion have testified.

In any case, since the CRC has to be interpreted in the light of and consistently with the Universal Declaration of Human Rights 1948 and the International Covenant on Civil and Political Rights 1966[39] then the question of the rights of the unborn child has to be resolved against a broader landscape than the CRC seen in isolation. Alston's contention that 'existing international human rights law' does not recognise the right to life of the unborn would, if it were true, help those who deny that the right to life of the unborn is recognised by the CRC. However, in this article, we will see that Alston's contention, far from being certain, is almost certainly false.

First, during the drafting of the International Covenant on Civil and Political Rights 1966 an amendment, to Article 6, submitted by Belgium, Brazil, El Salvador, Mexico, and Morocco[40] led to a discussion as to whether the right to life should be protected by law 'from the moment of conception'. 'Those supporting the amendment maintained that it was only logical to guarantee the right to life from the moment life began.'[41] The amendment was rejected.[42]

> It was pointed out that the legislation of many countries accorded protection to the unborn child. On the other hand, the amendment was opposed on the grounds that it was impossible for the State to determine the moment of conception and hence, to undertake to protect life from that moment. Moreover, the proposed clause would involve the question of the rights and duties of the medical profession. Legislation on the subject was based on different principles in different countries and it was, therefore, inappropriate to include such a provision in an international instrument.[43]

The toleration of abortion played no part in the rejection of the amendment.

Second, in the context of the CRC, Malta and Senegal proposed an amendment to draft Article 1 to explicitly protect the rights of the unborn child from conception.[44] These proposals were not rejected by the member states but were withdrawn by Malta and Senegal 'in the light of the text of preambular paragraph 6 as adopted' which referred to the rights of the child 'before as well as after birth'.[45]

Third:

> The representative of Italy observed that no State was manifestly opposed to the principles contained in the Declaration of the Rights of the Child and, therefore, according to the Vienna Convention on the Law of Treaties, the rule regarding the protection of life *before birth* could be considered as 'jus cogens' since it formed part of the common conscience of members of the international community.[46]

Jus cogens (or *ius cogens*) is a peremptory norm of general international law from which no derogation is permitted and which can be modified only by a subsequent norm of general international law having the same character.[47] The right to life of all human beings has the nature of an intransgressible norm already contained in the Universal Declaration of Human Rights 1948, the International Covenant on Civil and Political Rights 1966, and the Declaration of the Rights of the Child 1959. In other words, under international law, the unborn child is protected; and it was not permissible at this late stage to attempt to allow a liberal abortion agenda under the CRC.

Fourth, the Declaration on the Rights of the Child 1959, which carries the same preambular reference to the rights of the child before as well after birth, is part of Australian municipal law.[48] In his statement to the Senate, Senator Evans did not take account of these legal obligations. This, however, does not absolve the Commissions from taking seriously the issue of the rights of the unborn in the context of Australia's human rights obligations. Moreover, as has been established, these issues fall within the Commissions' Terms of Reference and must be addressed.

Finally, explicit protection is extended to the unborn child in the International Covenant on Civil and Political Rights 1966 and in the Convention on the Prevention and Punishment of the Crime of Genocide 1948. These protections will be discussed later in this chapter.

Having rehearsed these arguments in 1997,[49] one might have thought that they would have been taken seriously by academics interested in this area. Instead Alison Duxbury and Christopher Ward simply dismiss this position, without argument, and reassert Alston's position as if it had never been seriously challenged.

> It has been suggested that international law does recognise the right to life of the unborn child and therefore domestic cases should be argued with that in mind [reference to Fleming and Hains article]. However, at present it would appear that international human rights law does not recognise the *absolute* right to life of the unborn child.[50]

This also begs the question as to why Duxbury and Ward qualified the term 'right to life' with the word 'absolute' when it applies to the unborn. What point are they trying to make? Are they concerned that the recognition of the right to life of the unborn child would imply that the law of the land could not allow abortion in any case, including when there is a direct threat to the life of the mother? Is that why the word 'absolute' is used, to head off at the pass an unpalatable conclusion? That the pursuit of the truth may involve unpalatable conclusions is no reason to engage in obfuscations and distortions. And in any case the documents give no guidance as to how such a conflict between competing rights to life must be resolved.

As Duxbury and Ward continue their article it becomes clear that they do not pick up on some of the most important provisions of the various international human rights instruments which call into question the provisions of Australian (and British and American) law. More on that later.

9.1.2 The right to life of the unborn and international law

Within what limits may a state party provide for legal abortion? To find the answer to this question, full account has to be taken of the provisions of the United Nations Charter, the Universal Declaration of Human Rights 1948 that seeks to amplify Article 55 of the United Nations Charter, and the International Covenant on Civil and Political Rights 1966. Article 55 commits the United Nations to 'promote respect for, and observance of, human rights and fundamental freedoms for all without distinction as to race, sex, language, or religion'.[51]

The Universal Declaration of Human Rights 1948 is founded upon the notion that there are human values and these values are inherent in the human individual. In the Preamble, the Declaration states that 'the foundation of freedom, justice, and peace in the world' is the 'recognition of the inherent dignity and of the equal and inalienable rights of all members of the human family'.[52]

As far as the Declaration is concerned there are human values *inherent* in all members of the human family because of their 'inherent dignity'. Since 'dignity' is about true worth or excellence ['dignus' in Latin means 'worthy'], and, in the context, human worth, then the claim for the inherent dignity of human beings is a claim for basic human values.

Further, the Preamble links human dignity, human values with human rights that it describes as 'inalienable rights', rights of which we may not be deprived and cannot deprive ourselves. I must not be sold into slavery, and I am to be restrained from selling myself into slavery.

These human rights which reflect human values must, says the Preamble, 'be protected by the rule of law' otherwise humankind may be driven, 'as a last resort, to rebellion against tyranny and oppression'. This protection of the rule of law is necessary not only for human beings to live together peaceably within the State, but also so that nations may live together in peace.

The Universal Declaration of Human Rights 1948 presents itself to the world as 'a common standard of achievement for all peoples and all nations' and as a guide for every structure in society and for every individual, in order that the rights identified in the Declaration may have 'their universal and effective recognition and observance' secured.

Article 1 of the Declaration asserts certain things about human beings that affect the understanding of the rest of the document. Human beings, it says, 'are born free and equal in dignity and rights'. This value of equality of human beings, this injunction not to show preference between individuals in the recognition of 'the rights and freedoms set forth in this Declaration', is further specified in Article 2. In particular, in the entitlement to the rights and freedoms in the Declaration

278 ❖ COMMON GROUND?

there is to be no distinction of any kind, 'such as race, colour, sex, language, religion, political or other opinion, national or social origin, property, birth or other status'. In this way the Declaration excludes discrimination against the elderly and the very young, the physically and mentally disabled, and the chronically ill. All have equal claim to the rights and freedoms enunciated in the Declaration.

Article 3 of the Declaration begins the articulation of the human values to be defended in terms of human rights. 'Everyone has the right to life, liberty and the security of person.'Thus, human life is held to be both inviolable and inalienable. The Declaration does not begin with hard cases or exceptions, but with the general proposition that concerns the value of human life. Noting the order of the rights articulated is also interesting — life first, then freedom [liberty], and then security of person. Unless the State can guarantee the right to life then there are no meaningful rights to freedom or to security of person. The right to life is logically prior to considerations of the quality of the individual's life.

Does this right to life extend to the unborn child? When Article 3 of the Universal Declaration of Human Rights 1948 was being drafted there were several proposals for the provision of an explicit protection for the unborn child.[53] These proposals were certainly debated. 'In the event, none of the relevant proposals was pushed to a vote and the final text stated only that "everyone had the right to life …" .'[54]

The fact that the matter was not pushed to a vote does not mean that one can conclude that the rights of the unborn child are not covered by the Universal Declaration of Human Rights 1948. The text clearly states that everyone has the right to life, and that what is meant by 'everyone' is 'every member of the human family'[55], that is, all human beings. Here is the heart of the matter. Some of those nations who opposed an understanding of the CRC's Preambular reference to 'the child, by reason of his physical and mental immaturity' needing 'special safeguards and care, including appropriate legal protection, before as well as after birth,' as including abortion did so on the basis of attitudes which violate explicit provisions of the Universal Declaration of Human Rights 1948 and the International Covenant on Civil and Political Rights 1966.

That opposition was on the basis that:

> *an unborn child is not literally a person* whose rights could already be protected, and that the main thrust of the Convention was deemed to promulgate the rights and freedoms of every human being after his birth and to the age of 18 years.[56]

These are mere assertions of opinion, opinion that is not universally shared in the way that the various human rights instruments are universally agreed. In fact they are opinion which is in conflict with universally agreed human rights instruments.

Michel Meslin, however, has shown that 'the concept of person is one of the most difficult concepts to define — even though it is always burdened with hopes and revendications. It is neither a simple fact, nor evident throughout history'.[57] The briefest of surveys of the literature provides ample evidence to support Meslin's contention. Concepts of personhood based upon science and philosophy abound. For some, personhood begins at syngamy. For others it is at fourteen days after fertilisation, twelve weeks, twenty-eight weeks, birth, three months after birth, and so on. There is no agreement in science or philosophy about when personhood begins or where it ends or how it should be defined. The only agreement one finds that human life begins at fertilisation, is in the embryological text books. It is the fertilisation of a human egg by a human sperm that produces a member of the human species, the human family.

9.2 Science and the beginning of human life

In most mammals, oocytes which are released during ovulation are arrested during Metaphase II of the meiotic

280 ❖ COMMON GROUND?

cell cycle, and subsequent fertilisation then triggers the completion of meiosis.[58] The movement of cilia and the contractions of the oviduct propel the egg towards the uterus. If the egg is not fertilised, the corpus luteum stops producing progesterone, which is required to prepare the uterus to accommodate the fertilised egg. The absence of progesterone causes a break in the lining of the uterine wall, and menstruation begins.[59] The uterus sheds its endometrium and expels it along with the egg during menstruation. It is thought that the endometrium is only receptive to embryonic implantation during a defined window, which spans cycle days 20–24.[60]

Human chorionic gonadotropin (hCG) is produced by the embryo soon after conception and then by the syncytiotrophoblast. Its role is to maintain corpus luteum function and subsequent progesterone and estrogen release, thus facilitating pregnancy and preventing menstruation.[61]

After fertilisation comes the initiation of cleavage. This refers to the series of mitotic cell divisions whereby the zygote, which is a single cell, is fractionated into numerous cells referred to as blastomeres. This first division or cleavage marks the initiation of development, and the zygote is now known as an embryo and is referred to as a blastula.[62] Subsequent divisions give rise to exponential increases in the number of cells whose differentiation potential gradually becomes narrower, as the zygote progresses towards the preimplantation blastocyst stage.

The second polar body, which is released by the oocyte as it completes meiosis represents the 'animal pole' of the zygote. The opposite side is referred to as the 'vegetal pole'. The animal-vegetal axis, in conjunction with the point of sperm entry, defines the orientation of the first cleavage of the zygote, which indicates that the morphogenetic program for cell fate determination is in place very early in development.[63]

Another crucial milestone in embryonic development is the generation of asymmetry, which delineates the orientation of the basic body plan. Recent work by R. Gardner reveals that the early embryo already shows some asymmetry even at the single cell zygote stage.[64]

Anthony Fisher has assembled other citations from many medical and biological textbooks, all of which underscore the scientific consensus that 'the human embryo is a genetically human, discrete, and alive unit, organically single and individual, with a self-contained power to organise his or her own growth, multiplication, and differentiation in a way that ordinarily leads to a human adult'.[65] R. Yanagimachi begins his essay on 'Mammalian Fertilization' with the statement: 'Fertilization in mammals normally represents the beginning of life for a new individual'.[66]

On the basis, then, of this standard text book definition of fertilisation, and in light of what we know of early embryo formation and development, it may reasonably be concluded that the embryo[67] is a 'new individual', genetically different from his or her parents, and containing all the necessary genetic information for further development. This embryological understanding of the beginning of human life has been expressed in various formulations. The Senate Select Committee On The Human Embryo Experimentation Bill 1985 [Australia] defined the human embryo:

> The Committee, in adopting the usage 'embryo' to describe the fertilised ovum and succeeding stages up to the observation of human form, means to speak of genetically new human life organised as a distinct entity oriented towards further development.[68]

The testimony of C.R. Austin to that Senate Select Committee, that the 'stage which marks the start of a person is a matter of opinion'[69] was matched by Roger Short's contention that the benchmark fourteen days, for which he argued, was nevertheless 'a prejudice' and 'purely arbitrary'.[70] It should be noted that although Austin's expertise is that of a scientist, his opinion is not a scientific opinion, but rather a philosophical opinion because he is referring not to the beginning of life biologically, but to his personal opinion on when it is reasonable to recognise the beginning of personhood.

In summary, then, the main results of fertilisation are:

a) *restoration of the diploid number of chromosomes*, half from the father and half from the mother. Hence, the zygote contains a new combination of chromosomes, different from both parents; b) *determination of the sex* of the new individual. An X-carrying sperm will produce a female (XX) embryo, and a Y-carrying sperm a male (XY) embryo. Hence, the chromosomal sex of the embryo is determined at fertilisation; c) *initiation of cleavage*. Without fertilisation the oocyte usually degenerates 24 hours after ovulation.[71]

There is a widespread assumption in the public debate and commonly among philosophers that the early human embryo is undifferentiated or unspecialised and therefore less human and with diminished moral worth. But the science challenges that view revealing that, in fact, the early human embryo specialises in complex, directed, and precise ways from the moment of sperm penetration of the egg and onwards. Moreover, there is a body of literature and research that indicates that specification of form and function begins at fertilisation.[72] The human embryo acts for his or her own survival, signalling the mother of his or her presence, modifying the mother's biological systems at the molecular level to ensure survival, and at the same time engaging continuous process of development. Fertilisation, implantation, and birth are simply particular stages in the human life cycle.

There is, then, every good scientific reason to conclude that the early human embryo is one of us, a member of the human family. So while there is no agreed basis for dividing up the human family into persons and non-persons, there is an agreement from science that from fertilisation we all share a common humanity, that we are all members of the 'human family', to use the words of the Universal Declaration of Human Rights 1948. This latter point has been conceded by strong supporters of the 'pro-choice' position, especially Peter Singer, Michael Tooley, and Helga Kuhse. It is simply that they do not believe that being a member of the human family is a sufficient reason to conclude that an individual has, by reason of that fact alone, the right to life. And history shows that attempts to disenfranchise some members of the human family from moral consideration has lead to justifications of intolerable abuses of human rights including slavery, genocide, abortion, infanticide, non-voluntary sterilisation, and non-voluntary and voluntary euthanasia of other human beings. It was precisely in reaction to these abuses of human rights that the United Nations was brought into being on the basis of its Charter.

In the current climate we need to appreciate that fashionable philosophical notions of human personhood, which are being used to justify abortion, are also being used to justify the killings of children up to three to *six months after birth*.[73] If the killing of a child *after birth* is considered to be in violation of our human rights obligations, then the killing of the child *before birth* on the same philosophical justification must also be considered a violation of that child's right to life.

9.3 Denying personhood used to justify abuse of human rights

The eugenic impulse to kill foetuses and other members of the human family who have disabilities is still in evidence in the twenty first century[74] and is used together with a utilitarian moral philosophy to deny personhood, and therefore moral consideration, to those classes of human beings who constitute a burden to the community, a burden which it is often unwilling to accept. Abortion can then be advanced to parents who may feel unable to cope with that burden alone and without the support of the wider community.

There is a connection between the self-interest of communities and the line to be drawn between persons and non-persons. That self-interest may be driven by eugenic, economic, social and political factors such that those persons a society wishes to exclude are deemed to be non-persons. History is replete with examples of this phenomenon. Thus could Chief Justice Taney of the United States Supreme Court exclude Dred Scott (a Negro slave) from personhood;[75] the Egyptian Pharaohs exclude the Israelites; Hitler exclude Jews, Gypsies, the 'degenerate' and the asocials from personhood;[76] the British tolerate the slave trade; and some European Australians liquidate and repress the Aborigines.

The notion that certain classes of persons are non-persons is a not uncommon opinion. The Canada Indian Act 1880 states that 'the term person means an individual other than an Indian'. In the Canada Franchise Act 1885, we learn that:

> [a person] is a male person, including an Indian and excluding a person of Mongolian or Chinese Race.' Here is progress; in only five years Indians were upgraded to personhood and Asians are called persons in the very clause denying them personhood. By 1925, Canadian legislation had determined that all races — and women — are persons. Changes in Canada continued. By 1980, the government had recognised the Inuit, or Eskimos, as Indigenous Peoples with entitlement to lands. And the nation had developed a cadre of advocates dedicated to the empowerment of the disadvantaged.[77]

The Universal Declaration of Human Rights 1948, following the United Nations Charter, rejects discrimination against any members of the 'human family', and requires the 'recognition of the inherent dignity and of the equal and inalienable rights of *all* members of the human family' (emphasis added). As far as human personhood is concerned, the Declaration does not allow discrimination on the basis of human personhood. Article 2 asserts firmly that '*everyone* is entitled to all the rights and freedoms set forth in this declaration, *without distinction of any kind* . . .' (emphasis added), and Article 30 commands that 'nothing in this Declaration may be interpreted as implying for any State, group, or person any right to engage in any activity or to perform any act aimed at the destruction of any of the rights and freedoms set forth herein.' Article 6 specifically deals with the matter of the division of human beings into persons and non-persons in these terms: 'Everyone has the right to recognition everywhere as a person before the law'.[78]

It is true that the practice of abortion is widespread and, in many countries, legal at least in some circumstances. There is, however, a mismatch between the human rights requirements of international law and the practice of individuals and nation states in the same way that there is a mismatch between the rights of women and the practice of individuals and nation states. It is interesting to note that, in their discussion of the common law tradition that a human being is not a person until birth, Duxbury and Ward make no reference to Article 6 of the UDHR or Article 16 of the ICCPR, that is, the very provisions in international law, which most call into account current Australian (and other Western) legal notions of personhood. One wonders why.

If the human rights of the unborn child are to be upheld in law there will need to be with it an acceptance of the obligation to provide the social, economic, and moral support that women need when faced with an unwanted pregnancy. The hard cases need to be seen as hard cases against the background of the inalienable right of the foetus to live (a right that the foetus shares with his or her fellow human beings) and the rights of everyone (in this context especially women) 'to a standard of living adequate for the health and well being of himself and of his family ... and the right to security in the event of unemployment ... or other lack of livelihood in circumstances beyond his control'. And further,

Motherhood and childhood are entitled to special care and assistance. All children, whether born in or out of wedlock, shall enjoy the same social protection.[79]

Article 6 (1) of the International Covenant on Civil and Political Rights 1966 guarantees 'every human being has the inherent right to life'. The right to life is the only right in the Covenant that is *expressly* stated to be 'inherent' to everyone. The Human Rights Committee[80] has described it as 'the supreme right'.[81] It is also one of the rights which cannot be derogated from,[82] even in a 'time of public emergency which threatens the life of the nation'.[83] In its General Comment,[84] on Article 6, the Human Rights Committee has noted that:

quite often the information given concerning article 6 has been limited to only one or other aspect of this right. *It is a right which should not be interpreted narrowly.*[85]

And the

expression *'inherent right to life' cannot properly be understood in a restrictive manner,* and the protection of this right requires that states adopt positive measures.[86]

That international law does envisage human rights protection for the unborn can be seen in the provision dealing with capital punishment in the International Covenant on Civil and Political Rights 1966:

Sentence of death shall not be imposed for crimes committed by persons *below eighteen years of age* and *shall not be carried out on pregnant women.*[87]

In this provision, a state may execute a woman only when she is not pregnant. The innocent are not to die along with the guilty.[88] Indeed the *travaux préparatoires* of the International Covenant on Civil and Political Rights 1966 makes this abundantly clear:

The principal reason for providing in paragraph 4 [now Article 6(5)] of the original text that the death sentence should not be carried out on pregnant women was to save the life of an innocent unborn child.[89]

Here is an explicit recognition in international law that the human rights enjoyed by all other members of the human family are also to be enjoyed by the unborn. This fundamentally humane principle was reflected in the common law in England and Australia when each country had the death penalty.[90] Again, Duxbury and Ward make no reference to this provision. If this account of international law is wrong then it behoves those who deny human rights to some human beings to deal with the provisions of international law that seem to be saying that the unborn do have human rights.

Abortion advocates, however, have asserted that when Article 1 of the Universal Declaration of Human Rights 1948 says that 'all human beings are born free and equal in dignity and rights', this means that 'persons are recognised in international law, as human beings having been born'.[91] This deduction is without merit in the light of the detailed arguments we have already adduced. It cannot, in good faith, reasonably be deduced from Article 1, read in the context of the whole of the document and in the light of the covenants, which have further specified human rights, that unborn human beings are not persons with rights. The natural meaning of the text, in the light of the other references in the relevant provisions of international law, is that human beings without distinction are born free and equal in dignity and rights because as members of the human family they have had that status from the beginning. The interpretation offered by abortion advocates is about as helpful as deducing from a statement that a baby is born human that it was not human before birth.

Lastly, the use of abortion as a means of genocide is raised in the Convention on the Prevention and Punishment of the Crime of Genocide 1948.[92] In Article 2 the Convention defines the 'odious scourge'[93] of genocide to include 'killing members of the group' and 'imposing measures intended to prevent births within the group'.[94] The latter inclusion explicitly recognises the right to life of the unborn. In the same article genocide is conceived in terms of an intention 'to destroy, in whole or in part, a national, ethnical, racial or religious group'. The question is, to what extent, if at all, does this apply to the practice of abortion in contemporary society?

Much depends on what should be understood by the term 'in whole or in part of a national group'. The moral justification most frequently advanced for abortion is that, as a group or category of human beings, the unborn are not persons and accordingly have no right to life to protect. But, as we have already argued, the unborn are part of the human family. And the human family is itself broken down into nation states or groups. The unborn are, then, a sub-group of a national group. If the unborn, contrary to Article 6 of the Universal Declaration of Human Rights 1948 and Articles 6 and 16 of the International Covenant on Civil and Political Rights 1966, are defined, as a group, as non-persons and therefore beyond moral and legal protection, does the crime of genocide apply to those countries that fail to give protection to that part of the national group?

Even more obviously, 'disabled persons' are recognised in international law as a group which forms part of a nation.[95] These persons 'have the same civil and political rights as other human beings'[96] and must be 'protected against all exploitation, all regulations and all treatment of a discriminatory, abusive or degrading nature'.[97] If it is legally permissible to end the life of unborn human beings with disabilities, and medical tests are routinely applied to pregnant women to discover any foetal abnormality, would this not amount to the crime of genocide against the disabled unborn?

The Genocide Convention speaks of 'imposing measures intended to prevent births within the group'. Does this mean that the Genocide Convention is limited only to cases where abortion is imposed *on women*? The answer to this question is 'No'. Since the Genocide Convention defines genocide in terms of 'killing members of the group', since 'measures intended to prevent births' clearly includes induced abortion, and since abortion involves the intentional killing of the unborn, then the Convention's reference to 'imposing measures' cannot be interpreted in a way that would limit its application to women who are forcibly aborted. And in any case, the Convention's definition of genocide includes 'killing members of the group'. This is sufficient by itself to raise serious questions as to whether the practice of abortion is genocide.

What often makes a group vulnerable to genocide is the denial of human rights, precisely what has occurred to the unborn in Australia and in many other countries.

The questions that supporters of legal abortion need to address, then, are these: how is it not genocide to define some members of the human family as non-persons, thereby allowing them to be directly and intentionally killed by induced abortion? How is it not genocide to legally prescribe and actively promote the induced abortion of human beings on the grounds of their actual or perceived disability? If it could be shown that homosexuality was genetically influenced, and homosexuality was thought of as a disability, would the routine abortion of homosexuals be considered the crime of genocide against homosexuals?

9.4 Final observations

The member nations of the United Nations are committed to the promotion of 'universal respect for, and observance of, human rights and fundamental freedoms for all without distinction as to race, sex, language, or religion'[98] by way of a pledge.

> All members pledge themselves to take joint and separate action in cooperation with the Organisation for the achievement of the purposes set forth in Article 55.[99]

What we have here is the idea of a *consensus gentium*, an agreement among the nations, consent to be bound by certain values expressed as human rights. This doctrine of consent involves the idea that the 'basis of obligation of all international law, and not merely of treaties, is the consent of States'.[100]

Australia, like all the other nations of the world, has bound itself to membership of the United Nations, to the United Nations Charter, to the Universal Declaration of Human Rights 1948, the Convention on the Prevention and Punishment of the Crime of Genocide 1948, the International Covenant on Civil and Political Rights 1966, the Convention on the Rights of the Child 1989, and the Declaration of the Rights of the Child 1959. *These documents contain strong commitments to the protection of human rights of all without any distinction whatsoever.* Discrimination because of age, personhood, status and disability are all examples of unjust discrimination, including when they are applied to unborn children.

There are, of course, other important obligations under international law which, as we have already suggested, will influence municipal law in many other areas of the law. However, it is hard to imagine a more neglected area of human rights discussion, from the perspective of international law, than the rights of the unborn.

What I find particularly disappointing is the signal failure of the academy to honestly come to grips with and deal with the arguments set out in this chapter. This paper was originally published nearly ten years ago in a reputable journal, but there seems to have been little reaction to its findings. It seems that people want to read documents through the prism of their own ideological commitments or, worse, simply ignore passages which seem to challenge popular pro-choice rhetoric.

For too long nations, committees of inquiry, and academics failed to discuss these issues, which they are obliged to discuss, and take full account of the provisions which challenge the widespread discrimination against the unborn. Any domestic cases involving the unborn including abortion, succession, medical negligence, or the criminal law must have regard to our obligations under international law. Put succinctly, there is a case to be heard for the unborn based on Australia's existing human rights obligations, obligations which apply to all member states of the United Nations. Now is the time to adjust practice to principle rather than to continue to compromise principles to bring 'principle' into line with practice.

Chapter 10

Public policy and abortion:
bad but better law

Nicholas Tonti-Filippini

The reality in Australia is that, either by judicial interpretation or by changes to statute law, abortion on demand is practised lawfully. The great majority of Australians do not want that legal status quo to change, even though, as we have seen (chapters two and three), abortion does not enjoy the same level of *moral* support. It is also the case that when the different reasons for abortion are explored the proportion in support of legalised abortion varies, depending on the gravity of the reasons. In those circumstances of great complexity and with only 40 per cent support for restricting abortion in some circumstances (see chapter three), it is unlikely that any of Australia's parliaments will accept proposals to prohibit abortion. However a majority of Australians are of the view that abortion happens too often. That raises the question about what to do about it.

We have discussed the evidence as to what is effective sex education. Effective sex education is the obvious path to take toward making abortion rare. We concluded on the basis of reviewing the evidence, that programs like the 'safe sex' programs that focus on avoiding or minimising harm have not been shown to be effective. Similarly there is little evidence that abstinence-only programs are effective. However, programs that present the facts *and* have values and behavioural components, like the pledge or delay-first-intercourse programs, have been shown to have some success.

In relation to Australian attitudes to sex education, the Sexton survey (chapter three) has established that the Australian community,

- is strongly supportive of sex-education programs in Australian schools;

- believes such programs to be a necessary strategy to reduce the numbers of unwanted pregnancies and with it the numbers of abortions in Australia;

- expects sex-education programs to reflect family values;

- expects that parents be involved in the development of the materials;

- is largely ignorant of the content of sex-education programs and the identity of their authors; and

- lacks confidence that education authorities would take their concerns about sex education seriously.

However, it would be unrealistic to think that effective sex education would prevent unplanned pregnancies altogether. The reality is that some women will become pregnant when they do not expect to, especially as all methods of family planning have a pregnancy rate associated with them.

There are proposals that are not prohibitive of abortion, but which involve instituting requirements for a more considered process than a woman simply being referred directly to a pregnancy-termination clinic. The idea behind these proposals is that women who initially move towards abortion may choose otherwise if they are offered adequate support, relevant information, and time to reflect on the decision.

Each of the contributors to this collection has taken what they would describe as a pro-woman and pro-life approach to the issue of abortion. There is however a tension in relation to being pro-life and pro-woman with regard to policy and legislative proposals that would permit women to choose abortion. Being pro-woman may be seen in those circumstances as a failure to act justly towards the unborn.

The purpose of this chapter is to consider some of those proposals to see whether they could be supported as a way of both respecting women and seeking to uphold respect for human life, including acting justly towards the unborn.

10.1 The question of cooperating in evil

10.1.1 *Evangelium Vitae*

In his encyclical letter, 'The Gospel of Life' (1995), the late Pope John Paul II clearly rejected law which permits abortion. He said that laws which legitimise the direct killing of innocent human beings through abortion or euthanasia are in complete opposition to the inviolable right to life proper to every individual; they thus deny the equality of everyone before the law (EV, n.72). He also made it clear that in the case of an intrinsically unjust law, such as a law permitting abortion or euthanasia, it is never licit to obey it, or to 'take part in a propaganda campaign in favour of such a law, or vote for it' (EV, n.73).

However, there remains the question of the situation that arises when a proposal is put that would improve the prospects of survival for the child before birth by decreasing the rate of abortion, even though still permitting abortion to occur in some circumstances. The Pope wrote:

> A particular problem of conscience can arise in cases where a legislative vote would be decisive for the passage of a more restrictive law, aimed at limiting the number of authorised abortions, in place of a more permissive law already passed or ready to be voted on. Such cases are not infrequent. It is a fact that while in some parts of the world there continue to be campaigns to introduce laws favouring abortion, often supported by powerful international organisations, in other nations — particularly

those which have already experienced the bitter fruits of such permissive legislation—there are growing signs of a rethinking in this matter. In a case like the one just mentioned, when it is not possible to overturn or completely abrogate a pro-abortion law, an elected official, whose absolute personal opposition to procured abortion was well known, could licitly support proposals aimed at limiting the harm done by such a law and at lessening its negative consequences at the level of general opinion and public morality. This does not in fact represent an illicit cooperation with an unjust law, but rather a legitimate and proper attempt to limit its evil aspects. (EV, n.73)

The Pope then provided an analysis of what constitutes formal cooperation and stated that from the moral standpoint, it is never licit to cooperate formally in evil.

Such cooperation occurs when an action, either by its very nature or by the form it takes in a concrete situation, can be defined as a direct participation in an act against innocent human life or a sharing in the immoral intention of the person committing it. (EV, n. 74)

10.1.2 Classical treatments of cooperation

The theological genesis of the principles of legitimate cooperation are thought to be in the teachings of St. Alphonsus Ligouri (1696–1787), bishop, Doctor of the Church, and founder of the Redemptorist Congregation. St. Alphonsus made a distinction between acting in a way that indicates agreement with the evil that another person does, and giving assistance to them in a way that does not indicate agreement with their intention to do evil.[1] For instance, there would be a difference between my supplying large quantities of food to a person and exhorting them to eat in a gluttonous way, and a grocer selling food to a person knowing that they are eating gluttonously. In the former case I would be formally cooperating in the evil of gluttony and in the second case only materially cooperating in their gluttony. The first is morally reprehensible, the second not so. Anthony Fisher expresses the distinction thus,

Though cooperating in the project, the agent in question is not the one most directly involved, conceiving, instigating, directing, coordinating, and actually engineering the operation. Rather she is in a secondary or subordinate role to the principal agent(s) and contributes something which facilitates the wrongdoing of the principal agent(s). What she wants to know is how close she can properly get to taking part, without becoming, as it were, an accessory, a conspirator. How involved can she be without becoming tainted by it.[2]

The traditional principles of cooperation are commonly explained in the following way:[3]

Formal cooperation occurs when a person or organisation freely participates in the action(s) of a principal agent, or shares in the agent's intention, either for its own sake or as a means to some other goal.

Implicit formal cooperation occurs when, even though the cooperator denies intending the object of the principal agent, the cooperating person or organisation participates in the action directly and in such a way that it could not be done without this participation. Formal cooperation in intrinsically evil actions, either explicitly or implicitly, is morally illicit.

Immediate material cooperation occurs when the co-operator participates in circumstances that are essential to the commission of an act, such that the act could not occur without this participation. Immediate material cooperation in intrinsically evil actions is morally illicit.

Mediate material cooperation occurs when the cooperator participates in circumstances that are not essential to the commission of an action, such that the action could occur even without this cooperation. *Mediate material cooperation* in an immoral act might be justifiable under three basic conditions:

- if there is a proportionately serious reason for the cooperation (i.e., for the sake of protecting an important good or for avoiding a worse harm); the graver the evil the more serious a reason required for the cooperation;

- the importance of the reason for cooperation must be proportionate to the causal proximity of the co-operator's action to the action of the principal agent (the distinction between proximate and remote); and

- the danger of scandal (i.e., leading others into doing evil, leading others into error, or spreading confusion) must be avoided.

10.1.3 Association with evil

More recent treatments of cooperation have added a condition in relation to association with or appropriation of evil. Germain Grisez gives the example of a typist taking dictation and typing for a company and discovering that the communications with which she is assisting contain lies. Such work he says may be considered morally acceptable cooperation. She is not the instigator of the lies. The lies are someone else's expression and reflect someone else's intent, not her own.

The problem though is that, in a sense, the evil appropriates her. If she is doing her job well, she will make suggestions to improve the text, making it more presentable. She may also make suggestions about the wording to make the expression clearer and more credible. One could envisage her becoming more and more associated with the project itself and its objectives.

The situation is similar for someone who works in an institution in which immoral practices occur. One would share in the goals of efficiency and effective practice for the institution generally, and it may be likely that one's efforts also result in more efficient and effective execution of immoral practices. One's activities risk becoming entwined in the moral evil.

The questions of appropriation and association are complex. In relation to proposals for policies to limit or to regulate the practice of abortion, similar questions arise. Some pertinent questions would be:

- Will the policy actually reduce the risks to unborn children?

- Does the policy imply approval of the practice of killing the unborn (in some circumstances)?

- Would the policy lead some to think that abortion is a legitimate solution?

- For those involved in counselling or related activities:

  - Would the policy mean an association with the practice of abortion and does that association imply approval?

  - Would the activity be causally related to achieving abortion in the sense of being a necessary step to achieving abortion?

10.2 Particular proposals

10.2.1 Counselling requirements

10.2.1.1 Independent counsellors

Until the 1970s in Australia, abortion was an activity that was illegal or at least on the fringes of unlawfulness. As it emerged as lawful, largely through unsuccessful prosecution, it was still a practice on the fringes of medicine and not entirely respectable. The practice carries a shadowy history and remains socially stigmatised. It is not easily discussed and experiences are seldom shared. In this respect, abortion is unlike other medical procedures in which one would be likely to know of others who had had similar experiences and would be inclined to discuss one's fears and concerns with others in the process of making a decision and then preparing for the consequences.

There has been debate in recent times over how much opportunity women approaching abortion have to consider the issue, how free they are of pressure from others to abort, especially their partners or immediate family and friends, how well informed they are about the procedure and any consequences of it, the support that they receive to explore other options, such as keeping the child or adoption or fostering, the financial and material support available. The Sexton research showed that there is 94 per cent support for voluntary counselling about alternatives and 64 per cent support for compulsory counselling about alternatives to abortion.

Normally when one has a surgical procedure, there are two stages to the process. First, you perceive a problem, and you see a general medical practitioner who identifies the nature of the problem. There is then a stage during which diagnosis is achieved, and the options for treatment discussed. Then there is a *decision-making phase*. Once a decision is made, a discussion then occurs with the surgeon about the actual procedure, what to expect at the time of the procedure, the likely consequences and the risks, the recovery phase and rehabilitation. The discussion with the surgeon at that point is a *pre-procedural phase*, rather than decision making.

Usually these phases are relatively gradual and take time. There is time between referral and appointment and the opportunity to adjust to the knowledge of the disease state, its significance, and the options. Then there is time to consider the chosen option and its significance and to adjust to that, before it occurs. Usually by the time one sees the surgeon, the decision has already been made and the surgeon's 'counselling' is largely about the practical aspects of the chosen surgical procedure rather than discussion of alternatives to surgery. For instance, one is not likely to discuss chemotherapy or radiotherapy with a surgeon.

One of the problems with the shadowy history of surgical abortion is that these phases may be overly short, because this is a problem to be hidden. There may also be an urgency born out of the fact that the pregnancy is developing and the prospects of hiding it diminish, as well as the reality that the humanity of the unborn child becomes more and more apparent as he or she develops. There may also be a tendency to simply want to be rid of the problem as soon as possible, to remove the complication to life plans. There may be a view that the more thinking that goes on about pregnancy, the more difficult it may be to terminate. Abortion may be more likely in the circumstances of panic, rather than the result of a considered decision.

The reality is that the time between confirmation of pregnancy and termination of pregnancy may be a very short time and usually does not involve a distinct *decision-making phase* and then a *pre-procedural phase* of counselling, with sufficient time and opportunities between to make good decisions.

The fear also is that the *decision-making counselling* provided may be offered by those in abortion clinics and thus not independent and objective. The thought is that it is more likely to be in the character of *pre-procedural counselling*, than decision-making counselling. There is also the problem of a conflict of interest if the clinic earns its income by providing the service. The exploration of possibilities for pregnancy support and discussion with those who offer those services would also be unlikely within a termination clinic.

The above considerations all lead to proposals for provision of independent pregnancy counselling. The aim of such counselling is to provide time and the opportunity for a considered decision, and discussion of the options and the support available. Such counselling is most effective when it is client-based, rather than directional. One does not assist someone who is in a panic by applying even more pressure to her. Rather, a good, life-affirming decision is more likely if the individual is able to talk through her perceptions and have the opportunity to calmly consider the options while being personally supported and offered accurate information by someone in whom she has confidence. It is important that such a person is not running either a pro- or anti-abortion agenda, but provides professional counselling that is genuinely supportive and informative and based on the client's needs for time and space to make a considered decision. It is not the function of such a service to be a referral agency. The counselling should be independent and not part of a directional process. Having had time and space to make a decision following confirmation of pregnancy, the next phase is that she seeks a medical consultation, whether or not she intends to continue with the pregnancy.

In Australia, there is little difficulty in locating clinics that provide pregnancy termination. What is lacking is adequate opportunity for the decision-making phase. And abortion is different in this respect from the normal course towards surgery when there are usually time, space, information, and discussion opportunities to make a considered and well-informed decision.

A proposal to make pregnancy counselling and support a normal part of dealing with pregnancy crisis would seem to be neutral in relation to the abortion issue. In that respect the proposal ought to be welcome to both sides of the abortion debate. For that consensus to be achieved, however, pregnancy counselling and support needs to be undertaken by those who are professionally qualified in a counselling discipline, and there should be professional standards of accreditation for pregnancy counsellors.

10.2.1.2 The German problem

In 1998, the German bishops, who had supported independent counselling services and had encouraged Catholic services of that nature, ran into the difficulty that attendance at pregnancy counselling was made mandatory as a step on the way to procuring an abortion. Before a woman could have an abortion, she was required to obtain a certificate stating that she had attended a pregnancy counselling service. The moral difficulty that arose, was that the issuing of a certificate was in fact a form of cooperation with the practice of abortion. It was argued that the certificate was in effect 'a licence to kill'.[4]

There is a problem if independent pregnancy counselling is a mandatory step in order to have an abortion. That then takes away the independent, objective nature and its function as a client-centred service. In effect, it becomes part of the project of seeking an abortion and becomes tied to it. It also makes nonsense of counselling if it is a mandatory requirement because it would change the client-centred, personally supportive nature of the service.

A better course would be to fund independent pregnancy counselling and support so that the services are available and accessible for women troubled by pregnancy. It might then be a requirement for doctors, prior to abortion referral, to offer women a referral to pregnancy-counselling services, in the same way that couples approaching the Family Court are asked to see a counsellor.

10.2.2 Information requirements

10.2.2.1 Medical risks of abortion and of pregnancy

The medical effects and sequelae of abortion are much discussed and debated. As an ethicist it is important not to allow one's own moral view to select evidence that suits. Usually the approach I take to an issue such as this is to seek out any fourth-level reviews of the studies done and then base ethical evaluation on the range of findings offered from the reviews of well-constructed studies. Usually a useful source for such reviews is the Cochrane collaboration.

However, in this case the Cochrane data base is not of much use except to indicate that little real evidence from trials has been gathered to draw conclusions. The reviewers found there was not enough evidence from trials to show which surgical methods for early pregnancy termination are safest and most acceptable to women. They conclude that outcomes such as women's satisfaction, the need for pain relief, or surgeons' preference for the instrument have been inadequately addressed. No data outcomes, such as fertility after surgical abortion, are available.[5] It is little wonder then that the pro-life and anti-abortion protagonists often debate this issue and there is a yawning gap between their comparative assessments.

Given that there is surgery and anaesthesia, there are obvious risks that apply. The literature lists uterine perforation, excessive blood loss, blood transfusion, febrile morbidity, incomplete or repeat uterine evacuation procedure, re-hospitalisation, post-operative abdominal pain, or therapeutic antibiotic use as sequelae. However, the relative probability of those events is not assessable on the evidence available.

The relative risks of chemical abortion are also not established by the evidence. The Cochrane review comparing medical with surgical abortion concludes that the available results were derived from relatively small trials. The compared results for four different interventions (prostaglandins alone, mifepristone alone, and mifepristone/ misoprostol and methotrexate/misoprostol versus vacuum aspiration). They concluded:

> Prostaglandins used alone seem to be less effective and more painful compared to surgical first-trimester abortion. However, there is inadequate evidence to comment on the acceptability and side effects of medical compared to surgical first-trimester abortions. There is a need for trials to address the efficacy of currently used methods and women's preferences more reliably.[6]

The debate over long-term sequelae such as breast cancer and post-abortion grief is also lacking conclusive peer-reviewed evidence with claims made on both sides. In reality, a woman considering abortion ought to be informed of the known medical risks, but little help can be given to her to assess the relative probability of those risks.

To be balanced, it ought also be said that there are risks and complications of pregnancy and side-by-side the medical risks of pregnancy and childbirth would seem to be greater. However, there is a major difference in perceptions of those risks because they are undergone for the sake of a child and becoming a mother. Usually that is seen positively and a benefit that far outweighs the suffering and the risks. The risks of abortion procedures may be seen differently precisely because they cause the end of that development.

10.2.2.2 Ultrasound images of foetus

Researchers at the National Institutes of Health published an article in the *New England Journal of Medicine* in 1983 in which they concluded:

> Viewing the foetal form in the late first or early mid-trimester of pregnancy, before movement is felt by the mother, may also influence the resolution of any ambivalence toward the pregnancy itself in favour of the foetus. Ultrasound examination may thus result in fewer abortions and more desired pregnancies.[7]

Pro-life protagonists have seized on this, and have advocated using ultrasound machines in pregnancy counselling. Pro-abortion protagonists have argued that ultrasound technology is being used as a tool to influence women's reproductive choices and thus to coerce and devalue women.

Ultrasound in itself simply provides information, and it does so in a non-invasive way and without apparent risk. In my own experience with my own children, this was a very positive event, reassuring, full of wonder and excitement, an aid to preparing both emotionally and in case of predicted medical complication. Information giving, provided that it is accurate and not selective, normally increases choice and reduces fear. To withhold information would normally be regarded as coercive.

In this case, the pro-abortion argument seems to be opposed to informed choice. Knowing the consequences of a proposed course of action may in a sense limit my choice in that there are some things I would not do if I knew their effects. But a choice made in full knowledge is in that respect a more autonomous choice. The pro-abortion approach to this is thus contrary to respect for autonomy and in that sense contrary to respect for the woman's dignity.

I am opposed to adding to the emotional burden of a woman in crisis about a pregnancy by displaying dismembered bodies of aborted foetuses, but providing accurate information about her pregnancy to a woman is positive, informative, and part of respecting her ability to discern an appropriate course of action. It is essential to overcoming her sense of lack of control and panic that she is able to feel fully informed. Knowledge counters fear.

10.2.2.3 Post-abortion grief

There is no shortage of literature on the emotional and psychological sequellae of termination of pregnancy. The narratives of women harmed by abortion are compelling. See for instance the collection edited by Melinda Tankard Reist.[8] The contributions by Brigid Vout, Selena Ewing and Marcia Riordan in our collection provide accounts of this phenomenon.

One of the factors that is obviously relevant is that abortion is often a conflicted decision. The most obvious conclusion to draw is that decisions during crisis in pregnancy need time and opportunity to reflect on the complex factors involved. Of particular moment in the accounts of post-abortion grief is the sense of a forced choice through pressure from others or from circumstance. For that, abortion providers must take some responsibility for not ensuring that their patients had the time and the opportunity to reflect on the options in an informed, calm, and supported way, away from the clinic and medical pressure, and with independent advice that responded to their state of mind and their needs.

10.2.3 Limiting indications

A possible way to limit abortion would be to require a second medical opinion that the abortion was necessary to protect the mother's health or life and to remove the profit incentive for providers by limiting abortion to public-health facilities. There is evidence that where such restrictions apply, more women continue with their pregnancies. Such circumstances apply in South Australia, which appears to have a much lower abortion rate than Victoria or New South Wales.

Whether such a restriction is achievable in the current political climate is a moot point. It also raises some questions to do with illegitimate cooperation if one supported legislation that carried the message that approved abortion in such circumstances. The question would seem to turn on whether, in supporting such legislation as being as much as can be achieved, one is also understood to hold that all deliberate killing of the unborn is immoral and all the unborn ought to have protection under the law.

10.2.4 Late-term termination of pregnancy

'Late-term termination pregnancy' would seem to refer to termination of pregnancy at a stage when the child would normally be capable of being born alive. The gestational age and maturity at which the latter is so is obviously relative to advances in medical capability and the availability of the technology. Variously 'late term' refers to that period of pregnancy which commences 20–24 weeks after the last menstrual period.

'Late-term termination of pregnancy,' in practice, also includes foeticide as distinct from the 'early induction of labour' which is usually used in the circumstances in which a pathological condition endangers the child or the mother during pregnancy and delivery is warranted in order to overcome the danger to the mother, the child, or both. A major medical difference when the child is capable of being born alive is the fact that the pregnancy can be ended without ending the life of the child. Foeticide is a distinct medical choice and may even be a distinct procedure before delivery (e.g., saline infusion into the uterus), during delivery (e.g., dismembering prior to extraction), or after partial breech delivery (suctioning of brain cavity during delivery — D&X).

The difference between foeticide and infanticide is not the age or maturity of the child but whether the death is caused before or after complete birth. Whether there is medical effort directed to preserve the health and life of the child, or whether the procedure is done in such a way as to ensure that life does not continue, is a medical decision (albeit based upon whether the mother has decided that the child should live or die). There are obviously different attitudes within the profession about whether late-term termination should properly be considered a medical option. The former US surgeon general, Dr C. Everett Koop stated in an article in the *New York Times* that with all that modern medicine has to offer, partial-birth abortions are not needed to save the life of the mother, and the procedure's impact on a woman's cervix can put future pregnancies at risk.[9]

Medical and paramedical attitudes to late-term termination of pregnancy are likely to be different, not only because the child may be capable of being born alive, but also because he or she will be larger, bone structures will have formed, and there is much discussion in the literature about foetal pain. Response to painful stimulus is evident, and there has been much discussion about whether general anaesthesia in the woman would also anaesthetise the child.[10]

The fact that there may be monitoring of foetal heartbeat and foetal movement, and recognition of signs of foetal distress will obviously affect the operating room personnel, particularly if the procedure is being aided by real-time ultrasonography. In such circumstances there is more likely to be an operating-room awareness of the existence of the child. The notion that this is just the removal of tissue is not likely to be sustainable.

There are significant psychosocial sequellae after second trimester termination of pregnancy. A significant follow-up study of eighty-four women, in West Scotland, who had had second-trimester terminations of pregnancy for foetal abnormality concluded that within the context of continuing medical care, professionals have a responsibility to learn about this new kind of grief and to recognise (keeping the couples' reticence in mind) the signs that may signal a need for professional mental-health intervention.[11] That there is such grief warrants exploration of whether there are matters that have been overlooked in the philosophical debate.

An Oxford study of seventy-one women who had had termination of pregnancy for foetal abnormality[12] found that in the month after termination of pregnancy, many had high levels of psychiatric morbidity (41 per cent) as determined by a standardised psychiatric interview, which is 4–5 times higher than in non-puerperal (10 per cent) and post-partum women (9 per cent) in the general population. Thirty-one per cent still felt guilty and angry thirteen months later. Of the seventy-one women, about a third saw the baby after the termination; and of those who did not, just under a third had wished that they had. Fourteen per cent arranged funerals for their babies.

The fact that women following late-term termination of pregnancy may wish to see and hold the body of their child, the particular kind of grief, the possibility of a need for a funeral and burial, and the fact (discussed later) that the cause of death (post-twenty weeks) may be required to be certified by the doctor are all indications that the medical circumstances for the women, and presumably their spouses, are distinct. There is much more required in the continuing medical management than would seem to be the case for first-trimester termination of pregnancy.

There is something of a medical consensus amongst those who accept the practice, that the indications for late-term terminations of pregnancy are narrower than for first-trimester termination. The Medical Board of the Australian state of Queensland reports that terminations are performed after twenty weeks for the following indications:

- risk to maternal life
- psychotic/suicidal maternal behaviour
- life-threatening illness
- lethal foetal abnormality
- gross foetal abnormality.[13]

There is doubt over whether late-term abortion is ever medically indicated as a treatment for psychotic/suicidal maternal behaviour. The procedure itself is a cause of psychiatric morbidity. The use of late-term termination of pregnancy for risks to maternal life and for life-threatening illness would presumably be met, if necessary, by early delivery. Foeticide at the same time is not a treatment for any condition of the mother. Further, in the various enquiries held into this matter, numerous gynaecologists have testified that medical conditions in the mother can always be managed without necessitating late-term termination of pregnancy.[14] Given that risks to maternal life in late-term pregnancy can be managed, and using early delivery if necessary, then there is no maternal *medical* indication for foeticide in those circumstances.

Life-threatening illness in the mother may raise the matter of whether she wants the child to survive her given that she is facing the possibility of her own imminent death, but foeticide in such a case is obviously not a *medical* necessity; the indication, if there is one, is social. Without that necessity such a procedure would, as is discussed below, be unlawful in many jurisdictions. In the Australian state of Victoria, it would be the offence of child destruction punishable by up to twenty years imprisonment.

There remains, then, the matter of late-term terminations of pregnancy for reasons to do with lethal or gross foetal abnormality. This is a new practice that has developed with the advances in antenatal diagnosis. In the medical literature it is highly controversial. No consensus has emerged over what would be considered a serious enough indication.[15] Finally the social and cultural implications of foeticide as a means of selecting what sort of people there should be has not yet been fully explored.

Some medical differences between early and late-term termination of pregnancy are:

- the fact that foeticide or child destruction is a distinct medical choice late term because the child can be delivered alive to an independent existence;

- the foetus is more developed, responds to painful stimulus, and has solid bone structures such that different procedures are required; and

- there are continuing and very different matters of grieving and psychiatric morbidity involved in the termination of a pregnancy when the child is mature enough to be capable of being born alive and the mother is likely to have begun to relate to him or her such that afterwards she may want to see and hold the body of her dead child.

These differences have profound personal significance for all those involved in late-term termination of pregnancy, but particularly the mother, her partner, and any other children she may have.

By the time late-term termination of pregnancy is contemplated, the pregnancy is likely to be known and discussed within the family. Other children, if any, are likely to be considering the coming of a new brother or sister. The profound significance of a decision to terminate late term cannot be overcome.

Infanticide, in our culture, is viewed with horror. When a mother kills a neonate, we regard it as such an horrific event, that we, our legislature, and our courts readily classify it as a result of a temporary mental state, not something that is likely to have been freely chosen.

One possibility that is discussed is that of creating an offence for killing a child who is sufficiently mature that he or she could have survived early induction of labour. The moral problem of cooperation arises if the means used to prohibit killing a viable child at the same time makes it lawful to procure early abortion. However, in the Australian circumstances in which abortion already is either by statute or by judicial precedent lawful, it would seem morally legitimate to propose an achievable restriction to prohibit the direct destruction or neglect of a child capable of being born alive.

The tension between values and legislation in Australia remains. However, the clarification of moral and medical issues outlined above assists in the process of seeking consensus – a process whereby both sides of the abortion debate, by acknowledging common values, see a way forward.

Chapter 11

Seeking a consensus

Nicholas Tonti-Filippini

John Fleming

There are several impediments in Australia that tend to make consensus difficult on any moral question. They include:

- a view that seeks to foster disagreement in order to substantiate the view that no policy on moral questions is achievable because no consensus is achievable;
- lack of objectivity in the reporting of scientific evidence and the polemical selective use of information that then maintains disagreements;
- attempts to exclude contributions to the policy discussion on the basis of a kind of bigotry that classifies positions in a nominalist way;
- divisions of opinion that declare lack of sincerity or of good will on the other side.

As a community, when we look at the rising incidence of sexually transmissible infection, the effect on children and young people of insecurity and instability at home, the continued high incidence of unplanned pregnancy and abortion, and the continuing levels of violence against woman and the abuse of children, we clearly need policy initiatives that address the social causes of the harm and the misery of these problems that have so far remained intractable. We do need to seek consensus on many of these matters that have been marked more by polemics than constructive solutions.

11.1 Morality and public policy

11.1.1 Stalling consensus

There are some common moral discussion stoppers in these debates. Often a discussion is stymied by claims such as:

- People disagree on solutions to moral issues.
- Who am I to judge others?
- Morality is a private matter.
- Morality is simply a matter for individual cultures to decide.

Claims such as these foster tend to provide a basis for the view that no policy on moral questions is achievable because no consensus is achievable.

People disagree on solutions to moral issues, but the point of moral discussion is to explore the differences, rather than to see difference as either necessary or irresolvable. There is something very adolescent about seeing difference of view as an end of discussion rather than the beginning of a discussion. The fact is that experts in many areas disagree on key issues in their fields, but that is why they publish scientific findings and hold scientific conferences. The differences do not stop the progress of science and nor should they stop the progress of moral discussion.

Despite differences of perspectives, and different belief structure and different starting points, we are all dealing with the same human reality. The international human rights movement attests to the fact that there are many moral issues on which people agree, and there are values that transcend or are common across cultures and religions.

It is also the case that disagreements may not be about substantial moral beliefs, but about non-moral facts of a matter, about the relative priorities of value that are actually held in common, or about simply disagreement to participate in the common project that we call a community.

The question, 'Who am I to judge others?' is important but misdirected. Tolerance of others and their moral decisions is important. But deciding whether something is the right course of action is not the same thing as judging a person. There is also a distinction between judging as condemning and judging as evaluating.

When we look at the questions of moral education that are so important to the issues of sexuality and abortion, then we can see that there is an urgent need to respond to the developing needs of young people to assist them in their moral formation so that they acquire the knowledge, skills, behaviour, and attitudes that will protect them from harm and allow their goodness to flourish without the restriction on their freedom of illness, disease, and choices that lack goodness and stunt development. The claim that morality is a private matter is often intended to stop discussion. Privacy is an important right, and people are entitled to keep their own counsel about their relationships and intimacies. However, sharing common purposes and thus a common morality is what establishes and to an extent defines a community. Some aspects of morality are thus essentially public. Even a social or sporting club needs commonly accepted rules of conduct. In relating to one another we need conventions about behaviour and social expectations. Further, being able to discuss and to reason about morality is important and allows us to recognise the harm that our choices may cause. Moral choices are not isolated personal preferences, but are to do with interpersonal relationships and living in community.

The relativist claim that morality is simply a matter for individual cultures to decide is confusion between describing a morality and adopting a morality. There are moral principles that transcend culture because they are based on shared human reality. We need to be able to discern whether a cultural practice should be changed, such as the cultural practice of female genital mutilation. Policy reform would be impossible if we were to take the view that culture is beyond criticism.

The education of the so-called Y-generation by baby boomers has given them a strong sense of positivism, that is, the belief that meaningful statements are either empirically verifiable (e.g., HIV causes AIDS) or analytic truths (e.g., one cannot make a round square). The new generation is positivist in that it tends to assert that value judgments are neither empirically verifiable nor analytic truths. They are merely expressions of feeling or emotions, in that they tend to make a distinction between prescriptive and descriptive meaning. Values, they would claim, must not be confused with facts.

The conviction that there are no moral truths is an easy prey for a particular kind of utilitarianism. If you begin with the belief that all moral beliefs are entirely subjective, just feelings, then you will crave some kind of rule for resolving all those differences of opinion. One such rule is a basic notion of consistency. This generation believes strongly in the injustice of discrimination. They want moral and policy decisions to apply equally to like situations. This is known as the principle of universalisability: if I hold that something is wrong in one situation, I must hold that it is also wrong in all relevantly similar situations.

This leads to what might be called universalised prescriptivism: the right moral judgment or policy is that which treats everyone's preferences as equally important and then seeks simply to do the best to satisfy as many preferences as possible giving weight to the relative strength of preferences. This is preference utilitarianism[1] and varies only slightly from classical utilitarianism, which taught that one should maximise happiness by maximising pleasure and minimising pain.

Utilitarianism is an aggregative theory and fails to acknowledge the 'separateness of persons'[2]. It focuses on overall consequences and not on individual human acts.

A person's moral identity is constituted by his or her commitments and moral integrity for which utilitarianism has no explanation. In utilitarianism my identity is subsumed into a kind of single personhood. There is no accounting for how my preferences are formed. The preferences of Mother Teresa and Saddam Hussein rank the same in the calculation. This approach, by focusing on consequences, ignores the virtues of agents and the fact that choices to act shape the identity of who I am. If I steal I make myself a thief; if I kill I make myself a murderer; in giving to another I make myself a lover.

There are some basic notions that we need to make better sense of human morality. First, morality is prescriptive — that is what defines it. It is about deciding what is right and what is wrong in a given situation. Second, moral norms are universalisable — that is a logical requirement. The present generation is right in recognising that morality should be consistent and not discriminatory or arbitrary. Third, morality is about freely chosen actions. We are responsible for our own choices. Fourth, morality is agent-centred — about the agent as well as about the outcome of the agent's actions. When we choose to act we create the person we are. When we act wrongly, we do so by acting contrary to the goodness of the human person. A wrong act is essentially a contradictory act. Fifth, morality is descriptive — it describes the agent's commitments (whether sentimental, rational, autonomous, heteronomous [determined by others], heteronomously theonomous [determined by God], or participatively theonomous [determined by our participation in God's love]), otherwise it has no content.

The authors of this chapter belong to the Catholic tradition, which is not a simple divine command or fundamentalist tradition. Pope John Paul II taught that we are called to be participatively theonomous. We do not invent morality, nor is morality arbitrarily imposed on us. Rather we are made to participate in God's love, made like God, made to understand who we are and to develop our own identity in God's image and likeness, and to do so by the way in which we give expression to our love for God and for each other. We obey God's law not through fear but because through that obedience we acknowledge that as human beings we are made to participate wisely in God's goodness, in God's love. In being made in the image and likeness of God, we are given reason; and through that reason we come to know God and thus know God's goodness; and in that knowledge we wish to share in God's goodness.

But not everyone accepts the existence of a God of love or even God exists at all. But what we all have in common is our humanity and the knowledge that happiness is found in relationships with others by being in communion with others, and human fulfilment finds expressions in the gift of self to community. Human love ought thus be central to an adequate moral theory as goal and motivation. Genuine love, though, is premised upon respect for human worth and dignity. Love requires protecting both the inviolability of the other and respecting the freedom of the other.

The paradox for moral theory lies in being both descriptive and universalisable. The desire to resolve the paradox is what drives moral conversation. We seek a morality that is universalisable, prescriptive, descriptive, agent-centred, and free. We seek understanding, and through that understanding to be better lovers.

11.1.2 Consensus and democracy

What stops a democracy from being totalitarian is not in fact that it is rule by majority or by consensus, but that it has embedded within, in its constitutional arrangements, the notion that it is not just rule *by* the people but also rule *for* the people. There is no guarantee of protection of minorities by simple poll driven policy making. The function of the state is to deliver policies that respect the inherent dignity and inalienable rights of every member of the human family.

This is rule *for* the people. However, in the polyvalent processes of a democracy, consensus certainly helps!

The goals of genuine policy reform in a democracy are thus to try to elevate moral thinking from self-interest and private agendas to a level where people can try to formulate principles for the good government of the whole of society. In that way, a consensus may be possible that is not simply a reflection of mutual self-interest between those who constitute the dominant parties, but rather a reflection of a genuine sense of shared respect for all members of the human family.

Democracy is a system for determining who shall govern. It is in that respect a means and not an end. Its worth as a system depends upon whether it actually delivers. We are entitled to look at a democratically elected government and to ask, not whether it has a so-called 'mandate' of a popular vote for its policies, but whether those policies are, in fact, good. There are higher values than mere popularity. When governments are judged by history, whether or not they were popular at the time is not usually the basis of assessment, but rather whether they achieved good, whether they provided leadership towards a better society, whether they upheld the dignity of every human person, respect for inviolable and inalienable human rights, and the adoption of 'the common good' as the end and criterion regulating political life.

Majority opinion is provisional and changeable. It can also be led. Good government recognises that it has a role in forming, not just following, opinion. In the BBC-TV comedy drama, 'Yes Prime Minister', the writers of the satire have the Prime Minister saying, 'I am the people's leader. I must follow them'.

A problem that we face in our generation is an attitude of scepticism that lowers the flags of respect for inherent human dignity and inalienable rights and asserts instead a subjectivism that denies that protected status to each member of the human family. It is in such a culture that young people are most vulnerable to having their youthfulness exploited, their bodies treated as mere objects, and their health and their dignity placed at risk.

If there are no transcendentals, if there are no underlying principles that guide democracy, then the democratic system is just a mere mechanism for regulating different and opposing interests on a purely empirical basis.[3] Even in participatory systems of government, the regulation of interests often occurs to the advantage of the most powerful, since they are the ones most capable not only of manoeuvring the levers of power but also of shaping the formation of consensus. In such a situation, democracy easily becomes an empty word.

Former British Prime Minister, the late Sir Winston Churchill is reported to have said:

> Many forms of government have been tried, and will be tried in this world of sin and woe. No one pretends that democracy is perfect or all-wise. Indeed, it has been said that democracy is the worst form of government except all those others that have been tried from time to time.[4]

There is some element of truth in this, but we ought not be satisfied therefore with whatever policy it is that the democratic process produces. Democracy is only as good as its capacity to listen to voices of dissent and for its collective will to seek peaceful and stable communities based on respect for the worth and dignity of each member. The Universal Declaration on Human Rights (1948) begins with the truth: 'Whereas recognition of the inherent dignity and of the equal and inalienable rights of all members of the human family is the foundation of freedom, justice and peace in the world, ...'

It is more than half a century since the cataclysmic events that led to the development of the international human rights movement and its basis in inherent human dignity.

The human memory of the need for such a basis seems to be short. There is a need to recover the basic elements of the ideal of a relationship between public policy and morality.

Civil law is more limited in scope than morality. Not all that is immoral ought be made unlawful. But a moral vision of the inviolability of the human person should inform the legislative and public policy processes. Public policy that lacks such a vision would have no legitimacy.

11.2 Bigotry, religion, church and state

A question that every intelligent participant in public debate faces is the question of how to conduct oneself in a pluralist debate and what are legitimate personal ambitions for that participation.

To expect to produce public policy to one's liking would be an aspiration to demagoguery or tyranny. More than that, it would offend against basic ideals of freedom.

Respect for the human person entails respect for religious freedom, for freedom of thought and expression. But more than that it means that persons should be immune from coercion on the part of individuals or of social groups and of governments with respect to their own beliefs and practices, whether privately or publicly, whether alone or in association with others, within due limits.

As beings with reason and free will we each have a personal responsibility to seek to know the truth and to adhere to it. That pursuit of truth is best served by protecting each person from external coercion, from anything that would impinge upon his or her psychological freedom. The right to religious freedom ought not to be impeded, provided that just public order is protected.

The search for truth is an inquiry that should be free and informed and developed by dialogue. Free moral discussion is thus a crucial part of that inquiry. This freedom is asserted by the Catholic Church:

> In all his activity a man is bound to follow his conscience in order that he may come to God, the end and purpose of life. It follows that he is not to be forced to act in manner contrary to his conscience. Nor, on the other hand, is he to be restrained from acting in accordance with his conscience, especially in matters religious. The reason is that the exercise of religion, of its very nature, consists before all else in those internal, voluntary and free acts whereby man sets the course of his life directly toward God. No merely human power can either command or prohibit acts of this kind.[5]

Human persons do not live in isolation but in community. There are then basic norms that are required for persons to live together harmoniously. Personal and social responsibility and the rights of others impose restraints and obligations as a matter of justice.

Society also has the right to defend itself against possible abuses committed on the pretext of freedom of religion. But governments should not be arbitrary or unfair in that respect. Government has responsibilities to safeguard the rights of all citizens and for the peaceful settlement of conflicts of rights, also out of the need for an adequate care of genuine public peace, which comes about when people live together in ways that respect the dignity and rights of each.

There is a need for a public morality, a set of norms that govern our relationships with each other based on the fundamental notion of equal respect for persons, our inherent dignity, and our inalienable rights. These notions constitute the basic components of the common good. Outside of these restraints and obligations of the common good, persons have freedom in full range. The freedom of the human person is to be respected as far as possible and is not to be curtailed except to protect this public morality.

A legitimate aim of involvement in public debate is to seek to develop policies that give expression to equal respect for persons. There are many differences of opinion as to what constitutes respect for persons and indeed what is meant by human dignity. That discussion is fruitful and worthwhile, and the contributions of a plurality of approaches deepen and strengthen understanding. Open public debate thus serves important functions.

The point is not to exclude considered perspectives from discussion, but to listen to each and to gain the insights that each brings. Bigotry is limiting and destructive of community precisely because it is an effort to isolate and exclude contributions from discussion. In recent times we have witnessed an extraordinary bigotry that has attempted to exclude religious perspectives from public discussion.

American jurist Ronald Dworkin asserts the essentially *religious* content of respect for the intrinsic value of human life. He argues that the state's enforcement of responsibilities to protect the intrinsic value of human life, would breach the First Amendment and the understanding that a state has no business prescribing what people should think about the ultimate value of human life, about why human life has intrinsic importance, and about how that value is respected or dishonoured in different circumstances.[6]

This argument is linked in Australia to the Australian Constitution. Section 116 provides:

> The Commonwealth shall not make any law for establishing any religion, or for imposing any religious observance, or for prohibiting the free exercise of any religion, and no religious test shall be required as a qualification for any office or public trust under the Commonwealth.

The meaning of section 116 was determined by the High Court of Australia in the famous 'Defence of Government Schools' (DOGS) case in 1981. Barwick C.J. states that: 'the establishment of religion must be found to be the object of the making of the law. Further, because the whole expression is "for establishing any religion", the law to satisfy the description must have that objective as its express and, as I think, single purpose'.[7]

The purpose of these provisions in the Australian Constitution is, then, to limit the role of the state, not the church or any other religious grouping. Having come from a society where the king nationalised religion and made the church a department of state under parliamentary control, persecuting and marginalising those whose religious opinions differed from those of the state, it is not surprising that the founders wanted a constitution which would allow maximum freedom of religion. Where religion is concerned, it is the church that needs protection from the hubris of politicians and not vice versa. The church did not impose religion upon England. England imposed its views on the church.

Moreover, the Australian Constitution does not exclude religious arguments, religious people, or the churches from public debate. The opposite is true. People are not to have their religious freedom infringed by the state and are to be permitted to express their religious opinions in the public square. The Australian Constitution itself recognises the legitimacy of religion in the public square when, in its preamble, it says that we, the Australian people, are 'humbly relying on the blessings of Almighty God'. This is further supported by the custom of the parliament to begin each day with prayer including the 'Our Father'.

Perhaps it is fairer to say that the Australian Constitution provides for the cooperation between church and state, religion and state. Michael Hogan, Research Associate in Government and International Relations at The University of Sydney, put it this way:

> Australia does not have a legally entrenched principle, or even a vague set of conventions, of the separation of church and state. From the appointment of Rev. Samuel Marsden as one of the first magistrates in colonial New South Wales, to the adoption of explicit policies of state aid for denominational schools during the 1960s, to the two examples mentioned above, Australia has had a

very consistent tradition of cooperation between church and state. 'Separation of church and state', along with 'the separation of powers' or 'pleading the Fifth', are phrases that we have learned from the US, and which merely serve to confuse once they are taken out of the context of the American Constitution.

What Australia does have is a principle of state *neutrality*, or equal treatment, when dealing with churches. This principle dates back at least to Governor Bourke (if not to Macquarie) in colonial NSW, and extends all the way into contemporary Australia where government monies at all levels go quite happily to the churches so that they can run schools, hospitals, employment agencies, social welfare bureaux and even drug injecting rooms. This principle of neutrality is not entrenched in either the State or Federal Constitutions, and has no legal standing. (Constitutionally, State governments could still conceivably nominate an established church; only the Commonwealth is forbidden to do so by Section 116 of its Constitution!) Ultimately, the strength of the principle comes from the conventions hammered out in colonial Australia that saw English and Scottish established churches deprived of their priority in government funding. It survives into the twenty-first century because no major party could seriously contemplate abandoning it.

The principle of state neutrality has coexisted in Australia with a strong secular tradition in politics.... For most of our history most Australians have been quite happy with the principle that governments should not favour one church over another.[8]

Notwithstanding the legal position, many politicians and others have behaved in a way that does not respect the Australian Constitution by demanding that bishops, priests, ministers, churches, and other religious bodies stop 'meddling' in politics. Such *ad hominem* attacks represent an egregious appeal to prejudice and unjust discrimination against certain people or institutions. It is also hypocritical in the strict sense because such advice is usually given by, but not expected to apply to, those whose religion is variously described as secular, 'humanist', atheistic or agnostic.

Examples of publicly expressed religious bigotry by significant members of the press, political establishment, and others abound. The views of Christians are associated with fundamentalism, that unenlightened and ignorantly dogmatic religion, which is impervious to science, reason, and compassion. Alex Mitchell, columnist for Sydney's *The Sun Herald*, exemplified the crudest expression of anti-Catholic bigotry when accounting for the way in which NSW Senators voted against a private member's bill to overturn the ban on therapeutic cloning in 2006. Senators Ursula Stephens and Steve Hutchins were described as coming 'from the darkest recesses of the NSW right', while Senators Bill Heffernan and Concetta Fierravanti-Wells were 'mediaevalists' who 'took their stand somewhere around the fifteenth century when the Spanish Inquisition was in full swing'.[9]

Senator Amanda Vanstone, in supporting therapeutic cloning, said, 'There are different views on when life begins, but no religion has the right to seek to have its view legislated.' Never mind that Senator Vanstone then voted to have her own religious views legislated. Each politician had to vote, and Vanstone cast her vote according to her own opinion. But she was wrong to tell politicians of a different religious opinion to her own that they did not have the same right to seek to persuade the parliament to a particular point of view. There is nothing in the Australian Constitution to justify the denial of equal rights to free speech on the basis of a person's religious or other opinions.

The Hon. Tony Abbott was constantly questioned about his objectivity and even his right to be able to hold the office of Minister for Health because he is a Catholic. This was a constant theme in the debate over the abortion drug RU-486. And the same line of questioning of his religious views continued in relation to the therapeutic cloning debate.

Question:
Do you get the feeling that every time you open your mouth on these issues of conscience or ethics people — your critics — impugn your motives because of your religious faith?

Tony Abbott:

I think that it's noteworthy that no one was demanding that religion be kept out of politics when Bruce Baird, Barnaby Joyce, and Stephen Fielding opposed the Government's immigration bill but, on this particular issue, there are enormous demands, including from prominent members of the Labor Party, that 'religion' be kept out of politics.

Now, the truth is that I certainly haven't injected religion into politics, and I don't believe on the stem cell issue or the cloning issue anyone has injected religion into politics. The arguments that I've used, and other opponents of change in this area have used, are all based on human values. They're not based on religious teaching.

Question:

But it's a religious issue. Stem cells is a religious issue, and you could easily argue that case as well, couldn't you?

Tony Abbott:

Well, I—my arguments are not based on religious teaching. They're not based on Scripture; they're not based on what the Pope or the Archbishop of Canterbury or the Dalai Lama has said—they're based on what I think are decent human values that can be apprehended by anyone, regardless of his or her religious views.[10]

Abbott exemplified the classical Catholic approach to debating moral issues in the public square when he insisted that he was arguing on the basis of agreed 'human values' (the wrongfulness of killing the innocent), and the scientific account of when human life begins. He does not appeal to the data that is the sole preserve of revelation.

To make it clear that people should discount views contrary to those held by the elites, media outlets commonly describe dissenters as 'devout Catholic' or 'fundamentalist.' We have yet to see anyone from the elites described as 'atheist' or 'agnostic'. Which begs the question, 'Why not?' All human beings are influenced by their personal religious and philosophical commitments. Why is this only to be considered a problem for Christians? The attempt to define out of public debate contributors who come from selected religious viewpoints (but not others) exemplifies how deeply anti-religious and sectarian bigotry goes especially among those who would regard themselves as 'enlightened', even 'educated'.

When Christians, either as individuals or in company with others of similar mind, take part in public discussion, they do so simply as citizens expressing a view about the common good and the principles that are needed to protect the common good. They are behaving responsibly by taking their civic role seriously, provided of course that they conduct themselves properly within the norms of the Australian democratic system. This caveat also applies to those who substitute intelligent argument and debate for *ad hominem* attacks which invite people to disregard fellow citizens on the basis that of unjust religious discrimination.

The view that human life is to be protected is implied by the simple idea of equal respect for persons. It is legitimate to argue about who is a person, but that is not essentially a religious debate, even if religious people may be inclined to be more sensitive to the need to protect those who are most vulnerable on the fringes of life. The Australian Constitution protects religious freedom, including freedom of association and of expression. The right to be involved in public debate is protected. It is manifestly unjust and extraordinarily bigoted to claim that religious people ought not to be permitted to contribute or that their contribution ought not to be considered. At the same time, contribution to public debate needs to be aware of the sensitivities of others. Public policy advances through seeking points of agreement and being careful to respect areas of disagreement. There is a role for what John Rawls calls 'public reason', this is a discussion that takes place on the basis of agreed fundamental principles.

However it is important that there is also continued discussion of those fundamental principles, as well as discussion on the application of them, and it is appropriate in a pluralist society that all perspectives are brought to bear upon that discussion in a considered way.

Finally, we appeal to the media, to politicians, and to the spokespersons for lobby groups to put an end to attaching labels to people as a way of dismissing their opinions in advance of them being given a fair hearing. The blatantly ideological manner in which debate on fundamental issues of concern to the community is typically carried out in Australia reflects badly on those who engage such tactics. And the community does not like it. On abortion, for example, our research makes it clear that Australians want more debate, more informed debate, but not more bitter debate. The recent debates on abortion in the federal parliament were met with anger by those who wanted no debate on the basis that the issue had already been discussed and settled, and that a new debate would provide an unproductive opportunity for others to rehearse again their well established moral positions. What we have tried to do in our research and in this book which reports and discusses it is to try and see if both sides can engage the issues that really trouble the community as a whole and the women who seek abortion or who have already experienced abortion to see if there can be better social policy.

The Australian Government, under the leadership of John Howard and assisted by his Health Minister Tony Abbott, has been prepared to listen to this approach as have significant sections of the Australian Labour Party and some Independents. Accordingly we now have before us new initiatives that are in accordance with our research, that is, the wishes of the Australian community. These initiatives include:

a) the allocation of new money so that medical practitioners can have better opportunity to give time to women seeking an abortion to ensure they have all the information they need from a medical point of view to make the best decision they can; and

b) the allocation of funding to permit women to receive counselling on alternatives to abortion from appropriately credentialed counsellors.

If Australians really want women to have access to legal abortion despite their deeply conflicted views on the subject, they also want them to use that access only as a last resort. In the end, Australians accept the essence of both the pro-choice and the pro-life arguments. That being the case, these new initiatives are to be commended and may even lead to a society where there is better understanding across ideological divides and less inclination to uncritically demonise the 'opposition'. It may well turn out that both sides of the debate have more in common on this issue than many believe. In which case, social policy on this and other issues can continue to be revisited for the common good and the wellbeing of all Australian citizens.

Notes

Chapter 1

[1] Some academic writers in the field of bioethics argue that the foetus is not a 'person' and, lacking moral status, has no human rights to be protected. On this account there is no moral wrong in abortion.

[2] See, for example, the screening of 'My Foetus' on the 20 April 2004 on Britain's Channel 4 and subsequently on Australian television.

[3] Nicolle Dixon, *Abortion Law Reform: An Overview of Current Issue,* Research Brief No 2003/09, 2003 (Parliament of Queensland: Parliamentary Library) 10.

[4] For a fuller discussion of these figures see John I. Fleming & Daniel Ch Overduin, *Wake Up, Lucky Country* (Adelaide: Lutheran Publishing House, 1982) 29–31.

[5] See Annabelle Chan et al, 'Pregnancy Outcome in South Australia 2002', (Department of Human Services, Epidemiology Branch, Pregnancy Outcome Unit, November 2003) 39.

[6] Barbara Baird, ' "I Had One Too ...": An Oral History of Abortion in South Australia Before 1970' (Flinders University of South Australia: Women's Studies Unit, 1990) 13.

[7] Kerrilie Rice, *Abortion Issues Paper*, Policy and Research Office, Women's Health Victoria. January 2005.

[8] Rice, *Abortion Issues Paper.*

[9] [1939] 1 KB 687. For convenience, subsequent citations from this case will refer to the report or the case carried in the *Australian Law Journal* in 1938.

[10] *Australian Law Journal* vol.12 (14 October 1938) 212.

[11] It is interesting to note that in cases where the mother was at risk of being sentenced to death for a capital offence, the British Parliament passed *an Act to prohibit the passing of the sentence of death upon expectant mothers, and for other purposes therewith of 1931.* The purpose of this Act was to prevent even the passing of a death sentence, whereas previously the requirement had been (but not the practice) to delay carrying out the death sentence until after the child had been born. This Act put into statute law the existing practice of not actually executing the mother even though, strictly speaking, she was granted only a reprieve. This Act further justifies McNaghten's opinion that the law protected the life of the unborn child.

[12] *Australian Law Journal* vol.12 (14 October 1938) 169, emphasis added.

[13] *Australian Law Journal* vol.12 (14 October 1938) 169.

[14] 'Part of the reason for the increasing use of the pill, especially by younger women, was the changing levels of sexual activity and changing attitudes of doctors towards prescribing the pill – especially for unmarried women.'   David de Vaus, *Diversity and Change in Australian Families: Statistical Profiles* (Melbourne: Australian Institute of Family Studies, 2004) 193.

[15] Fleming & Overduin, *Wake Up, Lucky Country*, 34.

[16] Public and Environmental Health Service, South Australian Health Commission Department of Obstetrics and Gynaecology, The Queen Elizabeth Hospital, *A South Australian Study on Contraception and Abortion* (Adelaide: March 1994) 60.

[17] *A South Australian Study*, 60.

[18] Fleming & Overduin, *Wake Up, Lucky Country*, 40–1.

[19] Fleming & Overduin, *Wake Up, Lucky Country*, 42–3.

[20] Nicolee Dixon, *Abortion Law Reform: An Overview of Current Issues*, Research Brief No. 2003/09 (Parliament of Queensland: Parliamentary Library) 8; and cf. L. Crowley-Cyr, 'A Century of Remodelling: The Law of Abortion in Review', *Journal of Law and Medicine* vol.7 no.3 (2000) 252–266, citing a number of cases including *R v Walker* no. 2 [1915] St R Qd 143.

[21] (1969) VR 667.

[22] Louis Waller, 'Necessary Abortions', *Australian Law Journal* vol. 44 (27 February 1970) 90.

[23] Anthony Fisher and Jane Buckingham, *Abortion in Australia* (Blackburn, Victoria: Dove Communications, 1985) 94.

[24] Fisher and Buckingham, *Abortion*, 94.

[25] Natasha Cica, *Abortion Law in Australia*, Research Paper 1 1998–1999, (Parliament of Australia: Parliamentary Library) 19, <http://www.aph. gov.au/library/pubs/rp/1998-99/99rp01.htm>. Cf. *CES and Another v Superclinics (Australia) Pty Limited and Others* (1995) vol.38 NSWLR 47.

[26] Fleming & Overduin, *Wake Up, Lucky Country*, 77.

[27] A full treatment of all the issues contained in this section may be found in Fleming & Overduin, *Wake Up, Lucky Country*, 67-85.

[28] Fleming & Overduin, *Wake Up, Lucky Country*, 79-80.

[29] Fleming & Overduin, *Wake Up, Lucky Country*, 83.

[30] A direct abortion is when the doctor directly removes the foetus from the womb in order to terminate the pregnancy. An indirect abortion occurs when, for example, a cancerous uterus is removed from a pregnant woman, to save the life of the mother. In the latter case the purpose of the act is not to remove the foetus but to remove a cancerous organ that

threatens life, the removal of the foetus being an indirect consequence of that act.

[31] Nicolee Dixon, *Abortion Law Reform: An Overview of Current Issues,* Research Brief No. 2003/09 (Parliament of Queensland: Parliamentary Library) 12. <http://www.parliament.qld.gov.au/Parlib/Publications_pdfs/books/200309.pdf>.

[32] Dixon, *Abortion Law Reform*, 13.

[33] Qld Law Reports 9, (1986) 8.

[34] Natasha Cica, *Abortion Law in Australia*, Research Paper 1, 1998–1999 (Parliament of Australia: Parliamentary Library) 19, < http://www.aph.gov.au/library/pubs/rp/1998-99/99rp01.htm>, 22, cited in Dixon, *Abortion Law Reform,*14.

[35] Dixon, *Abortion Law Reform*, 15.

[36] *The Age*, 2 May 1988, 7.

[37] Lisa Teasdale, 'Confronting the Fear of being "Caught": Discourses on Abortion in Western Australia', *UNSW Law Journal* vol. 22 no.1 (1999) 71.

[38] Western Australian Parliament, Legislative Council, *Parliamentary Debates* 1998 (10 March) 10.

[39] WA Parliament, *(Debates)* 1998, 616.

[40] WA Parliament, *(Debates)* 1998, 739.

[41] WA Parliament, *(Debates)* 1998, 768.

[42] WA Parliament, *(Debates)* 1998, 779–780.

[43] *Rogers v Whitaker* (1992) ALR 625.

[44] Alannah MacTiernan (LA), *Parliamentary Debates,* 1998, 1072.

[45] Eric Ripper (LA), *Parliamentary Debates,* 1998, 1071.

[46] June van de Kalshorst (LA), *Parliamentary Debates,* 1998, 1086.

[47] June van de Kalshorst (LA), *Parliamentary Debates,* 1998; Robert Bloffwitch (LA), *Parliamentary Debates,* 1998, 1345; Eric Ripper (LA), *Parliamentary Debates,* 1998, 1361.

[48] WA Parliament, *Debates,* 1998, 2514.

[49] WA Parliament, *Debates,* 1998, 2514.

[50] WA Parliament, *Debates,* 1998, 2517.

[51] WA Parliament, *Debates,* 1998, 2533.

[52] Leslie Cannold and Cait Calcutt, *The Australian Pro-Choice Movement and the Struggle for Legal Clarity, Liberal Laws and Liberal Access: Two Case Studies.* Paper prepared on behalf of Children by Choice and the Australian Reproductive Health Alliance, 9. <http://www.arha.org.au/occasionalpapers/OP%203%20-%20Aust%20Abortion.pdf>.

[53] Dixon, *Abortion Law Reform,* 33.

[54] Dixon, *Abortion Law Reform,33.*

[55] Australian Capital Territory Parliament, Legislative Assembly, *Parliamentary Debates,* (2002) 2585, emphasis added.

[56] ACT Parliament, *(Debates),* 2581.

[57] ACT Parliament, *(Debates),* 2621.

[58] ACT Parliament, *(Debates),* 2605.

[59] ACT Parliament, *(Debates),* 2002.

[60] ACT Parliament, *(Debates),* 2579.

[61] ACT Parliament, *(Debates),* 2622.

[62] ACT Parliament, *(Debates),* 2642.

[63] ACT Parliament, *(Debates),* 2521.

[64] ACT Parliament, *(Debates),* 2580.

[65] ACT Parliament, *(Debates),* 2586.

[66] ACT Parliament, *(Debates),* 1897.

[67] Bruce Montgomery, 'State Flies Women Out for Abortions', *The Australian,* 13 December 2001, 1.

[68] Bruce Montgomery, 'MPs Sit Late to Legalise Abortion', *The Australian,* 20 December 2001, 5.

[69] Dixon, *Abortion Law Reform,* 30.

[70] Angela Pratt, Amanda Biggs, and Luke Buckmaster, Social Policy Section, *How Many Abortions Are There in Australia? A Discussion of Abortion Statistics, Their Limitations, and Options for Improved Statistical Collection,* Research Brief, 9, 2005 (Parliament of Australia: Department of Library Services).

[71] Pratt, Biggs and Buckmaster, Social Policy Section, *How Many Abortions,* 15-16.

[72] Pratt, Biggs and Buckmaster, Social Policy Section, *How Many Abortions,* 14.

Chapter 2

[1] For example; *Bulletin,* Morgan-Gallup polls of 1995, 1996, and 1998; and the Market Facts Queensland Poll 2004. See also Katharine Betts, 'Attitudes to Abortion in Australia 1972-2003', *People and Place* vol.12 no.4 (2004).

[2] For example, the International Social Science Surveys in Australia, reported in Jonathan Kelley and M.D.R. Evans, 'Trends in Australian Attitudes to Abortion 1984 - 2002', *Australian Social Monitor* vol.6 no.3 (September 2003); the Newspolls of 1996 and 2004; the Australian Election Surveys 1987, 1990, 1993, 1996, 1998, and 2001; the Australian National University's *Australian Survey of Social Attitudes, 2004.*

[3] For example, the Morgan Polls and the Newspolls.

[4] This section is taken from The Sexton Marketing Group, *Public Attitudes in Australia Towards Abortion December 2004 Report* (28 December 2004) 4-7.

[5] Sexton Marketing Group, *Public Attitudes*, 8-9.

[6] This section is mainly derived from The Sexton Marketing Group, *Public Attitudes in Australia Towards Abortion December 2004 Report*.

[7] Question: The next issue was the idea of re-introducing the death penalty for committing the most serious crimes in Australia. Do you agree or disagree with this idea? (Is that *strongly* agree / disagree or *somewhat* agree / disagree?). Thirty-seven per cent strongly agreed, 16 per cent somewhat agreed, 13 per cent somewhat disagreed, and 29 per cent strongly disagreed. That is, 53 per cent agreed, 42 per cent disagreed, and 6 per cent were neutral.

Question: The next issue was whether same-sex couples should be allowed to adopt children. Do you agree or disagree with that view? (Is that *strongly* agree/disagree or *somewhat* agree/disagree?). Twenty-four per cent strongly agreed, 17 per cent somewhat agreed, 14 per cent somewhat disagreed, and 36 per cent strongly disagreed. That is, 41 per cent agreed, 49 per cent disagreed, and 10 per cent were neutral.

[8] When asked whether a 'women should have unrestricted access to abortion on demand, no matter what the circumstance', 62 per cent said they agreed. When later asked whether they agreed with the pro-abortion argument: 'choosing to have an abortion is a woman's right no matter what the reasons for making that choice', 69 per cent agreed.

[9] *The Bulletin*, Morgan poll of February 1998 (published in *The Bulletin* on 3 March 1998), replicating the Morgan-Gallup polls of February 1995 and February 1996, found that 65 per cent approved of the termination of unwanted pregnancies through surgical abortion (57 per cent in 1996 and 55 per cent in 1995); 25 per cent disapproved (33 per cent in 1996, 32 per cent in 1995); and 10 per cent were undecided (10 per cent in 1996, 13 per cent in 1995).

The *Australian Election Survey 2001* found 57.6 per cent believed that women should be able to obtain an abortion readily when they want one (Clive Bean, David Gow, and Ian McAllister, 'Australian Election Study, 2001', *Australian Social Science Data Archive*, <http://assda.anu.edu.au/codebooks/aes >). See also David de Vaus, *Diversity and Change in Australian Families: Statistical Profiles* (Melbourne: Australian Institute of Family Studies, 2004) 194-5.

The ANU *Australian Survey of Social Attitudes 2004* (conducted in 2003; <http://aussa.anu.edu.au/index.html>) found a much higher figure: 82 per cent. Broken down, 43 per cent 'strongly agreed' and 39 per cent 'agreed' with the proposition that 'a woman should have the right to choose whether or not she has an abortion'.

On the other hand, a lower figure was found in the Newspolls of September 1996 and December 2004. In these polls only 50 per cent were in favour of abortion being 'allowed under any circumstances'.

Similarly, Market Facts Queensland's telephone survey of three hundred respondents conducted in April 2004 found that 42 per cent of Queenslanders supported abortion on demand while 44 per cent opposed it.

[10] Australian Federation of Right to Life Associations, *What Australians Really Think About Abortion* (Canberra: Australian Federation of Right to Life Associations, 2006) 14.

[11] Legislative Council of South Australia, Committee Appointed to Examine and Report on Abortions Notified in South Australia, Thirty-Third Annual Report (2002).

[12] Item nn. 16525 and 35643.

[13] Angela Pratt, Amanda Briggs, and Luke Buckmaster, *How Many Abortions Are There in Australia? A Discussion of Abortion Statistics, Their Limitations, and Options for Improved Statistical Collection,* Research Brief n. 9. 2005 (Parliament of Australia: Department of Parliamentary Services) 4.

[14] Pratt, Briggs and Buckmaster, *How Many Abortions,* 14.

[15] Australian Bureau of Statistics, *Australian Social Trends 1998*, cat. n. 4102.0. Of the total number of known pregnancies, this figure represents about 27 per cent ending in an abortion, during that period.

[16] Australian Bureau of Statistics, *Births Australia 2003*, cat. n. 3301.0.

[17] This section is taken from The Sexton Marketing Group, *Public Attitudes in Australia Towards Abortion December 2004 Report* (28 December 2004).

[18] For example, the self-selecting Voteline telephone poll in Melbourne's *Herald Sun*, 9 November 2004, 17, in which 91.2 per cent of the 2 081 callers said 'Yes' to the question: 'Are there too many abortions in Australia?'

[19] This section is taken from The Sexton Marketing Group, *Public Attitudes in Australia Towards Abortion December 2004 Report,* (28 December 2004).

[20] Strongly pro-abortion, 55 per cent agree; somewhat pro-abortion, 71 per cent agree; and neutral, 80 per cent. Cf. those somewhat opposed to abortion, 90 per cent agree; and those strongly opposed to abortion, 94 per cent agree.

[21] Strongly pro-abortion, 59 per cent agree; somewhat pro-abortion, 77 per cent agree; and neutral, 84 per cent. Cf. those somewhat opposed to abortion, 89 per cent agree; and those strongly opposed to abortion, 88 per cent agree.

[22] This section is taken from The Sexton Marketing Group, *Public Attitudes in Australia Towards Abortion December 2004 Report* (28 December 2004).

[23] This section is taken from The Sexton Marketing Group, *Public Attitudes in Australia Towards Abortion December 2004 Report* (28 December 2004).

[24] This section is taken from The Sexton Marketing Group, *Public Attitudes in Australia Towards Abortion December 2004 Report* (28 December 2004).

[25] This section is taken from The Sexton Marketing Group, *Public Attitudes in Australia Towards Abortion December 2004 Report* (28 December 2004).

[26] Miranda Devine, 'Abortion Debate Takes on a New Life of Its Own', *Sydney Morning Herald*, 3 February 2005, <http://www.smh.com.au/news/Miranda-Devine/Abortion-debate-takes-on-a-new-life-of-its-own/2005/02/02/1107228765861.html>.

[27] This section is taken from The Sexton Marketing Group, *A Qualitative Focus Group Study of Public Attitudes to Abortion in Australia Report*, 10 March, 2005.

[28] This section is taken from The Sexton Marketing Group, *A Qualitative Focus Group Study of Public Attitudes to Abortion in Australia Report*, 10 March, 2005, 4-5.

Chapter 3

[1] This section is mainly derived from The Sexton Marketing Group, *Public Attitudes Towards Abortion Study–Stage 3 Survey Results* (26 October 2005).

[2] Sexton Marketing, *Public Attitudes,* (26 October 2005).

[3] Sexton Marketing, *Public Attitudes,* (26 October 2005).

[4] See conclusion to previous chapter, which deals with the first and second stages of the research project.

[5] Should a woman be able to ask for an abortion, without any prior counselling or discussion with anyone, and receive the abortion that day, or do you think there should be a compulsory cooling off or waiting period in which she has time to consider her decision more fully?

[6] This section is mainly derived from The Sexton Marketing Group, *Public Attitudes Towards Abortion Study–Stage 3 Survey Results,* (26 October 2005).

[7] Sexton Marketing Group, *Public Attitudes,* (26 October 2005).

[8] Sexton Marketing Group, *Public Attitudes,* (26 October 2005).

[9] Sexton Marketing Group, *Public Attitudes,* (26 October 2005).

[10] Sexton Marketing Group, *Public Attitudes,* (26 October 2005).

[11] Sexton Marketing Group, *Public Attitudes,* (26 October 2005).

[12] Media Release from The Hon. John Howard MP Prime Minister, & The Hon. Tony Abbott MP Minister for Health and Ageing, media release, 2 March 2006, ABB024/06.

[13] This section is mainly derived from The Sexton Marketing Group, *Public Attitudes in Australia Towards the Introduction of New Abortion Counselling Services, RU-486 and Embryonic Stem-Cell Research Report,* (3 February 2006).

[14] Sexton Marketing Group, *Public Attitudes,* (3 February 2006).

[15] Sexton Marketing Group, *Public Attitudes,* (3 February 2006).

Chapter 4

[1] Department of Health and Ageing, Commonwealth of Australia, *National Sexually Transmissible Infections Strategy 2005–2008*, < http://www.vicaids.asn.au/contentfilesuploaded/STI_strategy.pdf>.

[2] Douglas Kirby, 'Reflections on Two Decades of Research on Teen Sexual Behaviour and Pregnancy', *Journal of School Health* vol.69 no.3 (1999) 89–94.

[3] A. Mindel and S. Kippax, 'A National Sexually Transmitted Infections Strategy: The Need for an All-Embracing Approach', *The Medical Journal of Australia* vol.183 no.10 (2005) 502–3.

[4] Curriculum Corporation, Carlton, Victoria, 1994.

[5] Curriculum Corporation, Carlton, Victoria, 1994.

[6] Queensland Government, 2002.

[7] SIECUS, 1999, <http://www.siecus.org>.

[8] S.R. Skinner and M. Hickey, 'Current Priorities for Adolescent Sexual and Reproductive Health in Australia', *The Medical Journal of Australia* vol.179 (2003) 158–161.

[9] Australian Institute of Health and Welfare (AIHW), 'Australian Young People: Their Health and Wellbeing 2003', *Canberra: Australian Institute of Health and Welfare* (cat. n. PHE50); M. Chen and B. Donovan, 'Chlamydia Trachomatis Infection in Australia: Epidemiology and Clinical Implication', *Sexual Health* vol.1 (2004) 189–196.

[10] A. Smith et al., *Secondary Students and Sexual Health 2002: Report of the Finding from the 3rd National Survey of Australian Secondary Students, HIV/AIDS and Sexual Health, Research Report,*(Melbourne: La Trobe University, 2003).

[11] J.C. Amba et al., 'Fertility, Family Planning and Women's Health: New Data from the 1995 National Survey on Family Growth, National Centre for Health Statistics', *Vital Health Statistics* vol.23 (1997) 1–114.

[12] L.C. Cooper, N.L. Leland, and G. Alexander, 'Effect of Maternal Age on Birth Outcomes Among Young Adolescents', *Social Biology* vol.42 (1995) 22–35.

[13] W.C. Miller, C.A. Ford, and M. Morris, 'Prevalence of Chlamydial and Gonococcal Infection Among Young Adults in the United States', *Journal of American Medical Association* vol. 291 (2004) 2229–2236.

[14] A.E. Biddlecom, 'Trends in Sexual Behaviours and Infections Among Young People in the United States', *Sexually Transmitted Infections* vol.80 suppl. 2 (2004) 74-9.

[15] C.E. Kaestle et al., 'Young Age at First Intercourse and Sexually Transmitted Infections in Adolescent and Young Adults', *American Journal of Epidemiology* vol.161 no.8 (2005) 774–780.

[16] Ellen, J., Aral, S. & Madger, L. 1998, 'Do Differences in Sexual Behaviours Account for the Ratial/Ethnic Differences in Adolescents' Self-Reported

History of a Sexually Transmitted Disease?', *Sexually Transmitted Diseases*, vol.25, 125-9. Cf. H.R. Harrison, M. Costin, and J.B. Meder, 'Cervical Chlamydia Trachomatis Infection in University Women: Relationship to History, Contraception, Ectopy and Cervicitis', *American Journal of Obstetric Gynecology* vol.153 (1985) 244–251; Aral (1998).

[17] C.A. Ford et al., 'Predicting Adolescents' Longitudinal Risk for Sexually Transmitted Infection', *Archive of Pediatric and Adolescent Medicine* vol.159 (2005) 657–664.

[18] AIHW, 'Australian Young People'.

[19] S. As-Sanie, A. Gantt, and M. Rosental, 'Pregnancy Prevention in Adolescents', *American Family Physician* vol.70 no.8 (2004) 1517–1523.

[20] N. Grayson, J. Hargreaves, and E.A. Sullivan, 'Use of Routinely Collected National Data Sets for Reporting on Induced Abortion in Australia', *AIHW National Perinatal Statistics* vol.17 (2005) 34.

[21] R.L. Barbieri, 'Population Density and Teen Pregnancy', *Obstetrics & Gynecology* vol.104 no.4 (2004) 741–4.

[22] S. Dyson and A. Mitchell, 'Sex Education and Unintended Pregnancy: Are We Seeing the Results?' *Australian Health Review* vol.29 no.2 (2005) 135–9.

[23] K.D. Wagner et al., 'Attributional Style and Depression in Pregnant Teenagers', *American Journal of Psychiatry* vol.155 no.9 (1998): 1227–1233; B. Barnet et al., 'Association Between Postpartum Substance Use and Depressive Symptoms, Stress and Social Support in Adolescent Mothers', *Pediatrics* vol.96 no.4 (1995) 659–666.

[24] C.P. Bonell et al., 'Effect of Social Exclusion on the Risk of Teenage Pregnancy: Development of Hypotheses Using Baseline Data from a Randomised Trial of Sex Education', *Journal of Epidemiology & Community Health* vol.57 no.11 (2003) 871–6.

[25] C.J. Seamark and D.J. Pereira-Gray, 'Like Mother, Like Daughter: A General Practice Study of Maternal Influences on Teenage Pregnancy', *British Journal of General Practice* vol.47 (1997) 175–6.

[26] M.C. Jolly et al., 'Obstetric Risks of Pregnancy in Women Less Than 18 Years Old', *Obstetric Gynecology* vol.96 (2000) 962–6.

[27] J.A. Quinlivan and J. Condon, 'Anxiety and Depression in Fathers in Teenage Pregnancy', *Australian and New Zealand Journal of Psychiatry* vol.30 no.10 (2005) 915–920.

[28] R.P. Lederman, W. Chan, and C. Roberts-Gray, 'Sexual Risk Attitudes and Intentions of Youth Age 12–14 Years: Survey Comparisons of Parent-Teen Prevention and Control Groups', *Behavioural Medicine* vol.29 no.4 (2004) 155–163.

[29] P. Borgia et al., 'Is Peer Education the Best Approach for HIV Prevention in Schools? Finding From a Randomised Controlled Trial', *Journal of Adolescent Health* vol.36 no.6 (2005) 508–516.

[30] J. Milton, 'Sexuality Education and Primary School: Experiences and Practices of Mothers and Teachers in Four Sydney School', *ACHPER Healthy Lifestyle Journal* vol.51 no.4 (2004) 18–25.

[31] C.L. Somers and M.W. Eaves, 'Is Earlier Sex Education Harmful? An Analysis of the Timing of School-Based Sex Education and Adolescent Behaviours', *Research in Education* vol.67 (2002) 23–32.

[32] J.D.G. Goldman, 'Sexuality Education for Children and Pre-Schoolers in the Information Age', *Children Australia* vol.28 no.1 (2003) 17–23.

[33] J.D.G. Goldman and G.L. Bradley, 'Parents as Sexuality Educators of Their Children in the Technological Age?', *Australian Journal of Guidance and Counseling*, vol.14.no.2 (2004) 233–250.

[34] C.L. Somers and A.T. Surman, 'Sources and Timing of Sex Education: Relation with American Adolescent Sexual Attitudes and Behaviour', *Educational Review* vol.57 no.1 (2005) 37–54.

[35] S.L. Escobar-Chaves et al., 'Impact of the Media on Adolescent Sexual Attitudes and Behaviours', *Pediatrics* vol.116 no.1 suppl. S (2005) 303–326.

[36] S.C. Rostosky, B.L. Wilcox, and B.A. Randall, 'The Impact of Religiosity on Adolescent Sexual Behaviour: A Review of Evidence', *Journal of Adolescent Research* vol.19 no.6 (2004) 677–696.

[37] R.K. Jones, J.E. Darroch, and S. Singh, 'Religious Differentials in the Sexual and Reproductive Behaviour of Young Women in the United States', *Journal of Adolescent Health* vol.36 no.4 (2005) 279–288.

[38] J.F. Hagan et al., 'Sexuality Educational for Children and Adolescent', *Pediatrics* vol.108 no.2 (2001) 498–502.

[39] Pinkerton (2001).

[40] A. DiCenso et al., 'Interventions to Reduce Unintended Pregnancies Among Adolescents: Systematic Review of Randomised Controlled Trials', *British Medical Journal* vol.324 (2002) 1426–1433.

[41] J.D. Fortenberry, 'The Limits of Abstinence-Only in Preventing Sexually Transmitted Infections', *Journal of Adolescent Health* vol.36 (2005) 269–270.

[42] P. Goodson et al., 'Defining Abstinence: View of Directors, Instructors and Participants in Abstinence-Only-Until-Marriage Programs in Texas', *The Journal of School Health* vol.73 no.3 (2003) 91–5.

[43] J. Milton and L. Berne, 'Condom and Contraceptive Availability for Young People: Do Australian Teachers, Parents and School Counsellors Support Access in School Settings?' *ACHPER Healthy Lifestyle Journal* vol.51 no.1 (2004) 7–11; S. Yoo et al., 'A Qualitative Evaluation of the Students of Service (SOS) Program for Sexual Abstinence in Louisiana', *Journal of School Health* vol.74 no.8 (2004) 329–334; A. Martin et al., 'Early to Bed: A Study of Adaptation Among Sexually Active Urban Adolescent Girls Younger Than Age Sixteen', *Journal of American Academy of Child & Adolescent Psychiatry* vol.44 no.4 (2005) 358–367.

[44] G.H. Guyatt, A.DiCenso,V.Farewell,A. Willan & L.Griffith, 'Randomised Trial Versus Observational Studies in Adolescent Pregnancy Prevention', *Journal of Clinical Epidemiology* vol.53 no.2 (2000) 167–174.

[45] A. Visser and P. Van Bilsen, 'Effectiveness of Sex Education Provided to Adolescent', *Patient Education and Counseling* vol.23 (1994): 147–160; C. Jacobs and E. Wolf, 'School Sexuality and Adolescent Risk-Taking Behaviour', *Journal of School Health* vol.65 (1995) 91–5.

[46] K.K. Coyle et al., 'Draw the Line/Respect the Line: A Randomised Trial of a Middle School Intervention to Reduce Sexual Risk Behaviours', *Research and Practice* vol.94 no.5 (2004) 843–851.

[47] J.D. Woody, A.D. Randall, and H.J. D'Souza, 'Mothers' Efforts Toward Their Children's Sex Education: An Exploratory Study', *Journal of Family Studies* vol.11 no.1 (2005) 83–7.

[48] Jadad et al. (1996).

[49] T.A. Furukawa and G.H. Guyatt, 'Sources of Bias in Diagnostic Accuracy Studies and the Diagnostic Process', *Canadian Medical Association Journal* vol.174 no.4 (2006) 481–2.

[50] K.L. Wilson et al., 'A Review of 21 Curricula for Abstinence-Only-Until-Marriage Programs', *Journal of School Health* vol.75 no.3 (2005) 90–8.

[51] N.D. Brener et al., 'Reliability of the Youth Risk Behaviour Survey Questionnaire', *American Journal of Epidemiology* vol.141 (1995) 575–580.

[52] Guyatt et al., 2000.

[53] M. Silva, 'The Effectiveness of School-Based Sex Education Programs in the Promotion of Abstinent Behaviour: A Meta-Analysis', *Health Education Research, Theory & Practice* vol.17 no.4 (2002) 471–481.

[54] A.S. Detsky et al., 'Incorporating Variations in the Quality of Individual Randomised Trial into Meta-Analysis', *Journal of Clinical Epidemiology* vol.45 (1992) 255–265.

[55] S. Weller and K. Davis, 'Condom Effectiveness in Reducing Heterosexual HIV Transmission (Cochrane Review)', *The Cochrane Library* vol. 4 (2002).

[56] A. Grunseit et al., 'Sexuality Education and Young People's Sexual Behaviour: A Review of Studies', *Journal of Adolescent Research* vol.12 (1997) 421–453.

[57] Michael Resnick et al., 'Protecting Adolescents from Harm: Findings From the National Longitudinal Study on Adolescent Health', *Journal of the American Medical Association* vol.278 (10 September 1997): 823–832.

[58] Andrew S. Doniger, 'Impact Evaluation of the 'Not Me, Not Now' Abstinence-Oriented, Adolescent Pregnancy Prevention Communications Program, Monroe County, New York', *Journal of Health Communications* vol.6 (2001) 45–60.

[59] Elaine Borawski et al., *Evaluation of the Teen Pregnancy Prevention Programs Funded Through the Wellness Block Grant (1999–2000)*, Center

for Health Promotion Research, Department of Epidemiology and Biostatistics, Case Western Reserve University, School of Medicine (23 March 2001).

[60] Peter S. Bearman and Hanna Bruckner, 'Promising the Future: Virginity Pledges and First Intercourse', *American Journal of Sociology* vol.106 no.4 (January 2001) 861-2.

[61] Stephen R. Jorgensen, Vicki Potts, and Brian Camp, 'Project Taking Charge: Six-Month Follow-Up of a Pregnancy Prevention Program for Early Adolescents', *Family Relations* vol.42 no.4 (October 1993) 401-6.

[62] National Health and Medical Research Council, *National Youth Suicide Prevention Strategy. Setting the Evidence-Based Research Agenda for Australia: A Literature Review* (1999), <http://www.nhmrc.gov.au/publications/ synopses/mh12syn.htm>.

Chapter 5

[1] J.I. Fleming and S. Ewing, *Give Women Choice: Australia Speaks on Abortion* (Southern Cross Bioethics Institute, 26 April 2005) 3.

[2] D.C. Reardon, *Making Abortion Rare: A Healing Strategy for a Divided Nation* (Springfield, IL: Acorn Books, 1996) ix.

[3] Fleming and Ewing, *Give Women Choice*, 3.

[4] D.C. Reardon, *Aborted Women: Silent No More* (Springfield, IL: Acorn Books, 2002) 10-21.

[5] Caring Foundation Research, outlined by Paul Swope, 'Heart and Soul: A New Abortion Strategy', *Crisis* 17 (March 1999) 33-7.

[6] Swope, 'Heart and Soul', 35. Swope describes this as a 'distorted maternal instinct': 'These women want their baby to be happy and healthy, but they view their own situation as so alien to the proper environment for raising a child that it appears preferable to end the child's life in the womb.'

[7] Swope, 'Heart and Soul', 35.

[8] Paul Swope, 'Abortion: A Failure to Communicate', *First Things* 82 (April 1998) 31-5.

[9] The strongest pro-abortion arguments are that abortion gives women control over their lives (75 per cent); abortion is bad but sometimes justifiable (70 per cent) and abortion is a woman's right (69 per cent), Fleming and Ewing, *Give Women Choice*, 18.

[10] Other pro-life strategists concentrated on the argument that an 'all or nothing' approach to changing legislation and court rulings and even voting for political candidates, at most, removes pro-lifers from effective engagement with politics and, at the very least, means that many other pro-life initiatives are overlooked. This argument is not directly addressed here, but an example is Nathan Schlueter, 'Drawing Pro-Life Lines', *First Things* 116 (October 2001) 32-4.

[11] Swope, 'Heart and Soul', 33.

[12] Frederica Mathewes-Green, 'Doing Everything We Can', *Touchstone Magazine* vol.17 no.1 (January/February 2004).

[13] Swope, 'Heart and Soul', 35.

[14] Melinda Tankard Reist, *Giving Sorrow Words: Women's Stories of Grief After Abortion* (Sydney: Duffy and Snellgrove, 2000); Serrin M. Foster, 'Women Deserve Better Than Abortion', in *Respect Life Program, 2003* (Washington, DC, United States Conference of Catholic Bishops, 2003).

[15] Selena Ewing, *Women and Abortion: An Evidence Based Review* (Women's Forum Australia, 2005); Erika Bachiochi, 'How Abortion Hurts Women: The Hard Proof', *Crisis* 23 (June 2005) 23–7.

[16] Francis J. Beckwith, 'Choice Words: A Critique of the New Pro-Life Rhetoric', *Touchstone Magazine* vol.17 no.1 (January/February 2004); Scott Klusendorf, 'The Vanishing Pro-Life Apologist: Putting the Life Back into the Abortion Debate', *Christian Research Journal*, vol.22 no.1 (1999).

[17] Beckwith, 'Choice Words'.

[18] Frederica Mathewes-Green, *Real Choices: Listening to Women; Looking for Alternatives to Abortion* (Ben Lomond: Conciliar Press, 1994).

[19] Beckwith, 'Choice Words'.

[20] Beckwith, 'Choice Words'.

[21] Beckwith, 'Choice Words'.

[22] Mary Cunningham Agee, 'A Call to Effective Action: When Being Right Is Not Enough', (Washington, DC: United States Conference of Catholic Bishops, 2004). <http://www.usccb.org/prolife/programs/rlp/04agee.htm>.

[23] Fr Richard Hogan, 'An Introduction to John Paul II's Theology of the Body', (2003). <http://www.nfpoutreach.org/Hogan_Theology_%20Body1.htm>.

[24] Beckwith, 'Choice Words'.

[25] Terry Sclossberg, 'A Serious Moral Issue: A Response to Francis J. Beckwith', *Touchstone Magazine* vol. 17 no.1 (January/February 2004).

[26] Erin Dolan, 'Women's Forum Australia: The New Face of Anti-Abortionists', *Do Not Be Quiet* vol.7, (January 2006).

[27] L. Cannold, 'Understanding and Responding to Anti-Choice Women-Centred Strategies', *Reproductive Health Matters, vol.* 10 no. 19, (2002) 177.

[28] Cannold, 'Understanding and Responding', 176.

[29] Cannold, 'Understanding and Responding', 177.

[30] Cannold, 'Understanding and Responding', 177.

[31] Martha Brant, 'Politics of Choice', *Newsweek* (6 February 2006), <http://www.msnbc.msn.com/id/11590468/site/newsweek/page/0/>.

[32] Brant, 'Politics of Choice'.

[33] John Paul II, *Crossing the Threshold of Hope* (London: Jonathan Cape, 1994), 207, original emphasis: 'It is precisely the woman, in fact, who pays the highest price, not only for her motherhood, but even more for its destruction, for the suppression of the life of the child who has been conceived. The only honest stance … *is that of radical solidarity with the woman'*.

[34] John Paul II, *Evangelium Vitae* (The Gospel of Life), (Sydney: St. Pauls, 1995) n. 87.

[35] Cunningham Agee writes:

> In essence, we must remember that it is the mother in crisis — not the unborn child, no matter how infinitely valuable his or her life truly is — who has the power and responsibility to make a life-and-death decision. We cannot afford to overlook the fact that it is the mother who is being asked to accept the economic hardships, social embarrassment, and physical hardship of her unplanned pregnancy. It is the mother in crisis, far more than anyone else, who must hear compassionate words and credible offers of assistance if she is to persevere on the lonely path of protecting the life of her unborn child. (Cunningham Agee, 'A Call to Effective Action', in *Respect Life Program 2004* [Washington, DC: United States Conference of Catholic Bishops].)

[36] See finding by the Southern Cross Bioethics Institute in Chapter 2.12.

[37] Catholic Bishops of Australia, 'Catholic Bishops Propose Abortion Alternatives' (25 November 2004), <http://www.acbc.catholic.org.au/bishops/200411253.htm>.

[38] Foster, 'Women Deserve Better Than Abortion', 3.

[39] John Paul II, *The Gospel of Life*, n. 23.

Chapter 6

[1] SCBI, survey 'Give Women Choice', 2–5.

[2] Carey Gillam, 'Abortion Rights Groups Say Battle Being Lost', *Reuters News Service*, 29 January 2006.

[3] Joan Vennochi, 'Abortion's Changing Landscape', *Boston Globe*, 16 August 2005.

[4] Cathleen Cleaver, 'Moving Toward a Culture of Life' (Washington, DC: United States Conference of Catholic Bishops, Inc., 2001).

[5] Susan Wills, *Never Too Late for a Legal Abortion*, (28 January 2005), <http://www.usccb.org/prolife/publicat/issues/012805.html>.

[6] Wills, 'Never Too Late'.

[7] Wills, 'Never Too Late'.

[8] See UCLA Higher Education Research Institute Study (25 January 1999). <www.gseis.ucla.edu/heri/norms_pr_98.html>.

9 Susan Wills , 'Never Too Late'.

10 'Poll: Seventy Per cent Support Parental Involvement on Abortion', <http.//www.LifeNews.com>, 28 April 2005.

11 'Poll', <http.//www.LifeNews.com>.

12 Jeff Johnson, 'As Abortion Drops, Polls Show Americans Turning Pro-Life', <http.//www.cnsnews.com>, 16 January 2003.

13 Ceci Connelly, 'Number of Abortion Providers at Lowest in Three Decades', *The Washington Post*, 22 January 2003.

14 Paul Swope, 'Abortion: A Failure to Communicate', *First Things* 82 (1998) 31–5.

15 For a more detailed explanation, see Swope, 'Abortion'.

16 Pope John Paul II, *Evangelium Vitae* (The Gospel of Life), (Sydney: St. Pauls, 1995).

17 Pope John Paul II, *Crossing the Threshold of Hope* (London: Jonathan Cape, 1994), 206–7.

18 Frederica Mathewes-Green, *Real Choices: Listening to Women, Looking for Alternatives to Abortion* (Ben Lomond: Conciliar Press, 1994).

19 David Readon, *Making Abortion Rare: A Healing Strategy for a Divided Nation* (Springfield: Acorn Books, 1996), vii.

20 Swope, 'Abortion'.

21 Brigid Vout, 'New Approaches to Induced Abortion: Is Reframing the Pro-Life Message Clever or Dangerous?' Paper presented at the National Colloquium for Catholic Bioethicists, Melbourne, 1 February 2006.

22 Staff Reporter, Telegraph, Washington 'Hilary Woos Conservative Vote on Abortion', *The Age*, 27 January 2005.

23 Leslie Cannold, 'Understanding and Responding to Anti-choice Women-centred Strategies', *Reproductive Health Matters* 2002; vol.10 no.19 171-9.

24 Australian Catholic Bishops Conference, 'Catholic Bishops propose abortion alternatives', *Media Release,* 25 November, 2004.

25 Bishops Conference, *Media Release.*

26 Bishops Conference, *Media Release.*

27 Bishops Conference, *Media Release.*

28 Archbishop George Pell, <http://www.smh.com.au/news/National/New-church-push-to-lower-abortions/2004/12/27/1103996496190.html>.

29 Melinda Tankard Reist. 'Giving Sorrow Words: Women's stories of grief after abortion', (Sydney: Duffy and Snellgrove, 2000).

30 Selena Ewing, 'The insidious censorship of pro-life women', *The Age*, 16 February 2005. See the Women's Forum Australia website, < http://www.womensforumaustralia.org>.

[31] Hon. John Howard and Hon. Tony Abbott, 'Pregnancy Support Counselling', Media Release ABB024/06, 2 March 2006.

[32] Patricia Heaton, Promotional Material, *Feminists for Life of America*, <http://www.feministsforlife.org>.

Chapter 7

[1] S. Allanson and J. Astbury, 'The Abortion Decision: Reasons and Ambivalence', *Journal of Psychosomatic Obstetrics and Gynaecology* 16 (1995) 123–136.

[2] Allanson and Astbury, 'The Abortion Decision: Reasons and Ambivalence'; M. Törnbom et al., 'Decision-Making About Unwanted Pregnancy', *Acta Obstetrica et Gynecologica Scandinavica* 78 (1999) 636–641; L. Alex and A. Hammarström, 'Women's Experiences in Connection With Induced Abortion–A Feminist Perspective', *Scandinavian Journal of Caring Sciences* vol.18 (2004) 160–8; S. Allanson and J. Astbury, 'The Abortion Decision: Fantasy Processes', Journal *of Psychosomatic Obstetrics and Gynecology* vol.17 (1996) 158–167.

[3] J. Singer, 'Options Counselling: Techniques for Caring for Women With Unintended Pregnancies', *Journal of Midwifery and Women's Health* vol.49 (2004) 235–242.

[4] V.L. Poole et al., 'Changes in Intendedness During Pregnancy in a High-Risk Multiparous Population', *Maternal and Child Health Journal* vol.4 no.3 (2000) 179–182.

[5] L. Williams et al., 'Pregnancy Wantedness: Attitude Stability Over Time', *Social Biology* vol. 48.no.3 (2001) 212–233.

[6] A. Kero et al., 'Legal Abortion: A Painful Necessity', *Social Science and Medicine* vol.53 (2001) 1481–1490.

[7] H. Söderberg et al., 'Continued Pregnancy Among Abortion Applicants: A Study of Women Having a Change of Mind', *Acta Obstetricia et Gynecologica Scandinavica* vol. 76 (1997) 942–7.

[8] H. Söderberg, L. Janzon, and N.O. Sjöberg, 'Emotional Distress Following Induced Abortion: A Study of Its Incidence and Determinants Among Abortees in Malmö, Sweden', *European Journal of Obstetrics & Gynecology and Reproductive Biology* vol. 79 (1998) 173–8.

[9] B. Major et al., 'Psychological Responses of Women After First-Trimester Abortion', *Archives of General Psychiatry* vol. 57 (2000) 777–784.

[10] C. Husfeldt et al., 'Ambivalence Among Women Applying For Abortion', *Acta Obstetricia et Gynecologica Scandinavica* vol.74 (1995) 813–7.

[11] Törnbom et al., 'Decision-Making About Unwanted Pregnancy'.

[12] H. Söderberg et al., 'Continued Pregnancy Among Abortion Applicants: A Study of Women Having a Change of Mind', *Acta Obstetrica et Gynecologica Scandinavica* vol. 76 (1997) 942–7.

[13] M.J. Korenromp et al., 'Long-Term Psychological Consequences of Pregnancy Termination for Fetal Abnormality: A Cross-Sectional Study', *Prenatal Diagnosis* vol.25 (2005) 253–260.

[14] A. Kersting et al., 'Trauma and Grief 2-7 Years After Termination of Pregnancy Because of Fetal Anomalies–A Pilot Study', *Journal of Psychosomatic Obstetrics and Gynecology* vol.26.no.1 (March 2005) 9–15.

[15] Söderberg, Janzon, and Sjöberg, 'Emotional Distress Following Induced Abortion'; P.K. Coleman et al., 'The Psychology of Abortion: A Review and Suggestions for Future Research', *Psychology and Health* vol.20 no.2 (2005) 237–271; Törnbom et al., 'Decision-Making About Unwanted Pregnancy'; A. Kero, U. Högberg, and A. Lalos, 'Wellbeing and Mental Growth–Long-Term Effects of Legal Abortion', *Social Science and Medicine* vol.58 (2004) 2559–2569; Korenromp et al., 'Long-Term Psychological Consequences of Pregnancy Termination for Fetal Abnormality'.

[16] P.K. Coleman and E.S. Nelson, 'The Quality of Abortion Decisions and College Students' Reports of Post-Abortion Emotional Sequelae and Abortion Attitudes', *Journal of Social and Clinical Psychology* vol.17 no.4 (1998) 425–442.

[17] Korenromp et al., 'Long-Term Psychological Consequences of Pregnancy Termination for Fetal Abnormality'.

[18] L. Pulley et al., 'The Extent of Pregnancy Mistiming and Its Association With Maternal Characteristics and Behaviours and Pregnancy Outcomes', *Perspectives on Sexual and Reproductive Health* vol.34 no.4 (2002) 206–211.

[19] G. Barrett and K. Wellings, 'What Is a 'Planned' Pregnancy? Empirical Data From a British Study', *Social Science and Medicine* vol.55 (2002) 545–557.

[20] L.V. Klerman, 'The Intendedness of Pregnancy: A Concept in Transition', *Maternal and Child Health Journal* vol.4 no.3 (2000) 155–162.

[21] M.R. Sable and M.K. Libbus, 'Pregnancy Intention and Pregnancy Happiness: Are They Different?', *Maternal and Child Health Journal* vol.4 no.3 (2000) 191–6.

[22] Barrett and Wellings, 'What Is a 'Planned' Pregnancy?'.

[23] Barrett and Wellings, 'What Is a 'Planned' Pregnancy?'.

[24] Williams et al., 'Pregnancy Wantedness'.

[25] Barrett and Wellings, 'What Is a 'Planned' Pregnancy?' 545–557.

[26] Barrett and Wellings, 'What Is a 'Planned' Pregnancy?' 545–557.

[27] R. Petersen et al., 'How Contraceptive Use Patterns Differ by Pregnancy Intention: Implications for Counselling', *Women's Health Issues* vol.11 no.5 (September/October 2001) 427–435.

[28] F.E. Skjeldestad, 'When Pregnant–Why Induced Abortion?', *Scandinavian Journal of Social Medicine* vol 22. no.1 (1994) 68–73; Allanson and Astbury, 'The Abortion Decision: Reasons and Ambivalence'; A. Kero and A. Lalos,

'Ambivalence–A Logical Response to Legal Abortion: A Prospective Study Among Women and Men', *Journal of Psychosomatic Obstetrics and Gynecology* vol.21 no.2 (2000) 81–91; M.C.A. White-Van Mourik, J.M. Connor and M.A. Ferguson-Smith, 'The Psychosocial Sequelae of a Second-Trimester Termination of Pregnancy for Fetal Abnormality', *Prenatal Diagnosis* vol.12 (1992) 189–204.

[29] Allanson and Astbury, 'The Abortion Decision: Reasons and Ambivalence'.

[30] Skjeldestad, 'When Pregnant–Why Induced Abortion?'.

[31] A. Bankole, S. Singh, and T. Haas, 'Reasons Why Women Have Induced Abortions: Evidence From 27 Countries', *International Family Planning Perspectives* vol.24 no.3 (1998) 117–127, 152.

[32] Kero and Lalos, 'Ambivalence–A Logical Response'; P. Adelson, M. Frommer, and E. Weisberg, 'A Survey of Women Seeking Termination of Pregnancy in New South Wales', *Medical Journal of Australia* vol.163 (1995) 419–422; A.M.A. Smith et al., 'Sex in Australia: Reproductive Experiences and Reproductive Health Among a Representative Sample of Women', *Australian and New Zealand Journal of Public Health* vol 27. no.2 (2003) 204–9.

[33] Specified medical conditions, 0.4 per cent; foetal abnormality, 2.1 per cent; and rape, 0 percent of all abortions in 2002 in South Australia. Parliament of South Australia, *33rd Annual Report of the Committee Appointed to Examine and Report on Abortions Notified in South Australia for the Year 2002* (2004).

[34] Allanson and Astbury, 'The Abortion Decision: Reasons and Ambivalence'.

[35] Allanson and Astbury, 'The Abortion Decision: Reasons and Ambivalence'.

[36] Adelson, Frommer, and Weisberg, 'A Survey of Women Seeking Termination of Pregnancy in New South Wales'; M. Larsson et al. 'Reasons for Pregnancy Termination, Contraceptive Habits and Contraceptive Failure Among Swedish Women Requesting an Early Pregnancy Termination', *Acta Obstetrica et Gynecologica Scandinavica* vol.81 (2002) 64–71; Allanson and Astbury, 'The Abortion Decision: Reasons and Ambivalence'.

[37] Adelson, Frommer, and Weisberg, 'A Survey of Women Seeking Termination of Pregnancy in New South Wales'.

[38] Adelson, Frommer, and Weisberg, 'A Survey of Women Seeking Termination of Pregnancy in New South Wales'; A. Sihvo et al., 'Women's Life Cycle and Abortion Decision in Unintended Pregnancies', *Journal of Epidemiological and Community Health* vol. 57 (2003) 601–5.

[39] Patricia Karvelas and Cath Hart, 'Age Emerges as Abortion Factor', *The Australian*, 10 November 2004, 2.

[40] Skjeldestad, 'When Pregnant–Why Induced Abortion?'.

[41] H. St. John, H. Critchley, and A. Glasier, 'Can We Identify Women at Risk of More Than One Termination of Pregnancy?', *Contraception* vol.71 (2005) 31–4.

[42] Larsson et al., 'Reasons for Pregnancy Termination, Contraceptive Habits and Contraceptive Failure'.

[43] Allanson and Astbury, 'The Abortion Decision: Reasons and Ambivalence'.

[44] Adelson, Frommer, and Weisberg, 'A Survey of Women Seeking Termination of Pregnancy in NewSouth Wales'; Sihvo et al., 'Women's Life Cycle and Abortion Decision'.

[45] W.A. Fisher et al., 'Characteristics of Women Undergoing Repeat Induced Abortion'. *Canadian Medical Journal* vol.172 no.5 (1 March 2005) 637–641; S. Phillips, 'Violence and Abortions: What's a Doctor to Do?', *Canadian Medical Journal* vol. 172 no.5 (1 March 2005) 653–4; Alex and Hammarström, 'Women's Experiences in Connection With Induced Abortion'.

[46] Kero et al., 'Legal Abortion: A Painful Necessity'; F.E. Skjeldestad, 'Induced Abortion: Effects of Marital Status, Age and Parity on Choice of Pregnancy Termination', *Acta Obstetrica et Gynecologica Scandinavica* vol.73 (1994) 255–260.

[47] Kero et al., 'Legal Abortion: A Painful Necessity'.

[48] Alex and Hammarström, 'Women's Experiences in Connection With Induced Abortion'; Alex and Hammarström, 'Women's Experiences in Connection With Induced Abortion'; Söderberg et al., 'Continued Pregnancy Among Abortion Applicants'; Fisher et al., 'Characteristics of Women Undergoing Repeat Induced Abortion'.

[49] C.D. Kroelinger and K.S. Oths, 'Partner Support and Pregnancy Wantedness', *Birth* vol.27 no.2 (2000) 112–9.

[50] J.B. Stanford et al., 'Defining Dimensions of Pregnancy Intendedness', *Maternal and Child Health Journal* vol.4 no.3 (2000) 183–9.

[51] A. Evans, 'The Influence of Significant Others on Australian Teenagers' Decisions About Pregnancy Resolution', *Family Planning Perspectives* vol.33 no.5 (2001) 224–230.

[52] Söderberg et al., 'Continued Pregnancy Among Abortion Applicants'.

[53] F. Bianchi-Demicheli et al., 'Contraceptive Practice Before and After Termination of Pregnancy: A Prospective Study', *Contraception* vol. 76 (2003) 107–113.

[54] L. Williams et al., 'Pregnancy Wantedness: Attitude Stability Over Time', *Social Biology* vol.48 no.3 (2001) 212–233.

[55] Allanson and Astbury, 'The Abortion Decision: Reasons and Ambivalence'.

[56] Fisher et al., 'Characteristics of Women Undergoing Repeat Induced Abortion'; S. Glander et al., 'The Prevalence of Domestic Violence Among

Women Seeking Abortion', *Obstetrics and Gynecology* vol.91 (1998) 1002–6; A.J. Taft, L.F. Watson, and C. Lee, 'Violence Against Young Australian Women and Association With Reproductive Events: A Cross-Sectional Analysis of a National Population Sample', *Australian and New Zealand Journal of Public Health* vol. 28. no.4 (2004) 324–9; L.W. Hedin and P.O. Janson, 'Domestic Violence During Pregnancy: The Prevalence of Physical Injuries, Substance Use, Abortions and Miscarriages', *Acta Obstetrica et Gynecologica Scandinavica* vol.79 (2000) 625–630; J. Keeling, L. Birth, and P. Green, 'Pregnancy Counselling Clinic: A Questionnaire Survey of Intimate Partner Abuse', *Journal of Family Planning and Reproductive Health Care* vol.30 no 3 (2004) 165–8; T.W. Leung et al., 'A Comparison of the Prevalence of Domestic Violence Between Patients Seeking Termination of Pregnancy and Other General Gynecology Patients', *International Journal of Gynecology and Obstetrics* vol.77 (2002) 47–54.

[57] Coleman et al., 'The Psychology of Abortion'.

[58] Keeling, Birth, and Green, 'Pregnancy Counselling Clinic'.

[59] Keeling, Birth, and Green, 'Pregnancy Counselling Clinic'.

[60] J. Webster, J. Chandler, and D. Battistutta, 'Pregnancy Outcomes and Health Care Use: Effects Of Abuse', *American Journal of Obstetrics and Gynecology* vol.174 no.2 (February 1996) 760–7.

[61] Taft, Watson, and Lee, 'Violence Against Young Australian Women'.

[62] Glander et al., 'The Prevalence of Domestic Violence Among Women Seeking Abortion'.

[63] Glander et al., 'The Prevalence of Domestic Violence Among Women Seeking Abortion'; Hedin and Janson, 'Domestic Violence During Pregnancy'; Keeling, Birth, and Green, 'Pregnancy Counselling Clinic'; J. Woo, P. Fine, and L. Goetzl, 'Abortion Disclosure and the Association With Domestic Violence', *Obstetrics and Gynecology* vol.105 (2005) 1329–1334.

[64] E.R. Wiebe and P. Janssen, 'Universal Screening for Domestic Violence in Abortion', *Women's Health Issues* vol.11 no.5 (September/October 2001) 436–441.

[65] Wiebe and Janssen, 'Universal Screening', 436–441.

[66] L.E. Saltzmann et al., 'Physical Abuse Around the Time of Pregnancy: An Examination of the Prevalence and Risk Factors in 16 States', *Maternal and Child Health Journal* vol.7. no.1 (March 2003): 31–43; J. Webster, S. Sweett, and T.A. Stolz, 'Domestic Violence in Pregnancy: A Prevalence Study', *Medical Journal of Australia* vol.161 (1994) 466–470.

[67] Webster, Sweett, and Stolz, 'Domestic Violence in Pregnancy'.

[68] D. Walsh and W. Weeks, 'What a Smile Can Hide', a report prepared for *The Support and Safety Survey: The Social, Economic and Safety Needs of Women During Pregnancy*, Women's Social Support Services, Royal Women's Hospital, Brisbane, August 2004.

[69] A. Taft, 'Violence Against Women in Pregnancy and After Childbirth: Current Knowledge and Issues in Health Care Responses', *Australian Domestic and Family Violence Clearinghouse Issues Paper* 6 (2002).

[70] R.O. De Visser et al., 'Sex in Australia: Experiences of Sexual Coercion Among a Representative Sample of Adults', *Australian and New Zealand Journal of Public Health* vol. 27 no.2 (2003) 204–9.

[71] Kero et al., 'Legal Abortion: A Painful Necessity'.

[72] D. Reardon, J. Makimaa, and A. Sobie, eds., *Victims and Victors: Speaking Out About Their Pregnancies, Abortions and Children Resulting from Sexual Assault* (Springfield, IL: Acorn Books, 2000).

[73] T.K. Sundari Ravindran and P. Balasubramanian, ' "Yes" to Abortion but "No" to Sexual Rights: The Paradoxical Reality of Married Women in Rural Tamil Nadu, India', *Reproductive Health Matters,* vol. 12 no.32 (2004) 88–99.

[74] L. Bonari et al., 'Perinatal Risks of Untreated Depression During Pregnancy', *Canadian Journal of Psychiatry* vol.49 no.11 (2004) 726–735.

[75] S.M. Marcus et al., 'Depressive Symptoms Among Pregnant Women Screened in Obstetric Settings', *Journal of Women's Health* vol.12 no.4 (2003) 373–380.

[76] J. Evans et al., 'Cohort Study of Depressed Mood During Pregnancy and After Childbirth', *British Medical Journal* vol. 323 (4 August 2001) 257–260.

[77] G.A. Burgoine et al., 'Comparison of Perinatal Grief After Dilation and Evacuation or Labor Induction in Second Trimester Terminations for Fetal Anomalies', *American Journal of Obstetrics and Gynecology* vol.192 no.6 (2005) 1928–1932.

[78] L.E. Ross et al., 'Mood Changes During Pregnancy and the Postpartum Period: Development of a Biopsychosocial Model', *Acta Psychiatrica Scandinavica* vol.109 (2004) 457–466.

[79] Bonari et al., 'Perinatal Risks of Untreated Depression During Pregnancy'.

[80] Evans et al., 'Cohort Study of Depressed Mood During Pregnancy and After Childbirth'.

[81] Marcus et al., 'Depressive Symptoms Among Pregnant Women Screened in Obstetric Settings'.

[82] <http://www.beyondblue.org.au/index.aspx?link_id=4.65>.

[83] Söderberg, Janzon, and Sjöberg, 'Emotional Distress Following Induced Abortion'.

[84] Kero, Högberg, and Lalos, 'Wellbeing and Mental Growth'.

[85] Törnbom et al., 'Decision-Making About Unwanted Pregnancy'; Coleman et al., 'The Psychology of Abortion'.

[86] Coleman et al., 'The Psychology of Abortion'.

[87] A. Kolker and B.M. Burke, 'Grieving the Wanted Child: Ramifications of Abortion After Prenatal Diagnosis of Abnormality', *Health Care for Women International* vol.14 no.6 (1993) 513–526; White-Van Mourik, Connor and Ferguson-Smith, 'The Psychosocial Sequelae of a Second-Trimester Termination of Pregnancy for Fetal Abnormality'; V. Davies et al., 'Psychological Outcome in Women Undergoing Termination of Pregnancy for Ultrasound-Detected Fetal Anomaly in the First and Second Trimesters: A Pilot Study', *Ultrasound in Obstetrics & Gynecology* vol.25 (2005) 389–392; S.H. Elder and K.M. Laurence, 'The Impact of Supportive Intervention After Second Trimester Termination of Pregnancy for Fetal Abnormality', *Prenatal Diagnosis* 11 (1991) 47–54; Korenromp et al., 'Long-Term Psychological Consequences of Pregnancy Termination for Fetal Abnormality'; M. Sandelowski and J. Barroso, 'The Travesty of Choosing After Positive Prenatal Diagnosis', *Journal of Obstetric, Gynecologic, and Neonatal Nursing* vol.34 (May/June 2005) 307–318; A. Kersting et al., 'Grief After Termination of Pregnancy Due to Fetal Malformation', *Journal of Pyschosomatic Obstetrics and Gynecology* vol.25 no.2 (June 2004) 163–9; Kersting et al., 'Trauma and Grief 2-7 Years After Termination Of Pregnancy Because of Fetal Anomalies'; C. Zeanah et al., 'Do Women Grieve After Terminating Pregnancies Because of Fetal Anomalies? A Controlled Investigation', *Obstetrics and Gynecology* vol.82 (1993) 270–5; K.A. Salvesen et al., 'Comparison of Long-Term Psychological Responses of Women After Pregnancy Termination Due to Fetal Anomalies and After Perinatal Loss', *Ultrasound in Obstetrics & Gynecology* vol.9 no.2 (February 1997) 80–5; K. Leithner et al., 'Affective State of Women Following a Prenatal Diagnosis: Predictors of a Negative Psychological Outcome', *Ultrasound in Obstetrics and Gynecology* vol.23 no.3 (March 2004) 240–6.

[88] Söderberg, Janzon, and Sjöberg, 'Emotional Distress Following Induced Abortion'; N. Russo and J.E. Denious, 'Violence in the Lives of Women Having Abortions: Implications for Policy and Practice', *Professional Psychology Research and Practice* vol.32 (2001) 142–150.

[89] V.M. Rue et al., 'Induced Abortion and Traumatic Stress: A Preliminary Comparison of American and Russian Women', *Medical Science Monitor* vol.10 no.10 (2004) SR5–16.

[90] Major et al., 'Psychological Responses of Women After First-Trimester Abortion'.

[91] A.C. Gilchrist et al., 'Termination of Pregnancy and Psychiatric Morbidity', *British Journal of Psychiatry* vol.167 (1995) 243–8.

[92] P.K. Coleman et al., 'The Psychology of Abortion: A Review and Suggestions for Future Research', *Psychology and Health* vol.20 no.2 (2005) 237–271.

[93] N. Press and C.H. Browner, 'Why Women Say Yes to Prenatal Diagnosis', *Social Science and Medicine* vol.45 no.7 (1997) 979–989; S. Markens, C. Browner, and N. Press, 'Because of the Risks: How Us Pregnant Women Account for Refusing Prenatal Screening', *Social Science and Medicine* vol.49 (1999) 359–369.

[94] L. Abramsky et al. 'What Parents Are Told After Prenatal Diagnosis of a Sex Chromosome Abnormality: Interview and Questionnaire Study', *British Medical Journal* vol.322 (24 February 2001) 463–6; C. Dunne and C. Warren, 'Lethal Autonomy: The Malfunction of the Informed Consent Mechanism Within the Context of Prenatal Diagnosis of Genetic Variants', *Issues in Law & Medicine* vol.14 no.2 (1998) 165–202; A. Brookes, 'Women's Experience of Routine Prenatal Ultrasound', *Healthsharing Women* vol.5 nos 3–4 (1994) 1–5.

[95] Dunne and Warren, 'Lethal Autonomy'.

[96] J.A. Hunfeld, J.W. Wladimiroff, and J. Passchier, 'Pregnancy Termination, Perceived Control, and Perinatal Grief', *Psychological Reports* vol.74 no.1 (Feb 1994) 217–8.

[97] T. Marteau and H. Drake, 'Attributions for Disability: The Influence of Genetic Screening', *Social Science & Medicine* vol.40. no.8 (1995) 1127–1132.

[98] Marteau and Drake, 'Attributions for Disability'.

[99] Lippman, cited in Marteau and Drake, 'Attributions for Disability'.

[100] Kolker and Burke, 'Grieving the Wanted Child'.

[101] White-Van Mourik, Connor, and Ferguson-Smith, 'The Psychosocial Sequelae of a Second-Trimester Termination of Pregnancy for Fetal Abnormality'.

[102] Elder and Laurence, 'The Impact of Supportive Intervention After Second Trimester Termination of Pregnancy for Fetal Abnormality'.

[103] Korenromp et al., 'Long-Term Psychological Consequences of Pregnancy Termination for Fetal Abnormality'.

[104] Kersting et al., 'Trauma and Grief 2-7 Years After Termination Of Pregnancy Because of Fetal Anomalies'.

[105] Sandelowski and Barroso, 'The Travesty of Choosing After Positive Prenatal Diagnosis'.

[106] Sandelowski and Barroso, 'The Travesty of Choosing After Positive Prenatal Diagnosis'.

[107] Kersting et al., 'Grief After Termination of Pregnancy Due to Fetal Malformation'.

[108] Sandelowski and Barroso, 'The Travesty of Choosing After Positive Prenatal Diagnosis'.

[109] Sandelowski and Barroso, 'The Travesty of Choosing After Positive Prenatal Diagnosis'.

[110] Zeanah et al., 'Do Women Grieve After Terminating Pregnancies Because of Fetal Anomalies?'

[111] Salvesen et al., 'Comparison of Long-Term Psychological Responses'.

[112] Leithner et al., 'Affective State of Women Following a Prenatal Diagnosis'.

[113] Davies et al., 'Psychological Outcome in Women Undergoing Termination of Pregnancy'.

Chapter 8

[1] This chapter was published as an article in *The National Catholic Bioethics Quarterly* vol.4 no.2 (2004) 275–288, and is reproduced here with permission.

[2] Willard Cates Jr., 'Contraception, Unintended Pregnancies and Disease: Why Isn't a Simple Solution Possible?' *American Journal of Epidemiology* vol.143.no.4 (1996); John Murtagh, *General Practice*, 2nd ed. (Melbourne: McGraw-Hill, 1998).

[3] Michael Christ, William V. Raszka Jr., and Christopher Dillon, 'Prioritizing Education about Condom Use among Sexually Active Adolescent Females', *Adolescence* vol.33 no.132 (Winter 1998) 735–744.

[4] D.C. Stewart, 'Contraception', in *Adolescent Medicine*, eds. A.D. Hofmann and D.E. Greydanus, 3rd ed. (Stamford, CT: Appleton & Lange, 1997), 566–588; G. Hewitt and B. Cromer, 'Update on Adolescent Contraception', *Obstetrics and Gynecology Clinics of North America* vol.27 no.1 March 2000) 143–162; American Academy of Pediatrics, Committee on Adolescence, 'Contraception and Adolescents', *Pediatrics* vol.104 no.5 (November 1999) 1161–6.

[5] Evelyn L. Billings and John J. Billings, *Teaching the Billings Ovulation Method*, part 2, *Variations of the Cycle and Reproductive Health* (Melbourne: Ovulation Method Research and Reference Centre, 1997), 45, citing Erik Odeblad.

[6] See a review of the effects of oral contraceptive pills in Nicholas Tonti-Filippini, 'The Pill: Abortifacient or Contraceptive? A Literature Review', *Linacre Quarterly* vol.62 no.1 (February 1995) 5–28.

[7] I. Aref et al., 'Effect of Minipills on Physiologic Responses of Human Cervical Mucus, Endometrium, and Ovary', *Journal of Fertility and Sterility* vol.24 no.8 (August 1973) 578–583.

[8] G. Ugocsai, M. Rózsa, and P. Ugocsai, 'Scanning Electron Microscopic (SEM) Changes of the Endometrium in Women Taking High Doses of Levonorgestrel as Emergency Post-coital Contraception', *Contraception* vol.66. no.6 (December 2002) 433–437.

[9] Ugocsai, Rózsa, and Ugocsai, 'Scanning'. Note that there has been little research interest since early on in the oral contraceptive pill development in identifying the precise effects. The manufacturers have been content to be vague and not to distinguish between antinidation and contraceptive effects. The most recent product information simply states that the precise mechanism is unknown.

[10] This information was given to me by Emeritus Professor James B. Brown (Endocrinology, University of Melbourne), who himself was involved in the work on the estrogens and had worked with Pinkus at that time. Conversation with author, 5 March, 2004.

[11] Professor James B. Brown, conversation with author, June 2002.

[12] G. Sheffer-Mimouni et al., 'Ectopic Pregnancies following Emergency Levonorgestrel Contraception', *Contraception* vol.67 no.4 (April 2003) 267-9; D.A. Grimes and E.G. Raymond, 'Emergency Contraception', *Annals of Internal Medicine* vol. 137 no.3 (6 August, 2002) 180 - 9.

[13] Professor James Brown, conversation with author, June 23, 2002.

[14] The function of the crypts and the cervical mucus have been well described by E. Odeblad et al., 'The Dynamic Mosaic Model of the Human Ovulatory Cervical Mucus', *Proceedings of the Nordic Fertility Society* (Umea, Sweden, January 1978).

[15] W.S.B. Yeung et al., 'The Effects of Levonorgestrel on Various Sperm Functions', *Contraception* vol.66 no.6 (December 2002) 453-7.

[16] C. Kahlenborn, J.B. Stanford, and W.L. Larimore, 'Postfertilization Effect of Hormonal Emergency Contraception', *Annals of Pharmacotherapy* vol.36 no.3 (March 2002) 465-470.

[17] J.B. Brown, 'Timing of Ovulation', *Medical Journal of Australia* 2 (1977) 780-3; J.B. Brown et al., 'New Assays for Identifying the Fertile Period', *International Journal of Gynaecology & Obstetrics* 1.suppl. (1989) 111-122; J.B. Brown, J. Holmes, and G. Barker, 'Use of the Home Ovarian Monitor in Pregnancy Avoidance', *American Journal of Obstetrics and Gynecology* vol.165 no.6 (December 1991) 2008-2011; S.J. Thornton, R.J. Pepperell, and J.B. Brown, 'Home Monitoring of Gonadotropin Ovulation Induction Using the Ovarian Monitor', *Fertility and Sterility* vol.54. no.6 (December 1990) 1076-82; L.F. Blackwell, J.B. Brown, and D.G. Cooke, 'Definition of the Potentially Fertile Period from Urinary Steroid Excretion Rates: Part II: A Threshold Value for Pregnanediol Glucuronide as a Marker for the End of the Potentially Fertile Period in the Human Menstrual Cycle', *Steroids* vol.63 no.1 (January 1998) 5-13.

[18] Professor James B. Brown, conversation with author, 5 March, 2004.

[19] Odeblad et al., 'The Dynamic Mosaic Model'.

[20] See J.B. Brown in note 16 above.

[21] Odeblad et al., 'The Dynamic Mosaic Model'.

[22] E.L. Billings, 'The Simplicity of the Ovulation Method and Its Application in Various Circumstances', *Acta Europaea Fertilitatis* vol.22 no.1 (January–February 1991) 33-6; J.J. Billings, 'The Validation of the Billings Ovulation Method by Laboratory Research and Field Trials', *Acta Europaea Fertilitatis* vol.22 no.1 (January–February 1991) 9-15; E.L. Billings and Ann Westmore, *The Billings Ovulation Method* (Melbourne: Anne O'Donovan P/L, 1998).

[23] The three major trials of the Billings Ovulation Method (BOM) (used to avoid pregnancy):

a) World Health Organization (WHO) (1977–1981) Task Force on Methods for the Determination of the Fertile Period, Special Programme of Research, Development and Research Training in Human Reproduction. Multicenter–Auckland, Dublin, San Miguel, Bangalore and Manila. 869

women, 10,215 cycles of use, 2.2 method-related pregnancies per hundred woman-years in initiates (2.8 when initial phase excluded). 'A Prospective Multicentre Trial of the Ovulation Method of Natural Family Planning: I. The Teaching Phase', *Fertility and Sterility* 36 (1981) 152ff; 'A Prospective Multicentre Trial of the Ovulation Method of Natural Family Planning: II. The Effectiveness Phase', 36 (1981) 591ff.

b) Indian Council of Medical Research Task Force on NFP (1995). States of Uttar Pradesh, Bihar, Rajasthan, Karnataka and Pondicherry. 2,059 women, 32,957 woman-months of use, 0.86 Method-related pregnancies per hundred woman-years in initiates. 'Field Trial of Billings Ovulation Method of Natural Family Planning', *Contraception* vol.53 no.2 (February 1996) 69–74.

c) Jiangsu Family Health Institute (1997). China. 1,235 women, 14,280 woman-months of use, No method-related pregnancies in initiates (5 user-related pregnancies). Shao Zhen Qian and De-Wei Zhang, 'Evaluation of the Effectiveness of a Natural Fertility Regulation Program in China', *Bulletin of the Ovulation Method Research and Reference Centre* vol.24 no.4 (2000) 17–22.

[24] World Health Organization Task Force on Methods for the Determination of the Fertile Period, Special Programme of Research, Development and Research Training in Human Reproduction, 'A Prospective Multicentre Trial of the Ovulation Method of Natural Family Planning: III. Characteristics of the Menstrual Cycle and of the Fertile Phase', *Fertility and Sterility* 40 (1983) 773–8.

[25] D.B. Dunson, B. Colombo, and D.D. Baird, 'Changes with Age in the Level and Duration of the Menstrual Cycle', *Human Reproduction* vol.17 no.5 (May 2002) 1399–1403.

[26] D. Blake et al., 'Fertility Awareness in Women Attending a Fertility Clinic', *Australian and New Zealand Journal of Obstetrics and Gynaecology* vol.37 no.3 (1997) 350.

Chapter 9

[1] This chapter draws significantly on an earlier article which I co-authored with Michael Hains and which was published in the *Australian Bar Review* 16, n. 2 (November 1997) 181-98.

[2] *Charter of the United Nations*, Art. 56.

[3] *Charter of the United Nations* Art. 55 (c).

[4] D.J. Harris, *Cases and Materials on International Law*, Fourth Edition, (London: Sweet and Maxwell, 1991), 18.

[5] D.J. Harris, *Cases and Materials,* 604.

[6] (1995) 183 CLR 273.

[7] The precise status of various Declarations and Conventions under Australian law is unclear, but it is fair to say that some uncertainty exists as to their status. At one extreme, if Parliament has merely approved and

repeated the treaty in legislation, without implementing it, the Act will give rise to no rights: see *Bradley v The Commonwealth* (1973) 128 CLR 557 at 582, noted (1974) 48 ALJ 368. However, the High Court subsequently in *Minister for Immigration and Ethnic Affairs v Teoh* (1995) 183 CLR 273 held that entry into a treaty by Australia creates a 'legitimate expectation' – in administrative law – that the Executive Government and its agencies will act according to the treaty, even where those terms were *not* incorporated in Australian law (cf the proposed Administrative Decisions (Effect of International Instruments) Bill 1997). At the other extreme where a Convention has been implemented, it gives rise to enforceable rights beyond that of legitimate expectations, e.g., the Racial Discrimination Act 1975 (Cth.) (implementing the International Convention on the Elimination of All Forms of Racial Discrimination) and the Sex Discrimination Act 1984 (Cth.) (implementing the Convention on the Elimination of All Forms of Discrimination Against Women). The Declarations and Conventions attached as schedules to the Human Rights and Equal Opportunity Commission Act 1986 (Cth.) fall between these two extremes. Thus their precise status under Australian law is unclear.

[8] *Minister for Immigration and Ethnic Affairs v Teoh*, (1995) 183 CLR 273, at 287, 315. Followed in *Krueger v The Commonwealth*, (1997) 146 ALR 126. Brennan J. in *Mabo (No. 2)*, (1992) 175 CLR 1, at 42, referred to international instruments as 'legitimate and important influences on the development of the common law, especially when international law declares the existence of universal human rights'.

[9] (1995) 38 NSWLR 47.

[10] (1971) 3 NSWDCR 25.

[11] (1996) 136 ALR 16 (SLA).

[12] Richard C Wilkins and Jacob Reynolds, 'International Law and the Right to Life, *Ave Maria Law Review* vol.4 no.1 (Winter 2006) 123–4.

[13] The Vienna Convention on the Law of Treaties 1969 applies to the interpretation of the Convention on the Rights of the Child because it entered into force after 27 January 1980, the operative date of the Vienna Convention. The Vienna Convention expressly provides that it does not apply retrospectively (see Article 4).

[14] Australia has approved and repeated the United Nations' Charter in the Charter of the United Nations Act 1945 (Cth.). However the Act does not *implement* the United Nations Charter into municipal law: see *Bradley v The Commonwealth* (1973) 128 CLR 557, at 582, noted (1974) 48 ALJ 368. See also *Minister for Immigration and Ethnic Affairs v Teoh* (1995) 183 CLR 273, at 286–287, 298, 304, 315.

[15] The Proclamation of Teheran, Final Act of the International Conference on Human Rights, Teheran, 22 April to 13 May 1968, U.N. Doc. A/CONF. 32/41 (1968) notes:

> 2. The Universal Declaration of Human Rights states a common understanding of the peoples of the world concerning the inalienable and inviolable rights of all members of the human family and constitutes an obligation for the members of the international community.

[16] Peter Bailey, *Human Rights, Australia in an International Context* (Sydney: Butterworths, 1990), 111.

[17] On 22 December 1992 the Federal Attorney General declared, under section 47 of the Human Rights and Equal Opportunity Commission Act 1986 (Cth.), that the Convention on the Rights of the Child was an 'international instrument' concerning 'human rights and freedoms' under the Act.

[18] See note **7 above.**

[19] Alison Duxbury and Christopher Ward, 'The International Law Implications of Australian Abortion Law', *UNSW Law Journal* vol.23. no.2 (2000)17.

[20] Art. 2(b) of the Vienna Convention on the Law of Treaties 1969 defines:'ratification', 'acceptance', 'approval' and 'accession' [to] mean in each case the international act so named whereby a state establishes on the international plane its consent to be bound by a treaty.

[21] Australia signed the Convention on 22 August 1990 and ratified it on 17 December 1990.

[22] Preamble, Convention on the Rights of the Child 1989, GA res. 44/25, annex, 44 UN GAOR Supp. (No. 49) at 167, UN Doc. A/44/49 (1989).

[23] Convention on the Rights of the Child, Art. 6 (1).

[24] Convention on the Rights of the Child, Art. 6 (2).

[25] Convention on the Rights of the Child, Preamble.

[26] At signature or ratification, a state may, but not afterwards, make a reservation or interpretation: Paul Sieghart, *The International Law of Human Rights* (Oxford: Clarendon Press, 1983), 36. Article 2(d) of the Vienna Convention on the Law of Treaties 1969 defines a reservation to mean: 'a unilateral statement, however phrased or named, made by a State, when signing, ratifying, accepting, approving or acceding to a treaty, whereby it purports to exclude or to modify the legal effect of certain provisions of the treaty in their application to that State'.

[27] According to United Nations ratification information, Australia only placed one reservation on the Convention on the Rights of the Child, being:

> Australia accepts the general principles of Article 37. In relation to the second sentence of paragraph (c), the obligation to separate children from adults in prison is accepted only to the extent that such imprisonment is considered by the responsible authorities to be feasible and consistent with the obligation that children be able to maintain contact with their families, having regard to the geography and demography of Australia. Australia, therefore, ratifies the Convention to the Oxford extent that it is unable to comply with the obligation imposed by Article 37 (c). (United Nations, *Treaty Series*, vol. 999, p. 171; and vol. 1057, p. 407)

[28] Australia, Senate 1989, *Debates*, (26 October 1989) 2309.

[29] For example, Malta and Senegal. In the United Nations ratification information concerning the Convention on the Rights of the Child, Ecuador expressly declared:

> In signing the Convention on the Rights of the Child, Ecuador reaffirms … [that it is] especially pleased with the ninth preambular paragraph of the draft Convention, which pointed to the need to protect the unborn child, and believed that that paragraph should be borne in mind in interpreting all the articles of the Convention, particularly Article 24. While the minimum age set in Article 38 was, in its view, too low, [the Government of Ecuador] did not wish to endanger the chances for the Convention's adoption by consensus and therefore would not propose any amendment to the text. [Doc. A/RES/44/25]

The Holy See also declared:

> that the Convention represents an enactment of principles previously adopted by the United Nations, and once effective as a ratified instrument, will safeguard the rights of the child before as well as after birth, as expressly affirmed in the Declaration of the Rights of the Child [Res. 136 (XIV)] and restated in the ninth preambular paragraph of the Convention. The Holy See remains confident that the ninth preambular paragraph will serve as the perspective through which the rest of the Convention will be interpreted, in conformity with article 31 of the Vienna Convention on the Law of Treaties of 23 May 1969. [Doc. A/RES/44/25]

According to a UN Glossary of Terms:

> states make 'declarations' as to their understanding of some matter or as to the interpretation of a particular provision. Unlike reservations, declarations merely clarify the state's position and do not purport to exclude or modify the legal effect of a treaty. Usually, declarations are made at the time of the deposit of the corresponding instrument or at the time of signature.

These two quotes were the only references in the formal ratification information concerning the unborn.

[30] Sharon Detrick, comp. and ed., *The United Nations Convention on the Rights of the Child, A Guide to the 'Travaux Préparatoires'* (Dordrecht: Martinus Nijhoff Publishers, 1992), 109, emphasis added.

[31] Article 1 of Convention on the Rights of the Child states: 'For the purposes of the present Convention, a child means every human being below the age of eighteen years unless, under the law applicable to the child, majority is attained earlier'.

[32] Detrick, *The United Nations Convention*, 110.

[33] Detrick, *The United Nations Convention*, 110.

[34] Carl August Fleischhauer, The Legal Counsel, 9 December 1988, 'Response of the Legal Counsel', E/CN.4/1989/48, Annex p. 144 Detrick, *The United Nations Convention*, 113.

[35] Philip Alston, 'The Unborn Child and Abortion Under the Draft Convention on the Rights of the Child', *Human Rights Quarterly* vol.12 (1990) 156, 177.

[36] Vienna Convention on the Law of Treaties 1969, Articles 2(1)(a) and 31(2).

[37] Vienna Convention on the Law of Treaties 1969, Article 32.

[38] Cf. evidence cited in Detrick, *The United Nations Convention*, 109.

[39] There was no mention of abortion in connection with privacy (Article 17) during the discussions on the *International Covenant on Civil and Political Rights 1966.*

[40] A/C.3/L.654.

[41] §112 A/3764.

[42] 30 votes against the amendment, 20 for and 17 abstentions: §119 A/3764.

[43] §112 A/3764.

[44] Malta proposed: 'In article 1, after the words "human being", add the words "from conception".[E/CN.4/1989/WG.1/WP.9]. Senegal's proposal was: 'According to the present Convention a child is every human being, *from his conception until at least,* the age of 18 years . . .' [E/CN.4/1989/WG.1/WP.17]

[45] Detrick, *The United Nations Convention*, 118.

[46] Detrick, *The United Nations Convention*, 109, emphasis added.

[47] Vienna Convention on the Law of Treaties 1969, Article 53.

[48] Human Rights and Equal Opportunity Commission Act 1986 (Cth.), Schedule 3.

[49] J. Fleming and M. Hains, 'What Rights, If Any, Do the Unborn Have Under International Law?' *Australian Bar Review* vol.16 (1997) 198.

[50] Duxbury and Ward, 'The International Law Implications', 17, emphasis added.

[51] *Charter of the United Nations*, Article 55(c).

[52] In *Secretary, Department of Health and Community Services v. J.W.B. and S.M.B.* (Marion's case.) (1992) 175 CLR 218 Brennan J. emphasised:

> The law will protect equally the dignity of the hale and hearty and the dignity of the weak and lame; of the frail baby and of the frail aged; of the intellectually able and of the intellectually disabled…. Our law admits of no discrimination against the weak and disadvantaged in their human dignity.

[53] Alston, 'The Unborn Child', 159.

[54] Alston, 'The Unborn Child', 159.

[55] Universal Declaration of Human Rights 1948, G.A. res. 217A (III), UN Doc A/810 at 71 (1948) Preamble.

[56] Detrick, *The United Nations Convention*, 109, emphasis added.

[57] Michel Meslin, 'Religious Traditions and the Human Person', in *Concepts of Person in Religion and Thought*, eds. Hans G. Kippenberg, Yme B. Kuiper, and Andy F. Sanders (Berlin: Mouton de Gruyter, 1990) 67.

[58] D. J. Wolgemuth, ' The Cell Cycle and Differentiation in the Reproductive System', in *Reproductive Medicine: Molecular, Cellular and Genetic Fundamentals*, ed. B.C.J.M. Fauser (New York: Parthenon Publishing Group, 2003) 61, 407.

[59] K. H. Hollen, *The Reproductive System* (Westport, CN: Greenwood Press, 2004) 14–15.

[60] L. C. Guidice, in Fauser, *Reproductive Medicine*, 440-1.

[61] C. R. Parker, 'Endocrinology of Pregnancy', in *Essential Reproductive Medicine*, eds. B. C. Carr, R. E. Blackwell, and R. Azziz (New York: McGraw Hill, 2005) 128–130.

[62] N.A. Campbell and J.B. Reece, *Biology*, 7th ed. (San Francisco: Benjamin-Cummings, 2004) 992–4.

[63] R.L. Gardner, M.R. Meredith, and D.G.Altman, 'Is the Anterior-Posterior Axis of the Fetus Specified Before Implantation in the Mouse?' *Journal of Experimental Zoology* vol. 264 (1992) 437–443.

[64] R.L. Gardner, 'Specification of Embryonic Axes Begins Before Cleavage in Normal Mouse Development', *Development* vol.128 no.6 (2001) 839–847.

[65] Anthony Fisher, *IVF: The Critical Issues* (Melbourne: Collins Dove, 1989), 133. Fisher refers to W.J. Hamilton and H.W. Mossman, *Human Embryology*, 4th ed. (Cambridge: Plenum, 1972); L.B. Arey, *Developmental Anatomy*, 7th ed. (Philadelphia: Saunders, 1975); B. Alberts et al., *Molecular Biology of the Cell* (New York: Garland, 1983); K.L. Moore, *Before We Are Born* (Philadelphia: Saunders, 1983); L. Nilsson et al., *A Child Is Born* (London: Faber & Faber, 1977).

[66] R. Yanagimachi, 'Mammalian Fertilization', *The Physiology of Reproduction*, eds. E. Knobil et al. (New York: Raven Press, 1988), 135.

[67] It is interesting to note that Langman's Medical Embryology, Sixth Edition, does not use the term 'pre-embryo', a term which is meant to refer to the entity up to 14 days. The comparative lawyer Albin Eser has suggested that:

> the naive (speaking from a normative-theoretical perspective) and rather simplistic efforts to get rid of the basic value problem through terminological "degradation" of the pre-implantation embryo to the status of "pre-embryo" or even to simple "seed" or "germ" should be abandoned. Rather than prejudicing the value questions involved through conceptual-terminological game-playing it would be better to concentrate on the question that is lastly decisive: To what extent does or should a species-specific human (since originating from human gametes) new entity of life — i.e., at least genetically capable of achieving the full potential of a human being — possess sufficient value to make us unwilling to allow for total freedom of choice with respect to maintaining or destroying this life? (A. Eser, 'Experiments with Embryos: Legal Aspects in Comparative Perspective', UK National Committee of Comparative Law 1987 Colloquium Legal Regulation of Reproductive Medicine [Cambridge], cited in Fisher, *IVF*, 173–4.)

[68] Senate Select Committee on the Human Embryo Experimentation Bill of 1986, *Human Embryo Experimentation in Australia* (Canberra: Australian Government Printing Service, 1986), xiii.

[69] C.R. Austin, *Human Embryos* (Oxford: Oxford University Press, 1989) 31.

[70] Senate Select Committee on the Human Embryo Experimentation Bill 1985, *Official Hansard Report*, in Senate Select Committee on the Human Embryo Experimentation Bill 1986, *Human Embryo Experimentation in Australia*, 2161–2. Professor R.V. Short was Chairman, Working Party on Human Embryo Experimentation, Australian Academy of Science, Canberra, Australian Capital Territory.

[71] T. W. Sadler, *Langman's Medical Embryology*, Sixth Edition, (Baltimore: Williams & Wilkins, 1990) 30.

[72] H. Pearson, 'Your Destiny From Day One', *Nature* 418 (2002): 14–5; K Piotrowska and Zernicka-Goetz, 'Role for Sperm in Spatial Patterning of the Early Mouse Embryo', *Nature* 409.6819 (2001) 517–521.

[73] Michael Tooley, *Abortion and Infanticide* (Oxford: Clarendon Press, 1983). Tooley argues that a child becomes a 'quasi-person' at around three months, after which time it might be thought wrong to kill the baby (see his conclusions on p. 424). Cf. Helga Kuhse and Peter Singer, *Should the Baby Live?*, (Oxford: Oxford University Press, 1985). esp. 131, where the authors describe Tooley's argument as 'basically sound'. For a refutation of Tooley, see Bernard Williams, *Ethics and the Limits of Philosophy* (London: Fontana Press/Collins, 1985) 114-5.

[74] It was also prevalent in the late nineteenth century and throughout the twentieth century. For example, 'Eugenics aims to secure better babies' (Margaret Sanger, 'Medical Journalists Advocate Birth Control', *Birth Control Review* 2.10 [October 1918]: 4) and 'we need not more of the fit, but fewer of the unfit ... Is it not time to protect ourselves and our children and our children's children? The propagation of the degenerate, the imbecile, the feeble minded should be prevented.' Margaret Sanger, 'Birth Control, Past, Present and Future', *Birth Control Review*, Vol. V, No. 5.8 (August 1921) 19.

[75] 'Prior to the American Civil War and the antislavery amendments, such decisions as *Dred Scott v. Sandford* relegated slaves to the legal status of non-persons in spite of clear biological evidence of their humanity'. John Warwick Montgomery, 'Abortion and the Law: Three Clarifications', in *New Perspectives on Human Abortion*, eds. Thomas W. Hilgers, Dennis J. Horan, and David Mall (Frederick, MD: University Publications of America, Inc., 1981), 284. Cf. *Dred Scott v. Sandford*, 19 Howard 393 (1857), and the Slavery Convention 1927, Article 1.

[76] See R. N. Proctor, *Racial Hygiene: Medicine Under the Nazis* (Cambridge, MA: Harvard University Press, 1988); also R J Lifton, *The Nazi Doctors: Medical Killing and the Psychology of Genocide* (New York, Basic Books, 1986).

[77] Hiram Caton and John I. Fleming, 'Afterword: An Allegory' in *Proceedings of the Bioethics Symposium: 'Limits on Care' of the Ninth World Congress on Intellectual Disability*, eds. Hiram Caton and John I. Fleming (Canberra: National Council for Intellectual Disability, 1992) 67–8.

[78] Cf. the International Covenant on Civil and Political Rights 1966, Article 16.

[79] Universal Declaration of Human Right 1948, Article 25.

[80] The Human Rights Committee is established under the International Covenant on Civil and Political Rights 1966 to implement the Covenant, see Part IV of the Covenant. Mr Ganji, a former Human Rights Committee member, has provided useful insight to the Committee's approach concerning Article 6. He has observed:

> In order to exercise any rights with which the Committee was concerned an individual had to exist; and in order to exist, he must die neither before nor after birth, and he must receive a minimum of food, education, health care, housing and clothing. There was undoubtedly an interconnexion between the right to life, the requirements of which were material and the right to exercise all other freedoms. (SR 67 pr. 78. Comments made during consideration of a report by the German Democratic Republic).

[81] GC 7(16), Doc. A/37/40, 94. Also in Doc. C/21/Add. I.

[82] International Covenant on Civil and Political Rights 1966, Article 4 (2).

[83] International Covenant on Civil and Political Rights 1966, Article 4 (1).

[84] International Covenant on Civil and Political Rights 1966, Article 40 (4).

[85] Human Rights Committee, 'Compilation of General Comments and General Recommendations Adopted by Human Rights Treaty Bodies', general comment 6, art. 6 (16th session, 1982), U.N. Doc. HRI\GEN\1\Rev.1 at 6 (1994) § 1.

[86] Human Rights Committee, 'Compilation', § 5, emphasis added.

[87] Article 6(5) of the International Covenant on Civil and Political Rights 1966, G.A. res. 2200A (XXI), 21 UN GAOR Supp. (No. 16) at 52, UN Doc. A/6316 (1966), 999 UNTS 171, emphasis added. See also the United Nations Safeguards Guaranteeing Protection of the Rights of Those Facing the Death Penalty 1984, Article 3.

[88] Marc J. Bossuyt, in the *Guide to the 'Travaux Préparatoires' of the International Covenant on Civil and Political Rights* (Martinus Nijhoff Publishers, 1987), observes:

Commission on Human Rights, 5th Session (1949), 6th Session (1950), 8th Session (1952):

> A/2929, Chapt. VI, §10: 'It would seem that the intention of paragraph 4 [5] which was inspired by humanitarian considerations and by consideration for the interests of the unborn child, was that the death sentence, if it concerned a pregnant woman, should not be carried out at all. It was pointed out, however, that the provision, in its present formulation, might be interpreted as applying solely to the period preceding childbirth. (E/CN.4/SR.311, p.7 [B])

Third Committee, 12th Session (1957):

> A/3764, §118 [actually §117]: 'There was some discussion regarding the meaning of paragraph 4 *[5]* of the draft of the Commission on Human Rights (E/2573, annex I B), which provided that the sentence of death should not be carried out on a pregnant woman. A number of representatives were of the opinion that the clause sought to prevent the carrying out of the sentence of death before the child was born [A/C.3/ SR.809, §27 (CHI); A/C.3/SR.810, §2 (B), §7 (IR); A/C.3/SR.812, §32 (RI); A/C.3/SR.814, §42 (CDN)]. However, other (sic) thought that the death sentence should not be carried out at all if it concerned a pregnant woman [A/C.3/SR.810, §14 (PE); A/C.3/SR.811, §24 (SA)]. The normal development of the unborn child might be affected if the mother were to live in constant fear that, after the birth of her child, the death sentence would be carried out'.

[89] Third Committee , 12th session (1957) §118, A/3764.

[90] In *R v. Wycherley* 173 ER 486, the accused woman had been found guilty of murder and was sentenced to death. When asked whether she had anything to say to stay the execution she replied: 'I am with child now'. A jury was empanelled and found that the woman was *not* pregnant. Nevertheless, the case highlights that the death penalty was stayed pending the resolution of the issue and logically would have been stayed until at least the birth had she been found to be pregnant.

[91] International Planned Parenthood Federation, *IPPF Charter on Sexual and Reproductive Rights*, 12.

[92] 78 UNTS 277, the Convention entered into force on 12 January 1951. The Convention was signed by Australia on 11 December 1948 and ratified on 8 July 1949. Australia has approved and repeated the Convention on the Prevention and Punishment of the Crime of Genocide 1948 in the Genocide Convention Act 1949 (Cth.). However, the Act does not *implement* the Convention into municipal law, see *Minister for Immigration and Ethnic Affairs v Teoh* (1995) 183 CLR 273, at 286–287, 298, 304, 315; and *Krueger v The Commonwealth*, unreported, High Court of Australia, 31 July 1997. Compare the comments of Justice Evatt who has argued:

> Quite apart from conventions that Australia ratifies, some parts of that international law can, as a matter of common law, apply in Australia without any further action on the part of anyone. I think the recent High Court case of *Teoh* may have referred obliquely to this, but it could have said more about the fact that under common law, customary rules, and particularly principles of human rights, such as the principle against genocide and so on, are part of customary international law. Naturally as such, they can be overruled by legislation, as any part of the common law can. But we should not think of international law as being an entirely separate thing from the law of Australia. Some parts of it we would recognise. [Report by the Senate Legal and Constitutional References Committee, 'Trick or Treaty? Commonwealth Power to Make and Implement Treaties', November 1995 at §6.6, see also §3.33.]

[93] Convention on the Prevention and Punishment of the Crime of Genocide 1948, Preamble.

[94] In *Thorpe v The Commonwealth [No 3]*, unreported, High Court of Australia, 12 June 1997, Kirby J. observed: 'The definition of "genocide" in the [Genocide] Convention is very broad'.

[95] Declaration on the Rights of Disabled Persons 1975, proclaimed by the General Assembly Resolution 3447 (XXX) of 9 December 1975. The Declaration is attached as Schedule 5 to the Human Rights and Equal Opportunity Commission Act 1986 (Cth.).

[96] Declaration on the Rights of Disabled Persons 1975, Article 4.

[97] Declaration on the Rights of Disabled Persons 1975, Article 10.

[98] United Nations Charter, Article 55(c).

[99] United Nations Charter, Article 56.

[100] *Parry and Grant Encyclopaedic Dictionary of International Law*, eds. Professor Clive Parry et al. (New York: Oceana Publications, Inc., 1986) 72.

Chapter 10

[1] St. Alphonsus Ligouri, *Theologia Moralita*, vol. 1, ed. L. Gaude (Typographia Vaticana), 357:

> Sed melius cum aliis dicendum, illam esse formalem, quae concurrit ad malam voluntatem alterius, et nequit esse sine peccato; materialem vero illam quae concurrit tantum ad malam actionem alterius, praeter intentionem cooperantis.

[2] Anthony Fisher, 'Co-operation in Evil', *Catholic Medical Quarterly* vol. 44 (February 1994) 15.

[3] < http://www.ascensionhealth.org/ethics/public/key_principles/cooperation.asp>.

[4] Bishop Karl Lehmann of Mainz, quoted in 'German Bishops in Urgent Talks About Abortion Advice', *The Tablet* (31 January 1998) 148–9.

[5] R. Kulier et al., 'Surgical Methods for First Trimester Termination of Pregnancy', *The Cochrane Database of Systematic Reviews* 3 (2006).

[6] L. Say et al., 'Medical Versus Surgical Methods for First Trimester Termination of Pregnancy', *The Cochrane Database of Systematic Reviews* 4 (2002). Art. CD003037.pub2. DOI: 10.1002/14651858.CD003037.pub2; M. Greene, *New England Journal of Medicine* vol.353 no.22 (1 December 2005) 2318.

[7] John Fletcher and Mark Evans, 'Maternal Bonding in Early Fetal Ultrasound Examinations', *New England Journal of Medicine* vol. 308 (17 February 1983) 392–393.

[8] Melinda Tankard Reist, *Giving Sorrow Words: Women's Stories of Grief After Abortion* (Sydney: Duffy and Snellgrove, 2000).

[9] 'Why Defend Partial-Birth Abortion?' *New York Times*, 26 September 1996.

[10] See for instance a survey of specialist opinion 'For Debate: Do Fetuses Feel Pain?' *British Medical Journal* 313.7060 (28 September 1996) 795–8.

[11] C.A. Margaret et al., 'The Psychosocial Sequellae of a Second Trimester Termination of Pregnancy for Fetal Abnormality Over a Two Year Period', in *Psychosocial Aspects of Genetic Counselling* (New York: John Wiley and Sons, 1992), 73.

[12] Susan Iles and Denis Gath, 'Psychiatric Outcome of Termination of Pregnancy for Foetal Abnormality', *Psychological Medicine* vol.23 (1993) 407–413.

[13] The Medical Board of Queensland, *Terminations of Pregnancies in Excess of 20 Weeks of Gestation: Project Information Paper* (July 1997) 4.

[14] See for instance, the enclosed letter from Professor John Bonnar et al., appendix 2.

[15] See, for instance, a debate carried out in *The Lancet*: *Lancet* 342 (21 August 1993); *Lancet* 342 (9 October 1993); *Lancet* 342 (6 November 1993).

Chapter 11

[1] For formal account of this basis for preference utilitarianism see R.M. Hare, *Moral Thinking: Its Levels, Method and Point Method* (Oxford: Oxford University Press, 1981).

[2] This point is well developed by John Rawls in *A Theory of Justice*, rev. ed. (Cambridge, MA: Belknap Press of Harvard University Press, 1999).

[3] Cf. John Paul II, Encyclical Letter *Veritatis Splendor* (6 August 1993), nn. 97 and 99 (*AAS* 85 [1993] 1209–1211).

[4] *Hansard*, 11 November 1947.

[5] Second Vatican Council, *Dignitatis Humanae* (1965), n. 3.

[6] Ronald Dworkin, *Life's Dominion* (New York: Knopf, 1993), 164.

[7] *Black v. The Commonwealth*, (1981) HCA 2, (1981) 146 CLR 559 (2 February 1981) 579, <http://www.austlii.edu.au/au/cases/cth/HCA/1981/2.html>.

[8] Michael Hogan, 'Separation of Church and State?' (16 May 2001), <http://www.australianreview.net/digest/2001/05/hogan.html>.

[9] Alex Mitchell, 'Faulkner Lone State ALP Senator to Back Cloning Legislation', *The Sun Herald*, 12 November 2006, 22.

[10] 'Doorstop Interview–Herceptin listed on the PBS', 22 August 2006, <http://www.health.gov.au/internet/ministers/publishing.nsf/Content/health-mediarel-yr2006-ta-abbsp220806.htm?OpenDocument&yr=2006&mth=8>.

Index of Proper Names